US POLITICS IN AN
AGE of
UNCERTAINTY

US POLITICS IN AN
AGE of
UNCERTAINTY

ESSAYS ON A NEW REALITY

Edited by Lance Selfa

Haymarket Books
Chicago, Illinois

Published in 2017 by
Haymarket Books
P.O. Box 180165
Chicago, IL 60618
773-583-7884
www.haymarketbooks.org
info@haymarketbooks.org

ISBN: 978-1-60846-853-9

Trade distribution:
In the US, Consortium Book Sales and Distribution, www.cbsd.com
In Canada, Publishers Group Canada, www.pgcbooks.ca
In the UK, Turnaround Publisher Services, www.turnaround-uk.com
All other countries, Ingram Publisher Services International,
IPS_Intlsales@ingramcontent.com

This book was published with the generous support of Lannan Foundation and
Wallace Action Fund.

Cover design by Rachel Cohen.

Printed in Canada by union labor.

Library of Congress Cataloging-in-Publication data is available.

10 9 8 7 6 5 4 3 2 1

CONTENTS

INTRODUCTION

Months after the event, the Electoral College's selection of Donald Trump as 45th president of the United States still has the power to shock on many levels. A transition from the first African American president to someone who made racism a cornerstone of his campaign is one element. Another is the fact that Trump triumphed against what appeared to be a solid "popular front" of most of American business, the media, the political establishment, and liberal activists lined up behind Democrat Hillary Clinton. Despite all of these factors—or perhaps, more accurately, because of them—the United States's dysfunctional political system delivered the world's most powerful office to the loser of the national popular vote for the second time in sixteen years.

Trump's election blindsided the political and media establishment. Even most of us on the left—who are much more attuned to the economic wreckage and despair on which Trump built his appeal—considered Trump's election a distant prospect. The *International Socialist Review*'s first postelection editorial noted:

> Very few of us on the left expected that the next president of the United States would be a corrupt, narcissistic billionaire swindler, an open sexist and self-confessed serial abuser, and a man the Far Right hails for his open racism and nationalist xenophobia. Donald Trump successfully positioned himself as a right-wing populist, anti-establishment candidate who would tear up free trade, deport immigrant "job-stealers," and restore good jobs for "real" Americans. And it worked.[1]

1

With this in mind, Haymarket Books decided to publish this reader. We've brought together contributions, written by socialists, on different aspects of US politics in this era of transition from Obama to Trump. Many of these texts appeared originally in publications such as *International Socialist Review, Jacobin, Dissent,* or *Catalyst.* Others are original to this volume. Although some of them were written or published after Trump's election, they generally do not speculate about the future course of a Trump administration. Instead, they attempt, as Trotsky once wrote, to "look reality in the face," in order to develop an understanding of what happened in 2016.

To be sure, each writer has a particular perspective on the election. And each emphasizes different points. And while the authors may not agree on each point, the collection develops general themes. One of these is the corrosive impact that forty years of free market policy and ideology, known as neoliberalism, has had on living standards and political imagination. Neoliberalism has devastated working-class lives and organizations, and narrowed mainstream political choices to liberal and right-wing populist versions of the same basic economic program.

Sharon Smith and Lance Selfa show how the Democratic Party's commitment to the neoliberal status quo, along with its own failure in government to address the real issues facing working-class Americans of all races and ethnicities, opened the door to Trump's right-wing populism. With the election seemingly offering a choice between a candidate who proclaimed that "America is already great" (Clinton) and one who—however disingenuously—promised to "make America great again," millions of voters opted for change. As Neil Davidson points out, this pattern, pitting what Nancy Fraser dubs "progressive neoliberalism" against right-wing populism, is a worldwide phenomenon, not just one observed in the United States.

Much postelection analysis and commentary focused on defining Trump's "base" as emanating from what the media and political professionals describe as the "white working class," a shorthand for "whites without four-year college degrees."[2] The contributions from Charlie Post, Mike Davis, Kim Moody, and Smith take up the question of the "white working class" from various angles. While it can't be denied that some layer of white workers—including people who had voted for Obama twice—voted for Trump, locating Trump's key support among white workers is sloppy and inaccurate. For one thing, as Davis shows, Trump's percentage of the white vote hardly differed from what Mitt Romney received in losing to Obama in 2012. Moreover, as Moody and Post point out, the population segment of "whites without a college degree" includes significant percentages of lower-level supervisors and small business owners who are normally thought of as the Republican rank-and-file. Plenty of analyses of the Trump vote suggest it represented more of a middle-class backlash than a working-class revolt, especially when one considers, as Smith does, the always-high level of working-class abstention in US elections.[3]

Another tendentious reading of the election—especially on the liberal side of the political spectrum—is the notion that the Democrats lost because they championed "identity politics," aimed at attracting groups of Blacks, Latinos, Muslims, women, and LGBTQ people, while eschewing a more inclusive "class" politics.[4] Most authors in this collection would disagree with this assessment. Other than projecting a kind of patina of "lean-in feminism" and the rhetoric of "diversity" common in Corporate America, Clinton and the Democrats have actually advanced—or acceded to—policies that have encouraged mass incarceration, the erosion of abortion rights, Islamophobia, and mass deportations.

Keeanga-Yamahtta Taylor's essay shows how "Obama's presidency was not a gift to African Americans; instead, it represented the painful continuity of racism, discrimination, and inequality that has always been at the center of Black life in America." Elizabeth Schulte contends that, while Trump and many of his Republican cohorts exude contempt for women, the Democrats' feeble attempt to pose themselves as the "lesser evil" on women's rights failed. The interviews with Deepa Kumar and Justin Akers Chacón remind us of how much the Obama and Bill Clinton administrations set in motion, or deepened, many of the policies that promote Islamophobia and "border security" and have now been placed in the xenophobic Trump administration's hands.

This brief introduction can't do full justice to the detailed and insightful analyses that each of the contributions collected here brings to an understanding of the 2016 election. These essays are offered with the knowledge that the social forces that drove the 2016 election remain with us still. For the left to build organizations and to project politics that can offer a real alternative to the working-class majority, we need to understand what these forces are.

Lance Selfa
October 2017

CHICKENS COMING HOME TO ROOST FOR THE DEMOCRATIC PARTY?

*How Neoliberalism Quietly Devastated
the US Working Class*

Sharon Smith

Amid the shock and horror following Donald Trump's election, mainstream news outlets all sounded the same alarm: white workers were getting their "revenge." Indeed, the headlines were stunningly similar. "How Trump Won: The Revenge of Working-Class Whites" (*Washington Post*);[1] "The Revenge of the White Man" (*Time*);[2] "Revenge of the Forgotten Class," (*ProPublica*);[3] "Revenge of the Rural Voter" (*Politico*);[4] "Why Trump Won: Working-Class Whites" (*New York Times*).[5]

In this way, the mainstream media created the postelection narrative, parroting Democratic Party leaders frantically seeking to blame someone (other than themselves) for Hillary Clinton's loss. They settled on the slice of white voters in key Midwestern swing states (Iowa, Wisconsin, Michigan, Pennsylvania, and Ohio) who voted for Trump. They labeled these voters "working class" based on the large number of Trump voters without a college degree—disregarding the fact that his supporters in the 2016 primaries earned an average of $72,000 per year, well above the median household income, indicating a solid middle-class component among Trump's core backers.[6]

Just weeks after the election, researchers Konstantin Kilibarda and Daria Roithmayr convincingly challenged the media's "blame the white working class" narrative. After studying the exit poll data in the Rust Belt swing states, they concluded, "Relative to the 2012 election, Democratic support in the Rust Belt collapsed as a huge number of Democrats stayed home or (to a lesser extent) voted for a third party. Trump did not really flip white, working-class voters in the Rust Belt. Mostly, Democrats lost them."[7] Voting analyst Nate Cohn reported that voter turnout fell significantly among people of color nationwide—and among Black residents in swing-state cities including Milwaukee, Cleveland, Detroit, and Philadelphia. In Detroit alone, turnout fell by 14 percent.[8]

Yet the blame game continued. Many Clinton supporters were openly contemptuous of the so-called white working class, also disparagingly labeled "low-information voters."[9] The *Daily Kos*, for example, reveled in its disdain: "Be Happy for Coal Miners Losing Their Health Insurance. They're Getting Exactly What They Voted For," its headline taunted.[10] On the other hand, some commentators criticized the Clinton campaign for purportedly front-loading "identity politics" (i.e., championing the rights of the oppressed)—speculating that this alienated white voters with "economic anxiety" who then had no choice but to reject Clinton and turn to Trump. Columbia University professor Mark Lilla put it perhaps the most crudely in the *New York Times*, claiming to "paraphrase" Bernie Sanders: "America is sick and tired of hearing about liberals' damn bathrooms," Lilla wrote.[11] (Fact check: Sanders declared his *support* for transgender bathroom rights in May 2016.)[12]

The mainstream debate thus counterposed "class" politics to so-called "identity" politics—as if combating class inequality and fighting racism, sexism, transphobia, and other forms of oppression are necessarily mutually exclusive. It also left hanging the issue of whether Clinton was a *genuine* fighter against oppression, or just cynically chasing the votes that her campaign mistakenly calculated could win her a majority in the Electoral College.

The working class is no longer (if it ever was) predominantly white and male, even though this remains the caricature. People of color will very soon become the majority in the US population, and are already close to 50 percent among younger generations.[13] Moreover, people of color have always been disproportionately represented within the working class and the poor, due to the economic consequences of racism. This demonstrates why combating oppression is (and always has been) a working-class issue, and will be vital to rebuilding a fighting class-based movement. Today's working class is multiracial, made up of multiple genders and nationalities, and many people with a variety of disabilities. While white male workers have suffered enormously in recent decades, Black people and other oppressed sectors of the working class have suffered yet more. There is no reason to counterpose their interests, when solidarity among all workers will advance the entire working class and all its oppressed members—if the movement champions the rights of all those who suffer oppression.

"Democrats for the Leisure Class"

Most in the media failed to ask the most important questions about the 2016 election before concluding that the white working class, especially in the "flyover country" of the Midwest, has become a bastion of reaction. How many of these same people voted for Obama four years earlier? Millions of them did, a fact the Clinton campaign discovered months before the November election. As Cohn described, "The [Clinton] campaign looked back to respondents who were contacted in 2012, and found large numbers of white working-class voters who had backed Mr. Obama were now supporting Mr. Trump."[14] It is also the case that self-described socialist Bernie Sanders experienced a groundswell of support in the Midwest during the 2016 primaries—winning the Michigan,

West Virginia, Indiana, and Wisconsin primaries—which all went to Trump in the general election.

The real story of the 2016 election is the sharp political polarization that allowed both Sanders and Trump to attract mass popular support during the primary season. The mainstream media, with its fleeting attention span, failed to appreciate this fact in its election postmortem. Although Sanders spoke from the left and Trump from the right, both candidates acknowledged the failures of the political status quo, which no other politicians had done for many decades. The centerpiece of Sanders's campaign message was that the Democratic Party establishment had sacrificed the interests of the working-class majority at the altar of its corporate donors. Trump succeeded in winning the nomination, but Sanders did not. Unfortunately, Sanders ran as a Democrat, but the party's powerbrokers had anointed Clinton as their neoliberal candidate from the beginning. There is no way to know what a Sanders vs. Trump contest would have produced, but it is very possible that Sanders would have energized Democratic voters in ways that Clinton could not in the general election.

The 2016 election elevated voting for "the lesser of two evils" to a new level, as Clinton and Trump were the two most unpopular candidates in recent decades—and undoubtedly many voters and nonvoters alike considered the election as a choice of which road to take to hell. The Clinton campaign's high-tech computer models couldn't motivate people to get to the polls on Election Day in what were once Democratic Party strongholds. The 2016 election merely highlighted how the Democrats had frittered away their traditional voting base over a period of decades—taking their votes for granted yet offering less than nothing in return, even as working-class living standards plummeted in the wake of the 2008 financial crisis.

As it happens, Bill and Hillary Clinton were among the key architects of the Democratic Party's open embrace of neoliberalism, beginning in 1985 with the founding of the Democratic Leadership Council (DLC), shifting the party and its loyalists steadily rightward in the process. The Rev. Jesse Jackson once called the DLC

"Democrats for the Leisure Class," and with good reason: its board of trustees, made up of major donors, included Koch Industries, Aetna, and Coca-Cola, while its executive board included Enron, AIG, Texaco, Chevron, and AT&T, among other corporate giants. The DLC spawned a generation of "New Democrats," to carry out its mission—reshaping the Democratic Party as (more openly) pro-business and much less liberal. As Robert Dreyfuss described in *The American Prospect,* "The DLC thundered against the 'liberal fundamentalism' of the party's base—unionists, blacks, feminists, Greens, and cause groups generally."[15] The DLC closed its doors in 2011, on the verge of bankruptcy, but it had already succeeded in its mission. The Clinton Foundation acquired its records, in a fitting conclusion.

The New Democrats had assumed that they could maintain the party's voting base by offering a "Republican-lite" alternative as the "lesser evil" at the voting booth. But, as the decades passed, the Democrats' voting base gradually hollowed out among those whose suffering steadily worsened, especially among young people with bleak futures—who also had no reason to be loyal to the Democrats. Many "low information voters" were very much aware that mainstream Democrats had turned their backs on them in search of a well-educated and higher-income constituency.

Together, the Clintons personify neoliberalism and its path of destruction for workers. In his 1996 State of the Union Address, Bill Clinton stole the Republican Party's thunder, declaring, "The era of big government is over." Reagan had invented the racist myth of the "welfare queen," but it was Bill Clinton who ended "welfare as we know it." He also oversaw the mass incarceration of Black and Latino nonviolent drug offenders in the name of the racist "War on Drugs"—while Hillary Clinton demonized young Black men with the racially charged term *super-predator* to bolster her husband's efforts. Trump called for building a one-thousand-mile wall at the Mexican border, but Bill Clinton had already built a three-hundred-mile security "smart fence" in the 1990s, and both Hillary Clinton and Barack Obama voted for a seven-hundred-mile fence in 2006 when they were in the Senate.

Hillary Clinton voted in favor of the PATRIOT Act, which enabled the massive roundup and deportation of Arabs and Muslims after 9/11 but did not generate a single charge of terrorism. Throughout her political career, she has without exception strongly supported US military intervention abroad, including the invasions of Iraq and Afghanistan, still wreaking death and destruction in those countries with no end in sight. Indeed, just hours before the Trump administration announced it had launched fifty-nine cruise missiles on a Syrian airfield on April 6, 2017, Clinton had argued that the United States "should take out [Assad's] air fields."[16]

Surely, many would-be Democratic voters viewed Hillary Clinton with skepticism in 2016, since the Clintons' record is well known. Perhaps her scripted commitment to Black Lives Matter activists seemed both insincere and hypocritical, as did her support for immigrants' rights. The hundreds of thousands of dollars she earned giving speeches to Goldman Sachs and other Wall Street vultures could not have sat well with those who lost their homes and jobs during the financial crisis while those same bankers got bailed out.

Clinton demonstrated just how out of touch she was with the working-class and once solidly Democratic base when she announced at a West Virginia campaign stop that she planned to "put a lot of coal miners and coal companies out of business"—without offering new training or help finding new jobs for those coal miners who would be displaced.[17] Her clueless comment sounded very much like Republican Mitt Romney's call in 2008 to "let Detroit go bankrupt" without regard to the mass unemployment such bankruptcy would cause.[18] As Cohn observed, "In retrospect, the scale of the Democratic collapse in coal country was a harbinger of just how far the Democrats would fall in their old strongholds once they forfeited the mantle of working-class interests."[19]

Nature abhors a vacuum, the old saying goes. The same dictum holds true in politics, and a left—or even a genuinely liberal—flank has been missing in mainstream US politics for decades, in large part because of the rightward shift of the Democratic Party helmed by the Clintons. Once Sanders was out of the picture and Clinton became the Democratic Party candidate in 2016, the vacuum was filled by Trump among millions who could not stomach to vote for another Clinton. As left-wing author Christian Parenti observed after watching many hours of Trump's speeches, "Contrary to how he was portrayed in the mainstream media, Trump did not talk only of walls, immigration bans, and deportations. In fact, he usually didn't spend much time on those themes." Mainly, Trump talked about bringing lost jobs back.[20]

There is no doubt that Trump fed the racism and sexism that already exists among large swathes of the white population, but he was also addressing the burning issue that Clinton ignored: the economic hardship of the working class, which has accelerated since the economic recovery began in earnest in 2010. Both these factors undoubtedly played a role in Trump's popularity. But it is also the case that roughly 28 percent of Latino and 27 percent of Asian votes went to Trump, according to exit polls.[21] Within the confines of the two-party system, voters are not given the opportunity to vote for their ideal candidate, but rather must settle for the one they perceive as the least harmful.

Clinton did, of course, win the popular vote by nearly three million yet lost the election. Only sixteen years earlier, Al Gore won the popular vote by roughly five hundred thousand, yet George W. Bush was elected president. The Electoral College in the so-called "world's greatest democracy" is inherently undemocratic. It is a holdover from slavery, originally designed to give disproportionate weight to Southern slave states in elections. It is no coincidence that the Constitutional Convention of 1787 that formed the Electoral College also determined that slaves (denied the right to vote) would be counted as three-fifths of a person for the sole purpose of inflating the representation of slaveholders.[22]

Why Nonvoters Matter

Yet, even after her surprise loss, Clinton accepted the results without questioning the legitimacy of the Electoral College, speaking volumes about the Party's commitment to preserving the political and social status quo that ultimately benefits both major parties, even when they lose elections. That status quo includes the power-sharing arrangement between the Democratic and Republican Parties, devised to prevent third parties from gaining a toehold. Voters unhappy with the state of politics are therefore given no other choice than to "kick the bums out"—only to replace them with the "bums" from the other party. The two-party system and its limited choices go a long way toward explaining why voters are used to backing candidates with whom they disagree on many issues, often as a vote against the other candidate. Perhaps for this reason, voter turnout in the United States is historically low overall.

Instead of focusing their discourse around white voters in swing states who voted for Trump, the media should have paid closer attention to the many millions of people who did not vote— *who far outnumber those who voted for either party in 2016, and as a group tend to hold more liberal views than the rest of the population.* This would give a much more accurate sense of the political leanings of the US population.

Voter turnout is strongly correlated to class position—extremely high among the wealthiest Americans and falling steadily as incomes decline. Policy analyst Sean McElwee showed that fewer than half of those with incomes of $20,000 or less voted in 2012, while those from households earning more than $75,000 voted at a rate of 77 percent.[23] In 2008, fully 99 percent of those in the top 1 and 0.1 percent of incomes voted. As he summarized, "Since the end of World War II, voter turnout has never risen above 65 percent of the electorate. Disproportionately, these non-voting citizens are low-income, young, less educated, and people of color."[24]

It is also worth bearing in mind (which mainstream commentators most often do not) the large number of voting-age people not allowed to vote, who are overwhelmingly poor and disproportionately made up of Black people and other people of color. The poor make up 55 percent of those who are not allowed to vote in presidential elections.[25] Fully four million people who are technically US citizens are excluded from representation by the Electoral College because they live in US territories, including Puerto Rico, which are ruled by the US government but denied the right to vote for president.[26] In addition, a total of 6.1 million Americans are barred from voting because of a prior felony conviction. One in every thirteen African Americans have lost their voting rights for this reason.[27] The 2016 election was also the first since the Supreme Court struck down key protections of the Voting Rights Act, leading to a surge in voting restrictions, including voter ID requirements, that have been shown to depress the votes of Black, Latino, poor, and transgender people.

In 2014, McElwee documented why those who have the right to vote decide not to do so—and this large sector of society leans left of the political mainstream. There are many reasons why low-income people face practical difficulties in exercising this legal right, including difficulty in getting time off work, childcare responsibilities, lack of transportation, and long waiting lines, among other reasons. But 41 percent of nonvoters also said, "My vote doesn't make a difference anyway," while 59 percent said, "Nothing ever gets done; it's a bunch of empty promises."[28] Likewise, the Rev. Charles Williams, pastor of King Solomon Baptist Church in Detroit and president of the National Action Network of Michigan, said that in 2016, especially among "young people and millennials," he heard, "I feel like I'm just voting for the lesser of two evils. That doesn't give you the push to vote."[29]

But McElwee's findings also confirmed that nonvoters tend to be more liberal than voters—favoring in much larger numbers policies that "make union organizing easier" and provide "more federal assistance for schools," and agreeing that "government should guarantee jobs" and "government should provide health insurance." And "while likely voters in the 2012 presidential election split 47 percent in favor of Obama and 47 percent in favor of Romney, 59 percent of nonvoters supported Obama and only 24 percent supported Romney."[30]

When the pro-Clinton super PAC Priorities USA surveyed Obama voters who switched to Trump, along with those who abstained from voting in 2016, it reported in May 2017 that Hillary

Clinton had "a Wall Street problem," and she was completely out of touch with the economic problems ordinary people faced. As the *Washington Post* reported, "A shockingly large percentage of these Obama-Trump voters said Democrats' economic policies will favor the wealthy—twice the percentage that said the same about Trump," while 53 percent said their vote was "more a vote against Clinton" than a vote for Trump. The pollsters concluded that "drop-off voters are decidedly anti-Trump," describing former Obama voters who didn't make it to the polls on Election Day.[31] Obama, soon after leaving office, accepted a fee of $400,000 for a single speaking engagement with Wall Street's Cantor Fitzgerald, underlining the Democrats' problem with ordinary people.

The Wreckage of Neoliberalism

The United States is strewn with the wreckage of neoliberalism, its landscape dotted with once-thriving communities built around manufacturing jobs where Walmart is now the biggest employer, setting the low standard for local wages. Well before Trump ever ran for president, the scale of class inequality in the United States was already the worst in the industrialized world. The *Allianz Global Wealth Report 2015*, using figures from 2014, reported that the United States possessed a larger amount of personal wealth than any other country, at 41.6 percent of the global wealth total. At the same time, the report found that the United States also had the largest concentration of overall wealth in the hands of the proportionately fewest people, leading it to call the United States "the Unequal States of America."[32]

In January 2017, the British business magazine the *Economist* reported that its Intelligence Unit, the research and analysis division of the *Economist* group, had downgraded the United States from a "full democracy" to a "flawed democracy"—based on low voter turnout, the degree of distrust that the population holds toward government institutions, and the high level of class inequality. "Popular trust in government, elected representatives, and political parties has fallen to extremely low levels in the US. This has been a long-term trend and one that preceded the election of Mr. Trump as the US president in November 2016," stated the report. It added, "[Trump] appealed to the angry, anti-political mood of large swathes of the electorate who feel that the two mainstream parties no longer speak for them."[33]

The neoliberal project over the last forty years has been entirely bipartisan, continuing unabated no matter which party occupied the White House. And both Hillary and Bill Clinton, alongside Republicans, played a major role in implementing it. The US ruling class began what was then called the "employers' offensive" in the mid-1970s, before anyone had coined the term *neoliberalism* to describe it. In 1974, *Business Week* put forward the corporate class's plan to shift the balance of class forces decisively in its favor: "It will be a hard pill for many Americans to swallow—the idea of doing with less so that big business can have more. Nothing that this nation, or any other nation, has done in modern economic history compares in difficulty with the selling job that must now be done to make people accept the new reality."[34]

That new reality was straightforward, thanks to a coalition of Democrats and Republicans in Congress: a green light for union-busting, corporate deregulation, regressive taxation, and so-called globalization—allowing capital to cross national borders unrestrained in the search for low-wage labor and maximum profits around the world. Meanwhile, the global working class was yet more tightly controlled when attempting to migrate through borders, whether these migrants were fleeing from war, poverty, and hunger or from violent dictators. The neoliberal agenda forced workers on a global scale yet more directly in competition with each other, in a race to the bottom.

Employers have always threatened to relocate their companies elsewhere as a tactic to keep workers from organizing unions and demanding higher wages. Throughout much of the twentieth century, this usually pitted workers in the northern United States against those in the nonunion southern part of the country. Neoliberal globalization extended this competition among workers far beyond US borders, as capitalists scoured the world in search of the cheapest wages and operating costs to maximize profits. Thus, the textile industry moved most of its operations to the southern United States by the mid-twentieth century, only to relocate to the Global South in the 1990s and 2000s.

Free trade agreements like NAFTA came to symbolize neo-liberalism's assault on the US working class, but they were just one part of its multipronged attack. And while outsourcing US jobs, especially to China, certainly played a role in the downward spiral of US wages, it's also true that increasing technology and automation allowed manufacturers to maintain and even increase output with far fewer workers. As labor activist and scholar Kim Moody argued:

> A more likely explanation for manufacturing job losses on the scale of the last thirty years or so, one that is internal to the workings of US capitalism and, indeed, capitalism generally, is to be found in the rise of productivity extracted after 1980 by the introduction of lean production methods, new technology, and capital's accelerated counteroffensive against labor—*an explanation based in class conflict itself* [emphasis added].[35]

But one of the most important goals of neoliberalism was simply crushing working-class organizations that could fight against lower wages. When Ronald Reagan took office in 1981, one of his first presidential actions was firing the striking members of the Professional Air Traffic Controllers' Organization (PATCO), crushing the strike and destroying the union—a union that had endorsed his campaign—and sharply escalating the employers' offensive. After that, employers were given free reign to force their workers to "give back" hard-earned wages and benefits during contract negotiations and to break unions by hiring professional union-busting firms, even when profits were high. It is not a coincidence that strike levels dropped significantly during the 1980s, falling steadily ever since. In February 2017, the Bureau of Labor Statistics reported that work stoppages over the last decade have been the lowest on record, noting that the "average number of major work stoppages by decade has declined over 95 percent since 1947."[36]

Amid this one-sided class war, union membership also fell sharply, from 20.1 percent in 1983 to 10.7 percent overall in 2016, and just 6.4 percent in the private sector, a level comparable to that before the labor upheaval of 1930s won the legal right to organize unions.[37] As of 2014, only 7.4 percent of young workers aged eighteen to twenty-nine were members of unions, even though 55 percent of them viewed unions favorably.[38]

Indeed, the war on unions escalated over the last decade, as Republican-dominated state legislatures went on an antiunion rampage in the Midwest, passing a wave of "right to work" laws that allow nonunion workers to withhold union dues even when they benefit from union contracts. Once a hallmark of the antiunion, low-wage South, twenty-eight states had adopted "right to work" by February 2017—including the Midwestern states of Indiana, Michigan, Wisconsin, West Virginia, Kentucky, and Missouri—with no end in sight.

The *Real State* of the US Working Class

The US working class was the highest paid in the world during the postwar economic boom, but its wages entered a downward spiral in the mid-1970s. Today it is the lowest paid among OECD countries, with the greatest proportion of low-wage jobs, defined as paying less than two-thirds of the nation's median income. Twenty-six percent of jobs in the United States fell into this category, earning less than $23,390 in the OECD's 2014 report.[39]

While most media reports have described US wages as "stagnating" over recent decades, the reality is far worse. Most middle-income earners have fallen off the face of the map, either advancing into the upper income tier or, more likely for the working- and lower-middle class, joining lower-income earners.[40] In addition, examining wages and incomes tells not even half the story about individuals in the lower-income tier, because so many more workers have joined that tier as the category of middle-income earners has hollowed out.

Far from its ostensibly "free market" ideology, neoliberalism has produced government austerity for the working class combined with economic welfare for the corporate class. This policy has taken many forms that have severely eroded working-class living standards, including regressive taxes (such as increased sales taxes); cuts in emergency heating and food-stamp subsidies; higher fees for everything from traffic tickets to public transportation; rising premiums and deductibles for health insurance coverage; higher rents; unaffordable childcare costs—among other expenses built into everyday life. Almost none of these is adequately incorporated into mainstream media analyses of the class divide.

The political establishment perhaps believed that shielding this reality from mainstream discourse would fool those suffering because of these policies. "Poverty Goes Down, Coverage Goes Up, and America Gets a Raise," announced MSNBC on September 13, 2016, about the Census Bureau finding that not only did all US incomes rise in the previous year, but incomes also grew the fastest for the poorest people.[41] We must ask whether this cheerful announcement fooled those workers whose lives have been turned upside down in recent decades. Even by the Census Bureau's own measurement, in 2015 median household income (which is the level at which 50 percent of the population makes more and the other 50 percent makes less) was lower than in 2007, and lower still than the all-time high in 1999. Further examination also reveals that people in rural areas didn't share in the increase, but rather experienced a 2 percent *decrease* in median income in 2015—which fell to just $44,657 for these households, far below the national median.

The Census Bureau generalizations about median income dramatically downplayed the deep concentrations of poverty that exist across the country. For example, North Dakota had the nation's biggest drop in child poverty between 2011 and 2016, but the poverty rate for Native American children, the majority living on reservations, is five times higher than for the rest of the state's children.[42] Likewise, buried within a *Detroit Free Press* article headlined "Michigan Posts Its Largest Income Gain since the Recession" is the admission that the majority Black cities of Flint and Detroit continue to have some of the highest poverty rates in the United States, at 40.8 percent and 39.8 percent, respectively. The child poverty rate is even higher—more than half of the children who lived in Detroit and Flint in 2015 lived in poverty, at a rate of 57.6 percent and 58.3 percent, respectively.[43]

The Census Bureau figures also ignore the enormous income disparities, often along racial lines, *within* individual cities. According to the Census Bureau, Washington, DC's median household income rose to $75,600 in 2015, but that breaks down to $120,000 for white households compared to just $41,000 for Black households. The poverty rate for the city's Black population is 27 percent—and 75 percent of all D.C. residents living in poverty are Black.[44]

There is yet another way that the Census Bureau's poverty statistics skew lower while its median income figures skew higher. In the introduction to its Current Population Survey, the Bureau makes the following caveat about its "sample" population: "People in institutions, such as prisons, long-term care hospitals, and nursing homes, are not eligible to be interviewed in the CPS. . . . People who are homeless and not living in shelters are not included in the sample." The list of those excluded from the survey thus includes millions of the most impoverished people in the United States. Despite the flaws in the Census Bureau's findings, they still show roughly one in four African Americans and Native Americans and more than one in five Latinos living under the official poverty line. One in five children overall are living in poverty by official standards, and 10 percent of US households are trying to survive on less than $13,300 a year.

But the most glaring problem with the Census Bureau's methodology is its appallingly low poverty threshold. If the poverty line were scaled upward to a more accurate level, the official poverty rate of the US population would certainly skyrocket statistically. The Social Security Administration developed the current poverty measure back in 1963, adopting a formula based on the minimum amount of money necessary to buy a subsistence level of food, using data from the 1955 Household Food Consumption Survey. On the assumption that food expenditures made up one-third of what a family of four needed to survive at the time, that amount was then multiplied by three to define the poverty line. This definition, using obsolete fifty-year-old consumption patterns and even more antiquated sixty-year-old prices (adjusted annually based on the consumer price index), is still in use today. If that formula (food expenses times three) was ever adequate for survival—and it most certainly wasn't in the era of Eisenhower—it is completely preposterous today. In 2015, the poverty threshold was set at just at $24,250 for a family of four and $11,770 for an individual. Even the Census Bureau recognizes some of the shortcomings of its formula. Since 2010, it has issued a "Supplemental Poverty Measure," adding income from sources such as Social Security, tax credits, and food stamps, while subtracting some expenses, such as work costs, medical care, and child-support payments. While those cloistered in the bubble of the federal bureaucracy seem to find its poverty threshold adequate for survival, anyone with at least one foot in the real world is aware that no family of four can make ends meet on $24,250 a year. Just as every household needs a budget measuring its income in relation to expenses, we should examine the actual cost of just a few major household necessities to give a cursory sense of whether that 5.2 percent rise in median household income in 2015 actually made a dent in falling working-class living standards:

Rent: According to Apartmentlist.com, using Census data from 1960 to 2014, median rent has risen by 64 percent after adjusting for inflation, while real household income only increased by 18 percent. Between 2000 and 2010, rents rose by 18 percent while household income fell by 7 percent.[45] As Apartmentlist.com concluded, "As a result, the share of cost-burdened renters [households spending more than one-third of their income on rent] nationwide more than doubled, from 24 percent in 1960 to 49 percent in 2014."

Childcare: The cost of childcare has nearly doubled since the 1980s—yet it is not considered a necessary household expenditure, even though 75 percent of mothers with children six to seventeen years old are in the labor force, as are 61 percent of mothers with children under three years old. In 2015, the average childcare cost rose to over $143 a week. As a result, fewer working parents can afford to pay for it. Those who cannot end up keeping children with relatives or trading off childcare shifts with a working co-parent, if there is one.[46] Whereas 42 percent of parents paid for child care in 1997, only 32 percent did so by 2011. *The poorest families spend the largest proportion—one-third of their income—on child care.*

Healthcare: The Supplemental Poverty Measure for 2015 showed that with medical expenses—including insurance premiums, copays, coinsurance, prescription drug costs, and other uncovered medical expenses—factored in, 11.2 million (or 3.5 percent) more people are living in poverty than the Census Bureau's Current Population Survey acknowledges. And we can expect the next survey's statistics to be even worse, as employers continue to push more insurance costs onto their employees. More and more employers are turning to plans with higher copays and so-called high-deductible plans, offering premiums workers can barely afford and deductibles of $1,000 or much more—meaning workers must pay these amounts before insurance kicks in even a penny toward their medical care. In 2016, *deductibles alone rose nearly six times faster than wages*, according to the 2016 Employer Health Benefits Survey of the Kaiser Family Foundation. According to the Commonwealth Fund, higher-deductible plans on average cost $5,762 for individuals and $16,737 for families.[47]

A Downward Spiral

A Georgetown University study on job creation showed that workers with a high school diploma or less lost the most income during the recovery, as more jobs go to those with at least some postsecondary education—likely reflecting a glut of "over-educated" applicants for low wage jobs. "Of the 7.2 million jobs lost in the recession," the Georgetown study states, "5.6 million were jobs for workers with a high school diploma or less. . . . On net, there are now more than 5.5 million fewer jobs for individuals with a high school education or less than there were in December 2007."[48] This downward trend began well before the Great Recession. A report by the Hamilton Project of the Brookings Institution found that between 1990 and 2003, *real median wages had already fallen by 20 percent for male workers without a high school diploma age thirty to forty-five*, and by 12 percent for women in the same category. As the *New York Times*, citing the report, concluded: "Less-educated Americans, especially men, are shifting away from manufacturing and other jobs that once offered higher pay, and a higher share are now working in lower-paying food service, cleaning, and groundskeeping jobs."[49]

But this decline in wages is tied to more than the decline in manufacturing jobs. As the *Times* article added, "Pay levels are declining in almost all of the fields that employ less-educated workers, so even those who have held onto jobs as manufacturers, operators and laborers are making less than they would have a generation ago." Inflation-adjusted annual pay for manufacturing jobs *fell from $33,600 in 1990 to $28,000 in 2013*. The greatest damage from neoliberalism was done early on, from the late 1970s through the early 1990s.[50] The average real hourly wages of production and nonsupervisory workers fell by 15 percent between 1973 and the mid-1990s, lowering the ceiling for working-class wages ever since. Wages briefly rose during the economic boom of the late 1990s— only to be derailed by the early 2000s when wages began to stagnate again. The Great Recession once again accelerated the decline.

The Trump administration will undoubtedly further immiserate the working class, given the opportunity. But the "out of touch" Democratic Party establishment does not offer a viable alternative to the class and social status quo, in which it has embedded itself. It is unfortunate that Sanders chose to run as a Democratic Party candidate when the party establishment ruled him out from the beginning, in favor of its anointed neoliberal candidate. Meanwhile, the working class is desperately seeking a voice in electoral politics. The only way the working class can advance in this dire situation is to rebuild its fighting tradition, the same tradition that built unions from the ground up in the 1930s. It worked then, and it is the only way forward today.

WE GOT TRUMPED!

Charlie Post

O n the night of November 8, 2016, I boarded a flight to London, on my way to the annual *Historical Materialism* conference. As the plane took off at 7:30 p.m., the polls across the United States were still open. I was confident that, when I arrived in London the next morning, Hillary Clinton would have been declared the president-elect of the United States. I believed that not only would Donald Trump be defeated, but that the Democrats might regain their majority in the Senate. Only three weeks before, I had predicted that Trump's middle-class, right-wing populist insurgency, which had temporarily captured the main party of capital in the United States, would go down in flames.[1]

Clinton was the clear favorite of the US capitalist class, who were repelled by Trump's nationalist hostility to neoliberal trade policies and the system of imperialist military-diplomatic alliances that guarantee US world domination, and his threats to deport all undocumented immigrants. According to the Center for Responsive Politics, Clinton received over 92 percent of corporate contributions in the 2016 election cycle, including over 80 percent

---

This essay first appeared in the Spring 2017 issue of the *International Socialist Review*. It was updated on March 14, 2017, and does not reflect developments since that date.

of the contributions from finance, insurance, and real estate; communications/electronics; healthcare, defense, and "miscellaneous business." Trump's support was limited to 60 to 70 percent of contributions from construction, energy, and natural resources, transportation, and agribusiness—which together accounted for less than 10 percent of total capitalist donations.[2] With such a huge war chest, I expected the Democrats to build a "get out the vote" machine across the United States that would deliver a victory for its unpopular candidate.

When the plane landed on the morning of November 9 and I turned on my phone, I was greeted by the unexpected—Trump had been declared the winner of the 2016 presidential election and the Republicans had maintained their majorities in both the House and Senate. The media had declared Trump's victory a "landslide," with his win of 304 Electoral College delegates, compared with Clinton's 227. The revolt of the "white working class" in the former industrial Midwest and Great Lakes region was credited for Trump's sweep.

What Really Happened?

I was not alone in my failure to foresee a Trump victory. Most of the political commentators in the United States and globally, based on preelection polling, had predicted a Clinton victory. How do we explain this unexpected turn of events?

First, we cannot overlook the fact that Clinton won the *majority of the popular vote*. She led Trump by approximately 2.9 million votes. If the United States had *direct election* of the president, Clinton would have been on her way to the White House. However, the Electoral College—created by slave owners and merchant bankers to prevent challenges to their class rule—allowed a popular *minority* to elect the President. As in many elections in the past forty years, *extremely small changes* in the participation and preferences of *minuscule portions* of the US electorate produced a sharp swing in electoral votes and the continued Republican majority in Congress.

While it initially appeared that voter participation rates dropped in 2016,[3] as paper ballots were counted, voter participation came within 1 percent of 2012 rates.[4] Clinton's vote was still about one million below Obama's last election. More importantly, voter participation among traditionally Democratic segments of the electorate fell.[5] African Americans dropped from 13 percent of all voters in 2008 and 2012 to 12 percent in 2016. In some predominantly African American communities, the drop was even more precipitous. In Milwaukee's Council District 15, which is 84 percent Black, voter turnout was nearly 20 percent lower than in 2012.[6] Households earning less than $50,000 per year, who made up 51 percent of the US population in 2014,[7] dropped from 41 percent of voters in 2012 to 36 percent in 2016. The percentage of households earning over $100,000, a mere 17 percent of the population, rose from 28 percent to 33 percent of voters between 2012 and 2016. Put simply, the electorate in 2016 was ever more disproportionately well-off than in the last three elections.

Within these key categories, there were also small, but significant, shifts in voter preference. While 60 percent of voters in households earning less than $50,000 a year voted for Obama in 2008 and 2012, Clinton's share of these voters dropped to 52 percent. Clinton only won 88 percent of the Black vote, down from 95 percent and 93 percent for Obama in 2008 and 2012. Especially alarming for the Democrats was their falling share of the Latino vote. Democratic pollsters had been confident that Trump's racist diatribes would allow Clinton to sweep this key sector. However, the Democrats' share of the Latino vote declined from 71 percent in 2012 to 65 percent in 2016. Finally, the percentage of union households voting Democratic fell from 58 percent in 2008 and 59 percent in 2012 to a mere 51 percent in 2016.

Trump's ability to retain the core sectors of the Republicans' voter base since 1980—primarily the traditional (self-employed and small businesses with less than ten employees) and new (professionals, managers, supervisors) middle classes, including evangelical Christians; and a minority of older, white workers—was clear in all the exit polling. However, Trump's margin of victory—greatly exaggerated in the fun-house mirror of the Electoral College—came from a tiny group of voters who had supported Obama in 2008 and 2012.[8] Of the 700 counties that had voted for Obama twice, nearly one-third (209) swung to Trump; and of 207 counties that Obama won once, almost 94 percent (194) went to Trump. The swing to Trump was concentrated in traditionally Democratic states of the Great Lakes and Midwest that had suffered the loss of manufacturing jobs and experienced a rise in the Latino population. However, Trump's victory was primarily a result of a sharp drop in the participation of traditionally Democratic voters, rather than a sharp swing to Trump. Trump did gain approximately 335,000 more votes than Romney among households earning less than $50,000 per year in Iowa, Michigan, Ohio, Pennsylvania, and Wisconsin. However, Clinton received *1.7 million* fewer votes than Obama among the same group.[9] It was these minuscule shifts in voter preference and participation that gave Trump his razor-thin margins in a number of key states: less than 0.25 percent in Michigan, less than 1 percent in Pennsylvania and Wisconsin, and less than 1.5 percent in Florida. According to one analysis, had about one hundred thousand Trump voters in these areas voted for Clinton instead, she would have swept the Electoral College.[10]

Put simply, Trump did not so much *win* the 2016 election, as Hillary Clinton *lost* it. Despite her enormous campaign treasury, Clinton did not build a "get out the vote" operation to mobilize traditional Democratic constituencies—African Americans, Latinos, and working-class households.[11] Instead, the Clinton campaign took these groups for granted, believing that they would have little or no choice but to turn out to defeat Trump. Time, funds, and energy were focused on "socially liberal" suburban, new middle-class professionals and managers. At a *Washington Post* symposium in July 2016, Chuck Schumer, the neoliberal Democratic senator from New York, was quite clear: "For every blue-collar Democrat we lose in western Pennsylvania, we will pick up two moderate Republicans in the suburbs in Philadelphia, and you can repeat that in Ohio and Illinois and Wisconsin."[12] Rather than knocking on doors in working-class and minority communities, and making a pretense of supporting the sort of social democratic policies championed by Sanders, the Clinton campaign targeted upper-middle-class suburbs, allowing her to win substantially more votes than Obama among households earning over $100,000.[13] Traditionally Democratic working-class voters were faced with the choice between a neoliberal who disdained working people and a right-wing populist who promised to bring back well-paying manufacturing jobs. Many stayed home and a tiny minority shifted their allegiances from the first African American president to an open racist and xenophobe.

The Social Foundations of Trumpism

The core of Trump's support, like that of Tea Party since 2009, is the older, white, suburban/exurban middle classes.[14] His success among non-college-educated whites—he won 52 percent of all voters without bachelor's degrees—appears to be concentrated among traditional small-business people (construction contractors, small shop keepers, etc.) and those supervisors (factory foreman, store and office managers, etc.) and semi-professionals (technicians, etc.) who do not require a college education. His success among households earning over $75,000 a year reflects the support of the managerial and professional elite of this class. Put another way, Trump's social base is that of the Republican Party since 1980—politically and socially conservative, older, white middle-class voters. However, the politics of these groups have *radicalized* since the economic crisis of 2008.

Prior to 2008, hostility to the democratic gains of racial minorities, women, and LGBTQ folks animated the hearts and minds of Republican voters. For most of the past four decades, these voters were willing to settle for symbolic concessions on these issues (restrictions, but not a legal ban on abortions; limiting access to contraception; local anti-LGBTQ ordinances) while loyally supporting the neoliberal agenda of the mainstream Republicans—those who traditionally represented the majority of capitalists in the United States.

The 2008 recession radicalized this base, leading them to challenge key components of the Republican establishment's agenda. Faced with declining living standards and the possibilities of downward social mobility into the working class,[15] the Tea Party, and later the Trump campaign, put forward a distinctively *populist* political and economic agenda. The new middle-class right wanted the wholesale deportation of undocumented immigrants, threatening the supply of cheap and vulnerable workers capitalists in agriculture, large-scale construction, garment, and other industries depend upon. They opposed the pro-corporate immigration reform proposals that would institute a permanent guest-worker program in the United States and offer a circuitous "path to citizenship" for the undocumented. The Tea Party was also willing to shut down the federal government—threatening the US public debt and the entire global financial system—to achieve their goals, alienating the major organizations of the capitalist class, the Business Roundtable and the US Chamber of Commerce.

While the Chamber helped defeat a majority of Tea Party supporters in the 2014 Republican congressional primaries, their middle-class supporters radicalized further in 2016. Not only were traditionally Evangelical Christian voters willing to support a thrice-divorced, profane billionaire who routinely made jokes about his penis size, but they rejected key elements of neoliberal economic and political policies for a *populist* nationalism. No significant segment of the capitalist class in the United States wants to dismantle the North American Free Trade Agreement or slap prohibitive tariffs on Chinese imports.[16] Nor is there a substantial group of capitalists willing to threaten the existing system of military and diplomatic alliances (NATO, alliances with conservative Arab and Muslim regimes, etc.) in favor of an "America First" foreign policy. It is the radicalized middle-class supporters of Trump who have embraced economic protectionism and diplomatic isolationism.[17] Caught between a decimated labor movement and an extremely aggressive capitalist class, parts of the middle classes globally have been drawn to a politics that scapegoat immigrants, unions, women, LGBTQ people, and people of color, fueling the growth of Trumpism in the United States, as well as the United Kingdom Independence Party, French National Front, Italian Five Star Movement, and similar formations across Europe.[18]

Recent sociological studies demonstrate how populist nationalism, with its deadly mixture of antielitism, racism, sexism, and homophobia, has provided a "mental road map of lived experience" for the middle classes since 2008. Theda Skocpol and Vanessa Williamson in *The Tea Party and the Remaking of Republican Conservatism* point to growing economic and social anxiety among the older, white middle classes, who see undocumented immigrants as threats to their "quality of life" and competitors for scarce social services, particularly Social Security pensions and Medicare.[19] Mass deportations and denying the undocumented any path to citizenship (and access to social services), combined with lower federal deficits, would protect the "earned" social benefits (Social Security, Medicare) upon which they rely. Arlie Russell Hochschild's *Strangers in Their Own Land* portrays people who believe they are "hard workers" who "play by the rules" and never ask for "handouts" (e.g., government subsidies) but are constantly falling behind socially and economically.[20] They are threatened both by powerful economic and social elites and "line jumpers"—undocumented immigrants, refugees, and African Americans, Latinos, and women who benefit from affirmative action.

The Marxist left has a rich analysis of the attraction of the middle classes—what Trotsky described as the "human dust"—to right-wing populist demagogues. Caught between the fundamental social classes, capitalists and workers, the middle classes are attracted to political "strongmen" who promise to defend the "little man" against the forces that squeeze them from above and below. However, the socialist left has had a more difficult time explaining the support of a minority of workers for right-wing politics. Why have approximately 40 percent of union households supported Republicans or other right-wing candidates (e.g., Ross Perot in 1992) in most of the elections since 1980?[21] Why did another, minute group of white, working-class voters embrace the nationalist populism of Trump?

For many on the left, working-class support for the right is some form of "false consciousness"—a mistaken identification of their own interests with those of their bosses as the result of capital's control of the means of ideological production (press, media, etc.) For others, working-class racism and sexism is the defense of some form of racial or gender "privilege" against threats from below. Both of these explanations are inadequate. "False consciousness" makes capital and its ideologists all-powerful, and portrays workers as passive consumers of capitalist ideologies. Simplistic notions of "defense of privilege" ignore the increasing precarity *all* workers face today.

Grasping the contradictory character of capitalist social relations of production allows us to explain the attraction of some workers to right-wing politics. The objective, structural position of workers under capitalism provides the basis for *both* collective, solidaristic radicalism *and* individualist, sectoralist, and reactionary politics. As Bob Brenner and Johanna Brenner pointed out in their 1981 analysis of Reagan's election,

> workers are not only *collective producers* with a common interest in taking collective control over social production. They are also *individual sellers of labor power* in conflict with each other over jobs, promotions, etc. This individualistic point of view has a critical advantage in the current period: in the absence of class against class organization, it seems to provide an alternative strategy for effective action—a sectionalist strategy which pits one layer of workers against another.[22]

As competing sellers of labor power, workers are open to the appeal of politics that pit them against other workers—especially workers in a weaker social position. Without the lived experience of mass, collective, and successful class organization and struggle, it should not surprise socialists that segments of the working class are open to right-wing politics.

Workers in the United States have experienced forty years of attacks on their living and working conditions. The labor movement has responded with one surrender after another, as concession bargaining and futile attempts to forge "labor-management cooperation" have destroyed almost every gain workers made through mass struggles in the 1930s and 1970s. Faced with an impotent labor movement that tails after an ever-rightward-moving Democratic Party, it is not surprising that a minority of older white workers are attracted to politics that place responsibility for their deteriorating social situation on *both* the corporate "globalists" *and* more vulnerable workers—African Americans, Latinos, immigrants, Muslims, women, and queer folk. Kirk Noden, writing in the *Nation*, grasps why the Republican right wins working-class votes:

> Two narratives emerged about the collapse of the industrial heartland in America. The one from the right has three parts: First, that industry left this country because unions destroyed productivity and made labor costs too high, thereby making us uncompetitive. Second, corporations were the victims of over-regulation and a bloated government that overtaxed them to pay for socialist welfare systems. Third, illegal immigration has resulted in the stealing of American jobs, increased competition for white workers, and depressed wages. . . . The second narrative, promoted by corporate Democrats, is that the global economy shifted and the country is now in transition from an industrial to a knowledge-based economy. This story tacitly accepts the economic restructuring of the heartland as inevitable once China and other markets opened up.[23]

Trump and his nationalist populist ideologues from Breitbart and the "alt-right" added a fourth element to the right's narrative— the role of globalizing corporations and "free trade." Given a choice between an elitist neoliberal who refused to speak to the realities of their lives (and rejected Sanders's social democratic program as "unrealistic") and a populist demagogue who offered an illusory *solution* to their problems, it is not at all surprising that a minority of white workers embraced Trump.[24] Trumpism is the fruit of decades of the politics of "lesser evilism," where the left tails after the labor officials who continually surrender to capital, while tailing after a rightward moving Democratic Party in the name of "fighting the right." Without a clear and potent, *independent,* working-class political alternative—one rooted in mass struggles in the workplaces and communities—more and more workers will see *no alternative* to the neoliberal capitalist offensive other than white populist nationalism.

Trump in Office

Not only were left and liberal commentators shocked by the election results, but so, it seems, was Trump himself. Like a drunken frat boy who wakes up after a bender to discover that he is now the CEO of a Fortune 500 company, Trump appears to be completely out of his depth. Ultimately, the chaos in his transition team and the behind-the-scenes struggles over key appointments was the result of the contradictory pressures pulling on Trump.[25] On the one hand, there are the establishment Republicans, with their ties to key segments of the capitalist class, whom Trump consistently denounced throughout his campaign. On the other, there are the alt-right nationalist-populists, who helped script his simultaneously anti-corporate, isolationist, and racist appeals. A situation of veritable "dual power" exists within Trump's team with his concurrent appointment of Republican National Committee Chair Reince Priebus as White House chief of staff, and his campaign manager, former Breitbart editor Steve Bannon, as senior counselor and strategist.[26] The Republican establishment is outraged that a "right-wing media provocateur"—an economic populist and "America First" critic of the US role in the world—has the ear of the President. The alt-right is deeply angered by Priebus's appointment, denouncing him as "the enemy within" and "everything the voters rejected."[27]

What are the politics of Breitbart and the alt-right? Despite their claims to the contrary, the alt-right is *racist*. They eschew the biological racism of openly white supremacist and fascist groupings, whom they refer to as the "1488ers"—a reference to a neo-Nazi slogans "We Must Secure the Existence of Our People and a Future for White Children" and "Heil Hitler." The alt-right instead embraces *cultural racism*—that certain groups have superior, and others inferior, values and behaviors—to justify the exclusion of non-European immigrants and the segregation of "cultural groups."[28] Trump and Breitbart have attempted to distance themselves from open white nationalists, like Richard Spencer, who originally coined the term *alt-right*, defining themselves as primarily *nationalists* and *populists*.[29]

In a multipart article in Breitbart, the pseudonymous "Virgil" argued that a successful Trump administration would need to achieve two goals. First, it must revamp US foreign policy, ending the subordination of America to its historic allies (NATO). Trump needs to put "America first" and "treat China and Russia as great powers to be dealt with as potential partners, not as bad actors to be 'reformed' by America." Second, Trump has to defend "blue-collar America" against the "globalist" corporate elite.[30] In an interview with the *Hollywood Reporter,* Bannon insisted: "I'm not a white nationalist, I'm a nationalist. I'm an economic nationalist. . . . The globalists have gutted the American working class and created a middle class in Asia. The issue now is about Americans looking to not get f-ed over."[31] Central to saving "blue-collar Americans" is the dismantling of neoliberal "free trade" deals and the deportation of *all* undocumented immigrants. The forces around Bannon are clear that they are at war with the Republican establishment, and, in particular, House Speaker Paul Ryan, over both cabinet appointments and economic and military policy.[32]

The battle over cabinet appointments has produced mixed results.[33] Most of Trump's appointees come from the extreme right of the Republican establishment. Betsy DeVos, the secretary of education, is a bitter foe of public education and teacher unions, but is a mainstream Republican on economic policies and did not support Trump's candidacy. Attorney General Jeff Sessions, a nasty racist and early Trump supporter, is well within the Republican consensus on trade and diplomatic alliances. Nikki Haley, his UN ambassador, broke with many southern Republicans' defense of the Confederate flag in the aftermath of the racist shootings in a Charleston church in 2015 and opposed Trump's populist nationalism. Elaine Chao, the second Bush's labor secretary and wife of

Senate Majority Leader Mitch McConnell, and Trump's pick for transportation secretary, is a consummate Washington insider. Scott Pruitt, the Oklahoma attorney general tapped to lead the Environmental Protection Agency, is a close ally of the energy companies and a climate change denier, but not an opponent of "free trade." General John F. Kelly, the homeland security secretary, shares the bipartisan consensus for "greater border security," but is not an advocate of wholesale deportations. Ben Carson, secretary of housing and urban development, advocates massive privatization of public housing, but is a mainstream neoliberal on trade.

Several supporters of the populist camp were nominated but face real limits on their ability to implement their politics. Tom Price, the choice for Health and Human Services, is a militant critic of Obamacare and "free trade." Mike Pompeo, nominee for director of the CIA, has been highly critical of "free trade" and is hostile to the United Nations. Michael Flynn, Trump's choice for national security advisor, is a former Democrat and Islamaphobe whose ties to Putin's Russia led to his resignation. Price appeared to have the greatest room to pursue his agenda of dismantling Obamacare, but now supports the mainstream Republican alternative, which not only preserves the popular aspects of the program (coverage for preexisting conditions and coverage for children to the age of 26) but provides massive tax subsidies to private healthcare corporations as well.[34] Pompeo will have to negotiate any changes in policy with the "professional staff" of the CIA.

Ultimately, the appointments to head the four most important cabinet offices—State, Defense, Commerce, and Treasury—will shape the Trump agenda. Trump chose two Wall Street financiers for Commerce and Treasury. Both Wilbur Ross at Commerce and Steven Mnuchin at Treasury, have made statements hostile to "free trade" in general and Chinese "currency manipulation" in particular. However, it is unclear whether they actually want to dismantle the neoliberal financial and trade policies of the past three decades. In fact, Trump has selected Iowa governor, Terry Branstad, a long-time advocate of free trade with China, as US ambassador to the

People's Republic.[35] James "Mad Dog" Mattis, the choice for secretary of defense, was critical of the Obama administration but has unswerving allegiance to NATO and the traditional US alliance system. The *actions* of Exxon Mobil CEO Rex Tillerson, Trump's secretary of state, are at odds with Trump's *pronouncements*—including Tillerson's moves to strengthen sanctions on Russia and to continue diplomatic engagement with China and his public commitments to NATO.[36]

In Congress, the populist nationalists will face resistance from the Republican establishment. Despite Trump's victory in the presidential election, the congressional Republican party is solidly pro-corporate. The US Chamber of Commerce announced that "95 percent of Chamber-endorsed candidates in House and Senate won."[37] This is reflected in Ryan's "A Better Way" legislative proposals.[38] Most of Ryan's proposals continue "business as usual," with new cuts to public education and social welfare and more deregulation of capital. However, in both "A Better Way" and in public statements, Ryan and the establishment Republicans in Congress have made clear their opposition to any retreat from "free trade" or the central military and political role of the United States in preserving and defending global capitalism. They are also adamantly opposed to mass deportations of undocumented immigrants, other than the "felons" already targeted by Obama, and support expanding guest-worker programs to provide cheap and vulnerable workers to capital in labor-intensive industries.[39] Despite the bitter opposition of the remnants of the Tea Party, Paul Ryan was overwhelmingly renominated for Speaker of the House by the Republican caucus.[40]

What's Next? Neoliberalism Is *Not* Dead!

Despite riding to the White House on the revulsion of a segment of the white middle and working classes to the political class ("Drain the swamp") and its commitments to neoliberal policies, the Trump administration will *continue* and *intensify* neoliberal attacks on working people, racial minorities, immigrants, women, and LGBTQ folks. Put another way, do not expect a sharp break with the forty-year-long *bipartisan* capitalist offensive. There is no question that the minor regulations placed on the financial industry after the economic meltdown of 2008 will be repealed, while new cuts to corporate taxes are on the agenda. Although Wall Street overwhelmingly supported Clinton in the elections, they appear willing to give the new administration "a chance."[41]

Similarly, there are few obstacles to Trump's removing the modest environmental regulations the Obama administration imposed. He can easily rely on the Office of Information and Regulatory Affairs, a creation of the Clinton administration, which has the final say on authorizing new regulations.[42] Both Trump and the Republican congressional leadership agree that the time is ripe to massively reduce funding for antipoverty programs like Head Start, Medicaid, and food stamps (which suffered their sharpest cuts under Obama).[43]

Trump will also intensify the Obama administration's policy of deporting "criminal" undocumented immigrants, utilizing the massive deportation apparatus created under Obama,[44] while back-pedaling on Trump's own promise of wholesale deportations and even hinting he may not roll back Deferred Action for Childhood Arrivals (DACA), which protect undocumented immigrants who arrived as children.[45] For all of Trump's "law and order" rhetoric, his policies will continue the Obama presidency's toleration of police killings. The first two African American attorney generals in US history, Eric Holder and Loretta Lynch, did not indict a single cop for violating the civil rights of the young Black men they have murdered. We can expect the Justice and Defense Departments to continue the sale of surplus military equipment to local police forces that began under Clinton. While the Democrats, who are the primary beneficiaries of union election contributions and support, will oppose a National Right to Work Act, they are unlikely to stop its serious consideration.[46]

Trump's nationalist-populist proposals will face much more

resistance both from congressional Republicans and the unelected, permanent professional bureaucracy in the executive branch of the federal government.[47] His infrastructure program, which relies primarily on tax credits to encourage private companies to rebuild and repair roads, bridges, and the like, rather than massive federal spending, may well pass Congress. However, it is unlikely to provide the sort of Keynesian stimulus that would create the "good paying jobs" that many of his middle- and working-class supporters hoped for.[48] However, on the key populist elements of his program—repealing neoliberal trade pacts, wholesale deportations of undocumented immigrants, and a realignment of US foreign policy toward Putin's Russia—Trump will either continue to backpedal or face concerted opposition.

Trump has already backpedaled on some of his more populist and nationalist proposals. Not only is Trump no longer threatening to indict Bill and Hillary Clinton, but he has also waffled on calls for withdrawing from the Paris climate accord (which would require congressional approval) and reinstituting waterboarding and other forms of "enhanced interrogation" (torture).[49] Other key elements, like the renegotiation or withdrawal from NAFTA or the imposition of tariffs on companies moving production abroad, will likely require the cooperation of Congress to implement. The repeal or restructuring of Obamacare and the building of a wall on the US-Mexico border also require congressional approval. Other policies, like the suspension of immigration from "terror-prone areas" (having abandoned a blanket ban on Muslim immigrants), ending foreign trade "abuses," and leaving the negotiations for the Trans-Pacific Partnership, could be done through executive order.[50] However, it is clear that key congressional Republicans and key groups of capitalists organized in the Business Roundtable and the US Chamber of Commerce will oppose any and all attempts to undermine the neoliberal order.[51] Any attempt to realign US imperialist alliances away from traditional allies in Western Europe and the Middle East, in favor of Putin's Russia, will face resistance from the permanent officialdom of the State, Defense, Commerce, and Treasury Departments.[52] Put another way, Trump will face the same structural-institutional obstacles social democrats face when attempting to implement anticapitalist reforms through the capitalist state.[53]

The clearest indications of capitalist pushback on the Trump administration can be seen in his speech to Congress on February 28, 2017, and his enthusiastic support for Speaker Ryan's proposal to replace Obamacare. Trump's first speech to both houses of Congress was filled with Bannonite *rhetoric*—complete with attacks on "globalism" and NAFTA. Trump actually quoted Lincoln, who argued that protective tariffs are necessary to defend the living standard of American workers.[54] However, its *substance* affirmed Trump's willingness to accept the limits capital has placed on his actions. Despite calling on NATO partners to "meet their financial obligations," Trump reaffirmed US support for "NATO, an alliance forged through the bonds of two World Wars that dethroned fascism, and a Cold War that defeated communism." His calls for "fair trade," were not followed by calls for renegotiating NAFTA or ruling out future multilateral trade deals.

Most importantly, Trump embraced "a merit-based immigration system." This is the foundation of the McCain-Schumer bill that has been languishing in Congress since 2007, blocked by Tea Party populists who rejected any bill that includes provisions allowing undocumented immigrants to achieve legal status. The McCain-Schumer proposal does include a long and tortuous road to citizenship, which would involve millions returning to their countries of origin for indefinite periods before being allowed to come to the United States as legal immigrants who only then become eligible for US citizenship. The most important element of the plan, "merit-based immigration," would move the United States away from a system of nationality-based quotas that allow legal immigrants to become permanent residents and citizens. In its place would be a system where people with certain "skills"— not just those with computer science and engineering degrees, but workers in agriculture, construction, garment, and other low wage industries—to come to the United States to work for defined periods of time. Put another way, the United States would move toward a guest-worker program, where immigrants would be allowed to come to the United States to work, have no legal rights (in particular the right to unionize), and be forced to return to their country of origin when their employers no longer need them. The main supporter of this proposal is the National Immigration Forum—a coalition that includes the US Chamber of Commerce, executives from agribusiness and the healthcare industry, religious leaders, heads of police departments, and the leaders of two of the largest US trade unions, the Service Employees International Union (SEIU) and the American Federation of Teachers (AFT).[55]

Trump's enthusiastic support for Ryan's plan to replace the Affordable Care Act also demonstrates his support for a neoliberal solution to healthcare. While dropping the individual mandate and replacing income with age-based tax breaks to purchase individual plans, Ryan's proposal would preserve Obamacare's large public subsidies for private insurance companies.[56] However, key aspects of the plan are still opposed, from different directions, by the remnants of the Tea Party in Congress and the healthcare industry. For the Tea Party Republicans, the Ryan-Trump proposal is "Obamacare lite," and the tax subsidies to pay for individual health insurance create another monstrous "entitlement program."[57] On the other side, the healthcare industry—major insurers, hospital associations, and the American Medical Association—are joining Democrats in denouncing the end of individual mandates and the restructuring of Medicaid, with the federal government substituting fixed-block grants (along the lines of Bill Clinton's 1996 "Welfare Reform Act") for federal funding of state expenditures on healthcare for the poor.[58] Ryan and Trump may well find themselves caught between the Democrats and the healthcare industry, which fears the loss of 24 million potential customers; and the Tea Party right, which welcomes a potential $337 billion reduction in the deficit over the next ten years but opposes any public funding of healthcare.[59] The end result will likely be a plan that will have much more in common with Obamacare than Trump and his nationalist-populist supporters promised.

Trump's vacillations and the opposition to his nationalist populist proposals portend a continued civil war within the Republican Party. In this battle, the Republican establishment, with its historic ties to old-line WASP capitalists, has all the advantages in a confrontation with the populist nationalists. The Republican leadership controls the party's purse strings and they are well situated to change the rules for the next presidential nominating race. They already have the Democrats' road map to prevent any future insurgency: the creation of unelected "super-delegates."[60] Trump's failure to "Make America Great Again"—the rollback of neoliberal trade deals, mass deportation of undocumented immigrants, and the revival of industrial employment—will disillusion many of his white middle- and working-class supporters. Without their support, the populist nationalists may find themselves marginalized in the Republican Party well before the 2020 election.[61]

The biggest danger issuing from Trump's victory comes not from the corridors of power, but from the streets. Small groups of organized fascists and individual right-wingers believe they have the "wind at their back," freeing them to assault people of color, immigrants, Muslims, queer folks, and leftists. Through November 16—just one full week after Trump's election—the Southern Poverty Law Center counted approximately *seven hundred* violent hate crimes in the United States.[62] The greatest number occurred in the three days following the election, but incidents continue to be reported from across the United States. Approximately 29 percent of the attacks targeted immigrants, 22 percent African Americans, 11 percent LGBTQ folks, 7 percent Muslims, and 5 percent women. Another 11 percent involved swastika vandalism, while less than 4 percent involved verbal or physical attacks on Trump supporters.

The fightback against Trumpism will have to take various forms—organized, collective anti-fascist defense against attacks; mass protest demonstrations; and, ultimately, in a struggle in the workplace. Strategically, new organizers need to understand that we cannot rely on either the Democrats or the forces of official reformism (labor officials, middle-class leaders of people of color, women, immigrants, LGBTQ folks, etc.) in these battles. With most leading Democrats, from Clinton to Sanders, arguing that we "need to give Trump a chance," any notion that the Democrats will tack to the left after their 2016 defeat is illusory. The "insurgent" bid of African American representative Keith Ellison (MN) for chair of the Democratic National Committee went down to defeat, following the routing of Representative Tim Ryan's (OH) challenge to Nancy Pelosi for House Democratic leader. While the labor officials and their allies may be more willing to mobilize against Trump than they were against Obama, we can expect them to "double down" on their support of the Democrats in the 2018 congressional election. Given the commitment of most of what passes for a left in the United States—social democrats and former Stalinists who share a commitment to a "strategic alliance" with the forces of official reformism—it will be an uphill battle to build movements capable of acting independently of the Democrats and their reformist supporters.

The spontaneous protests in many cities, the disruptions at the airports protesting Trump's de facto ban on Muslims entering the United States, and the March 8th Women's Strike are all promising beginnings. However, the danger is that these struggles, like the Wisconsin Uprising, Occupy, and Black Lives Matter, will be short-lived and leave little independent organization in their wake. The way forward for the left is rebuilding the militant minority—the layer of activists with a strategy and tactics that go beyond reformism, if not explicitly to revolution—in workplaces and social movements. Without such a layer rooted among broader layers of working people, the labor officials, Democratic Party politicos, and the middle-class leaders of the social movements will be able to continually derail and demobilize promising struggles—as they have for most of the last forty years.

WHO PUT DONALD TRUMP IN THE WHITE HOUSE?

Kim Moody

The media story in the days following the 2016 election was that a huge defection of angry white blue-collar workers from Rust Belt communities from their traditional Democratic voting patterns put Donald J. Trump in the White House in a grand slap at the nation's "liberal" elite. But is that the real story? While he didn't actually win the popular vote, Trump did carry the majority (58 percent) of white voters. Furthermore, he won the key "battleground" states in the Rust Belt that are the basis of the media story, which raises serious questions. The first question is, who were these white voters? Second, was this the major shift that sent Trump to victory or was there something else?

Exit polls taken during the primaries, when the Trump revolt began, showed the whole election process was skewed toward the better-off sections of US society and that Trump did better among them than Clinton. Looking at those voters in the general election from the 26 percent of US households earning more than $100,000, who are unlikely to be working class these days, we see that Clinton got 34 percent of her vote and Trump a slightly larger 35 percent of his from these well-to-do voters.[1] In other words, upper-income groups were overrepresented in the voting electorate as a whole, and both candidates drew a disproportionate part of their vote from the well-to-do, with Trump a bit more reliant on high-income voters. This, in itself, doesn't rule out a working-class shift to Trump, but the media's version of this is based on a problematic definition.

Aside from the narrower measure of the union household vote, which we will examine below, in most exit polls and media accounts of this blue-collar rebellion, white "working class" was defined as those white voters without a college degree. There are a number of problems with this definition. One problem is that a large majority of those without a college degree don't vote at all, so that any measure of patterns among those who do vote is a measure of a minority who, as we will see, are likely to be among the higher-income voters. Furthermore, as we will see below, people who don't vote are generally to the left of those who do on economic issues and the role of government. Hence the minority of little more than a fifth of the 135.5 million white Americans without degrees who voted for Trump do not represent this degreeless demographic very well. Another problem is that there are only about 18.5 million white, "blue-collar" production workers—the prototype of the defecting white industrial worker.[2] If we double this to account for adult spouses to make it just under 40 million, and assume that none of them have degrees, it still only accounts for a little more than a third of those white adults lacking the allegedly class-defining degree. Of course, there are another 14 million or so white, "service" workers who are working class, but, even if we bring them and their spouses in, we still account for only about half of the huge 70 percent of white adults in the United States who lack a college degree.

The other side of this definitional problem is that there are also millions of Americans who don't have a college degree, who are not working class, and who are actually more likely to vote than the "left behind" industrial workers. There are some 17 million small business owners without that degree. As a 2016 survey by the National Small Business Association tells us, 86 percent of small business owners are white, they are twice as likely to be Republicans as Democrats, almost two-thirds consider themselves conservative (78 percent on economic issues), and 92 percent say they regularly vote in national elections. Plus, they drew an average salary of $112,000 in 2016 compared to $48,320 for the average annual wage.[3] It is doubtful that any significant group of blue-collar workers can match that salary or level of voter turnout, even assuming these small entrepreneurs exaggerated their civic virtue. Add in the spouses and this classically petty-bourgeois group alone could more than account for all the 29 million of those lacking a college degree who voted for Trump.[4]

There are also 1.8 million managers, 8.8 million supervisors, and 1.6 million cops whose jobs don't require a college degree. To this we could add insurance and real estate brokers and agents, and so on.[5] Some may have a degree, but it is clear that there are tens of millions of nonworking-class people in the United States who lack such a degree, and who are more likely to be traditional and frequent Republican voters than a majority of white, blue-collar workers. Thus, the proportion of those without a college degree who are petty bourgeois or genuinely middle class, who are more likely to vote and to vote Republican, is clearly very large, and the equation of the missing degree with working-class status misleading. The relatively high income levels of much of Trump's vote point toward a majority petty-bourgeois and middle-class base for Trump, something *The Economist* concluded in its earlier survey of Trump primary voters when they wrote, "but the idea that it is the mostly poor, less-educated voters who are drawn to Mr. Trump is a bit of a myth."[6] The first point, then, is that Trump's victory was disproportionately a middle-class, upper-income phenomenon.

To test the extent to which white, blue-collar or related workers handed Trump victory, we will look at the swings in union household voting in national elections. This is far from perfect, of course, since only a minority of workers belong to unions these days, about half are public employees, and nonwhite workers make up a third of the total. Nevertheless, we can safely assume that any swings toward the Republicans came mostly from white union members and their families. It is important to bear in mind as well that the union household vote has declined as a percentage of the total vote in presidential elections from about 27 percent in 1980 to 18 percent in 2016. The impact of the union household vote has diminished, though not disappeared.[7]

Table I

Union Household Vote in Presidential Elections, 1976–2016

YEAR	DEMOCRATIC	REPUBLICAN
2016	51%	43% (6% other/no answer)
2012	58%	40%
2008	59%	39%
2004	59%	40%
2000	59%	37% (1% Buchanan, 3% Nader)
1996	60%	30% (9% Perot)
1992	55%	24% (21% Perot)
1988	57%	43%
1980	48%	45% (7% Anderson)
1976	62%	38%

Sources: Roper Center, "How Groups Voted," 1976–2012, http://ropercenter.cornell.edu /polls/us-elections/how-groups-voted/how-groups-voted/; "Election 2016: Exit Polls; President," CNN Politics, November 23, 2016, www.cnn.com/election/results/president.

Two things are clear from table I. First, an average of about 40 percent of union members and their families have been voting Republican in presidential elections for a long time, with the Democrats winning a little under 60 percent of the union household vote for the last four decades. Only in 1948 and 1964 did over 80 percent of union household members vote for the Democratic candidate, Harry Truman and Lyndon B. Johnson respectively.[8] Nevertheless, in 2016, a relatively small number shifted to Trump from 40 percent for the Republican in 2012 to 43 percent in 2016. These 3 percentage points represent a shift of just under 800,000 union household voters across the entire country, which is 3.5 percent of the more than 23 million of them who voted in 2016. Even more interesting is that the Democratic vote fell by seven points from 2012 to 2016 as union household members defected to a third party, refused to answer the question when surveyed, or didn't vote and weren't surveyed. While the unspecified "no answer" group of those surveyed lends some credibility to the theory of the "silent Trump voter," this drop nonetheless points to the fact that the Democrats have lost votes since 2012.

Putting this in historical context, Trump's shift of union household voters is actually less dramatic than the swing from 1976 to 1980 for Reagan and even less so than the fourteen-point desertion of union household voters from Carter in 1980, half of which went to independent John Anderson rather than Reagan in 1980, when the union-householders composed 26 percent of all voters.[9] In other words, Trump attracted both a smaller proportion and number of these voters than Reagan or Anderson. These same voters have swung between Democrats, Republicans, and high-profile third party candidates such as Anderson; Perot, who got 21 percent of union household voters in 1992; and Nader, who got 3 percent in 2000, for some time.[10] The meaning of the 2016 shift was more sinister to be sure, but it was also long in the making as the Democrats moved to the right.

This is not to say that the swing of union household or white, working-class voters away from the Democrats doesn't reflect the conservative social views, racism, and in the case of Clinton, sexism of many white, working- and middle-class people as well as their anger at their deteriorating situation. Nor is Trump the same as Reagan. Clearly Trump won almost 10 million union household votes, compared to almost 12 million for Clinton. We might assume that the broader nonunion, white, working-class electorate is even more conservative-leaning than union members, but since the level of education turns out to be a dubious measure of working-class status, we have no way of measuring just how many white, working-class people actually shifted from the Democrats, either in 2016 or at some point in the past. We only know that the numbers are significant, but that many are not as new to voting Republican as is often thought. This, of course, is not something to take comfort in, but it is an indication of the results of the Democratic Party's choice to emphasize higher-income people who are more likely to vote that began under Bill Clinton and the Democratic Leadership Council.[11]

Nevertheless, it seems clear that a significant number of white, working-class people who had voted for Obama in 2008 or 2012 voted for Trump—even if more just didn't vote. To get a closer look at how this might have worked across the Rust Belt, where the Democrats lost both the vote and the Electoral College, we will look more closely at Ohio and at heavily white and blue-collar counties that moved from Obama in 2012 to Trump in 2016.

In this Rust Belt state, the union household vote was a dramatic 54 percent for Trump. This was a huge change from 2012, when only 37 percent went for Romney and 60 percent for Obama. The Republicans lost Ohio in 2012, but won it in 2016 by 446,841 votes. This would seem to justify the media story. The total two-party vote, however, declined by 253,859 votes between 2012 and 2016, and the union household vote by 74,366. Trump's gain of 151,054 union household votes over Romney, and 166,867 more than Clinton, is obviously significant, but less so than the huge drop in the Democratic vote from 2012 to 2016, and not enough to explain Trump's majority. The Ohio Latino vote, alone, slumped from 10 percent of the total vote to 3 percent in 2016 according to the exit polls. In the actual results, Clinton got 433,547 fewer votes than Obama, while Trump got 179,598 more than Romney, not enough to absorb all the missing Democrats.[12] The biggest story here was the drop in Democratic voters.

Thus, the biggest shift was not to Trump, despite the large percentage of union household votes for him, but away from Clinton and the Democrats. The third-party vote increased by two-and-a-half times to 261,318, but not in a way that would have harmed Clinton, as the Libertarian took the lion's share. The Greens at about forty-five thousand were not a "spoiler" and couldn't have a made a difference. Clinton's overall loss of votes was almost two-

and-a-half times larger than Trump's gain.[13] Trump won Ohio because the total Democratic vote had declined more than the drop in the total two-party vote, and significantly more than the Republican increase. Furthermore, the 2016 Ohio electorate saw an increase in the proportion of higher-income voters. The Ohio electorate saw those earning $50,000 or more go from 59 percent in 2012 to 63 percent in 2016, while those earning $100,000 more increased from 28 percent to 30 percent. Trump got 57 percent of voters in the $100,000 plus income level, compared to 39 percent for Clinton.[14] This certainly smells like a petty-bourgeois/middle-class movement.

To examine the Ohio vote a little more deeply, we will look at four of Ohio's Rust Belt counties along Lake Erie, stretching from Cleveland to Toledo, both of which, like most cities, went Democratic in both 2012 and 2016. These four counties, Lorain, Erie, Sandusky, and Ottawa, all went for Obama in 2012 by a total of 124,330 to 98,564. In 2016, this vote was somewhat reversed, with Trump getting 113,081 votes to Clinton's 98,789.[15] Again, the two-party vote dropped by 11,024, while the loss of 25,541 from the Democratic column was larger than the shift of 14,517 to Trump and larger than his margin of victory in these four counties. Presumably, the story is similar in other blue-collar counties, such as those in northeast Ohio, home to Youngstown and the legendary GM Lordstown plants. What seems clear about these deindustrialized blue-collar counties is that disillusioned Democrats and demoralized labor leaders forced to "sell" Clinton as an establishment neoliberal could not prevent either the drop in Democratic voters or the shift to Trump, even though the latter was relatively small. A look at Lorain County, the largest of the four, will tell us more.

Lorain County's population of just over 300,000 is 80 percent white. It includes the small, upper-income Cleveland suburb of Amherst, the small, liberal-college community of Oberlin, a number of small farming communities and townships, as well as larger working-class Lorain City and Elyria City. The county's workforce is still 42 percent blue-collar. While it still has many employed industrial workers, the local Ford plant has closed, and employment at its biggest steel mill went from 15,000 jobs to fewer than 4,000 in 2014. This is, of course, the county where labor elected three independent candidates on the "Lorain Independent Labor Party" slate in 2014, due to disgust with the local Democrats.[16] In 2012 it chose Obama 78,112 to Romney's 58,092, a majority of over 20,000 votes. In the 2016 primaries, Bernie Sanders got almost as many votes in the Democratic primary (16,587) as Trump did in the Republican primary (16,776).[17]

In 2016 the county went narrowly for Trump—65,346 votes to Clinton's 64,958, a margin of just 388 votes. Voter turnout was down by 5,900 voters, but the Democratic vote dropped by over 13,000 votes from that in 2012. The fact that Lorain County is 80 percent white means a lot of white people voted for Clinton, but a significant number just stopped voting. Trump won not only the upper-income Cleveland suburb of Amherst, but all the more rural small towns and townships in the county, with the sole exception of the tiny college community of Oberlin. Trump's slight majority did not come from the two largest and most "proletarian" towns in the county: Lorain City and Elyria City, the two places where the Independent Labor candidates won in 2014. Lorain City is just over two-thirds white, while Elyria City is closer to 78 percent white. Thus, both have substantial white majorities, but also a significant African American and/or Latino population.[18]

Table II

Number of Votes per Candidate in the 2012 and 2016
General Elections: Lorain County, Lorain City, Elyria City

YEAR		LORAIN COUNTY	LORAIN CITY	ELYRIA CITY
2016				
	Clinton	64,958	14,502	10,834
	Trump	65,346	7,366	8,351
2012				
	Obama	78,112	19,040	14,505
	Romney	58,092	6,211	7,412
Increase in Republican Vote 2012 to 2016		+ 7,254	+1,155	+939
Decrease in Democratic Vote 2012 to 2106		-13,154	-4,538	-3,671

Sources: Lorain County Board of Elections, 2016, 2102, "General Election"; *New York Times,* 2012, "President 100% reporting," http://elections.nytimes.com/2012/results/states/ohio.

Both towns went for Obama by large margins: three-to-one in Lorain City and two-to-one in Elyria City in 2012, and for Clinton by smaller two-to-one and five-to-four margins respectively in 2016. As the figures in table II show, the turnout in 2016 was down by over 6,000 votes in these two towns, while the increase in the Republican vote for Trump of 2,094 votes was almost four times smaller than the drop in the Democratic vote of 8,209. In other words, the drop in the Democratic votes surpassed that of the decline in voter turnout and the increase in the Republican vote in these two heavily blue-collar towns. This is consistent with the larger statewide drop in the Democratic vote of 433,547 compared to the drop in the total two-party turnout in Ohio of over 250,000.

One can hardly avoid the conclusion that the Democrats lost the 2016 presidential election, and those for state office as well, in these and other similar Rust Belt counties due to the fact that former Democratic voters in Rust Belt states with relatively large white, blue-collar populations failed to turnout for Clinton and other Democrats, but did not necessarily vote for Trump. More failed to vote at all. While there was a swing among white, blue-collar and union household voters to Trump, it was significantly smaller than the overall drop in Democratic voters. Below we will see why.

While recent voter-suppression laws demanding state-issued photo IDs in some seventeen states, along with the racial cleansing of voter rolls in many states, have undoubtedly limited voting for Blacks, Latinos, and low-income whites, most nonvoters don't vote because they don't see anything compelling to vote for. At the same time, working-class voter participation has remained low in part because the political parties have reduced the direct door-to-door human contact with lower-income voters in favor of *purchased* forms of campaigning from TV ads to the new digitalized methods of targeting likely voters.[19] Vast amounts of personal data are accumulated by firms specializing in this, turned into voter-targeting algorithms, *and sold.* Among the firms specializing in voter targeting are Artistole, Xaxis, Voter Contact Services, and DSPolitical, the latter of which specifically serves Democratic campaigns. According to John Aristotle Phillips, the CEO of Aristotle, they can provide customers with "up to 500 different data points on each individual."[20]

The parties or campaigns that purchase this service, in turn, use it to spread targeted messages to specific groups or even individual voters mostly via the internet through various platforms, including Facebook, which apparently made a bundle off the 2016 election. Digitalized politics cost more and more money. As one recent academic study of voter mobilization said of these new techniques, "campaign consultants have a business interest in deploying these kinds of tactics and the fact that no one knows for sure whether such tactics generate votes allows sub-optimal campaign tactics to persist." Spending on digital political ads rose from $22 million in 2008 to $158 million in 2012 and is expected to hit $1 billion for the 2016 election and over $3 billion by the 2020 elections. No doubt these amounts will continue to soar as digital political ads are increasingly available for elections way down the ballot to the local level, according to the Democratic digital outfit DSPolitical.[21]

Aside from the soaring costs this invasive digital targeting adds to US elections and the further erosion of our privacy, it further removes political campaigning from any direct human contact. As reporters for the *Guardian* put it, "campaigns of the future will depend as much on being able to track people across screens and apps as knocking on doors or sending out flyers."[22] It's not that no doors are knocked on or phone calls made, but that it is the algorithm that decides the limited number of actual voters to be visited or called to turn out the vote. In practice, this has meant identifying those most likely to vote; that is, the better-off part of the population. The Get-Out-The-Vote campaign has become the Get-Out-The-Well-To-Do-Vote canvass. Most of the persuasion side of campaigning by these outfits is done online through ads on Facebook, YouTube, your smart phone, etc. The knowledge about local voters once in the head of the precinct captain is no longer needed, as far more data are fed through an algorithm that has your number. More importantly, the shaping of the political process, already an auction, is being even further outsourced to the profitmaking "expert" firms that provide this service. The result is that the proportion of relatively higher-income people in the electorate has grown, as the votes for both Clinton and Trump show.

In other words, despite all the vast amounts of money raised and deployed, all the digital and "expert" sophistication available to this "party of the people," and Clinton's allegedly massive "ground war" force in the "battleground" states, the Democratic Party as a whole cannot or no longer tries to mobilize enough of those among its traditional core constituencies—Blacks and Latinos, as well as white workers and union members—to win national and even state offices in these key states and possibly elsewhere, despite the demographic trends in its favor. While race was certainly a factor in Trump's appeal, the fact is, in much of the country, the Democrats at every level could not get the turnout of African Americans or Latinos they needed to balance out their losses among white voters of all classes. To be sure, Clinton won a majority of the popular vote nationally, perhaps, as John Nichols gloated in the *Nation,* an "unprecedented" majority that might run as high as two million by the time the official state votes are counted. [*Editor's note*: The final tally, according to certified results recorded for the Electoral College at the National Archives, showed a difference of 2.839 million votes in Clinton's favor.] The problem is that 1.5 million of that majority can be accounted for from Clinton's vote in New York City alone; that is, by just her majority over Trump, not her total vote.[23] The majorities in the coastal states of California and New York by themselves account for more than her net final majority count of 2.8 million. The rest of the country continues to see its Democratic vote stagnate or decline. Aside even from the digital demobilization, the reason is not hard to find.

The Democrats are and have been for decades the party of the (neoliberal) status quo, when millions of all races have seen their living standards shrink and future prospects disappear and, as a result, have come to despise the status quo. And, as not only the Clintons' social position, but the many millionaire Democrats in Congress (average wealth of a Democratic Representative is $5.7 million), and their business buddies demonstrate for all to see, they are part of the nation's elite. The decline in manufacturing jobs, the shrinking of union representation, the creation of more and more lousy jobs, the withdrawal of aid to the cities, etc. have created, not just "angry white men" who voted for Trump, but angry white, Black, Latino, and Asian men and women who, for good and sound reasons, no longer see the Democrats as their defenders. Many in the ranks of this legion have voted with their feet, and it wasn't to the polls. According to one estimate, over 100 million eligible voters didn't cast a ballot in the 2016 presidential election. In 2014, the last off-year congressional election, nonvoters numbered almost 128 million adult citizens—a majority of eligible voters.[24] And, the vast majority of these were middle-to-lower-income, working-class people.

Strong evidence that the Democrats can no longer motivate or mobilize the majority in much of the country is found in the fact that the millions of nonvoters are on average and in their majority politically to the left of those who do vote on key economic issues. As one study put it, "Nonvoters tend to support increasing government services and spending, guaranteeing jobs, and reducing inequality" more than voters and do so by about 17 percentage points. This includes whites as well as Black and Latino nonvoters. Furthermore, these nonvoters are as likely to support legal abortion and gay marriage as those who vote. Specifically, they are to the left of voters on economic issues in that a consistently higher percentage of them think the government should "make union organizing easier," increase funds to the poor and for schools, "guarantee jobs," and "provide health insurance."[25] In short, the Democrats cannot mobilize the forces needed to defeat the right, including Blacks and Latinos, in part because they cannot implement any policies capable of addressing the plight of the majority that might attract these left-leaning nonvoters.

In fact, nationally, the Democrats have been losing elections at just about every level since 2009. In that year, during the 111th Congress, the Democrats had 257 members in the House of Representative. By 2015, in the 114th Congress, that was down to 188 Democrats, the lowest number since the 80th Congress in 1947–49, over which time voter participation rates fell from 48 percent to 42 percent in off-year congressional elections. In 2016 the Democrats won back just six seats in the House.[26] Between 2009 and 2015, the Democrats lost 203 seats in State Senates and 716 in State Houses or Assemblies. An indication of what was to come in Ohio and Pennsylvania in 2016 could be seen in the loss of 21 Democratic seats in the state legislatures of each of these states between 2009 and 2015.[27]

This time, however, the falling Democratic vote meant the victory not of a run-of-the-mill conservative or even a Tea-Bagger, but of a racist demagogue bent on doing serious damage. And he already is. There will be resistance. Rather, there is increased resistance. And this will offer new possibilities for organizing, even in a more hostile atmosphere. At the same time, many, including not a few on the socialist left, will run for cover in the Democratic Party's "Big Tent," arguing now is not the time to take on the Democrats, that the great task is to elect a Democratic Congress, any Democratic Congress, in 2018 to rein in Trump just as the Republicans blocked Obama after 2010, and so on. It will not even be an argument for reforming the party, just stopping the Trump rampage. It will be a tempting and effective argument, particularly if Trump has, indeed, pulled out all the stops or hasn't already appointed someone to the Supreme Court. But such a political direction will only reinforce the Democrats' neoliberalism, digital-dependency, and failed strategies.

In addition to all the structures and money behind the Democrats at all levels and the reality of party discipline in most legislative bodies, there stands the mass of elected Democratic Party office holders. In what was surely a real-life test of their politics, Bernie Sanders's campaign for the presidency, they stuck with the neoliberal mainstream in their vast majority. While Sanders got nearly 13 million votes from rank and file Democrats, his support among Democrats in office was marginal, even among self-styled progressives: 10 out of 232 Dems in both houses of Congress endorsed Sanders; five of the 75 of his fellow members of the Congressional Progressive Caucus; 91 out of 3,170 Democratic state legislators; three of the 48 Democrats in New York's city council; only two of that council's 19 Progressive Caucus members; and so on.[28]

We had better bear in mind what this approach has *not* done for the past four decades and will not do in the coming years. It will not significantly or permanently increase voter turnout for working-class people, especially African American and Latino voters. The rate of voter turnout has fallen for the past few decades and particularly for off-year congressional elections. Both Black and Latino rates of voter participation in off-year elections, long below average, have nosedived since 2010 and did not recover in 2016 despite the threat of a Trump victory.[29] Nor will the off-the-rack centrist liberalism, much less neoliberalism, of the vast majority of

Democratic incumbents and most-likely candidates win back those white, working-class people or those in union households who have been voting Republican for decades, much less the recent angry Trump converts. Politics as usual have failed! Who put Trump in the White House? The Democrats.

THE GREAT GOD TRUMP
AND THE WHITE WORKING CLASS

Mike Davis

History has been hacked. Trump's "impossible" victories in June and November, together with the stunning challenge of Sanders's primary campaign, have demolished much of elite political wisdom as well as overthrowing the two dynasties, the Clintons and Bushes, that have dominated national politics for thirty years. Not since Watergate has so much uncertainty and potential disorder infected every institution, network, and power relationship, including the Trump camp itself. What was unimaginable recently has now come to pass: the alt-right has a foot inside the White House, a white supremacist controls the machinery of the Justice Department, the coal industry owns the Commerce Department, hedge funds dictate deregulation, oil makes foreign policy, and a wealthy school-wrecker is in charge of national education policy. Obscure Midwestern billionaires, like the DeVoses and Hendrickses, who have spent years transforming Michigan and Wisconsin into right-wing policy laboratories, are now cashing their support for the president elect into the kind of national influence once enjoyed by Rockefellers and Harrimans. Carbon has won the battle of the Anthropocene and *Roe v. Wade* has been put on the butcher's block. Out of an election that was supposed to register the increasing clout of women, millennials, antiwarming activists, and people of color, a geriatric far right has wrested policymaking power on a terrifying scale.[1]

Trump's victory, of course, may yet turn out to be the ghost dance of a dying white culture, quickly followed by a return to Obamian, globalist normalcy or, conversely, we may be heading into the twilight zone of homegrown fascism. The parameters of the next four years are largely unknown. Much depends on whether the Republicans succeed in incorporating the old industrial states of the upper Midwest into their midcontinental *reich* of solidly red southern and plains states. In this case, their gerrymandered electoral advantages, as the *National Review* recently pointed out, might override the popular vote for another decade.[2] But whatever the scenario, the issue of the utmost immediate importance to the left is whether or not the Sanders coalition, including the progressive unions that backed him, can be kept alive as an independent movement bridging the racial and cultural divides amongst American working people. An extraordinary restructuring of political camps, cadre, and patronage is taking place in an atmosphere of chaos and uncertainty, but we need to understand more clearly whether 2016 actually reflects, or necessarily anticipates, a fundamental realignment of social forces.

Breaking Bad

This is not going be an election on niceness.

—Donald Trump

The mainstream narrative, accepted by much of the right and the left, is that Trump rode a wave of white, working-class resentment, mobilizing traditional nonvoters as well as alienated, blue-collar Republicans and Democrats, some of whom were also attracted to Sanders. Political analysts, as well as Trump himself, emphasized the campaign's affinities with European right-nationalist movements that likewise claim to fight against globalization in the names of forgotten workers and small businesses. Endlessly cited have been exit polls that demonstrate Trump's extraordinary popularity amongst noncollege, white men, although the same polls indicate that he ran up his highest margins in middle-class Republican constituencies. (If the polls in Wisconsin and elsewhere are to be believed, moreover, a fifth of Trump voters had an unfavorable opinion of their candidate and held their noses when they checked his box.)[3] In any event he flipped a third of the counties that had voted for Obama twice. However, until the US Bureau of the Census's Current Population Survey releases its analyses of turnout demographics, political scientists can only speculate on whether changes in allegiance or changes in turnout were chiefly responsible for the results.[4] (Although turnout was slightly higher than in 2012, one hundred million eligible voters stayed away from the polls.)

What follows is skeptical interrogation of this narrative using county-level vote data to compare the 2016 presidential campaign with the 2012 campaign in older industrial regions of the Midwest and Appalachia.[5] A number of distinct voting patterns emerge, only one of which actually conforms to the stereotype of the "Trump Democrats." The phenomenon is real but largely limited to a score or so of troubled Rust Belt counties, from Iowa to New York, where a new wave of plant closure or relocation has coincided with growing immigrant and refugee populations. Election punditry has consistently conflated blue-collar votes long captured by Republican presidential candidates with the more modest and localized defection of working-class Democrats to Trump. Several hundred thousand white, blue-collar Obama voters, at most, voted for Trump's vision of fair trade and reindustrialization, not the millions usually invoked. I'm not suggesting that these substantial beachheads cannot be expanded in the future by continued appeals to white identity and economic nationalism, but merely that have been overinterpreted as the key to Trump's victory.

The true "miracle" of the mogul's victory, apart from his cunning success in manipulating negative media coverage to his advantage, was capturing the entirety of the Romney vote, without any of the major defections (college-educated Republican women, conservative Latinos, Catholics) that the polls had predicted and Clinton had counted upon. As in an Agatha Christie mystery, Trump eliminated his dazed primary opponents one after another with murderous innuendo while hammering away on his master themes of elite corruption, treasonous trade agreements ("greatest job theft in the history of the world"), terrorist immigrants, and declining white economic opportunity. With the support of Breitbart and the alt-right, he essentially ran in Patrick Buchanan's old shoes.

But if visceral nationalism and white anger gave him the nomination, it was not enough to ensure that the big battalions of the GOP, especially the evangelicals who had supported Ted Cruz, would actively campaign for him. Trump's stroke of genius was to allow the religious right, including former Cruz cheerleaders David Barton and Tony Perkins, to draft the Republican program and then, as surety, to select one of their heroes as his running mate. As the *New York Times* editorial board epitomized "the most extreme platform in memory," its "retrograde positions [included] making no exceptions for rape or women's health in cases of abortion; requiring the Bible to be taught in public high schools; selling coal as a 'clean' energy source; demanding a return of federal lands to the states; insisting that legislators use religion as a guide in lawmaking; appointing 'family values' judges; barring female soldiers from combat; and rejecting the need for stronger gun controls."[6] To ensure implementation of this agenda, Trump promised to recompose the federal judiciary with evangelical fellow travelers, beginning with the vacancy left by the death of Justice Antonin Scalia.

At the same time, Rebekah Mercer, sometime "queen of the alt-right," whose family super PAC had been Cruz's largest backer, seconded Trump her crack political team: pollster Kellyanne Conway, Citizens United head David Bossie, and Breitbart chair Stephen Bannon. ("It would be difficult to overstate Rebekah's influence in Trump World right now," one insider told *Politico* after the election.)[7] This fusion of the two antiestablishment Republican insurgencies, subsidized by the Mercers and other hedge-fund billionaires, was the crucial event that many election analysts overlooked. They exaggerated the blue-collar "populist" factor while underestimating the equity acquired by the right-to-life movement and other social-conservative causes in Trump's victory. With the Supreme Court at stake and Mike Pence smiling from the dais, it was easier for the congregation to pardon the crouch-grabbing sinner at the head of the ticket. Trump, as a result, received a larger percentage of the evangelical vote than Romney, McCain, or Bush, while Clinton underperformed Obama among Catholics, including Latinos.[8] Against all expectations, Trump also improved on Romney's performance in the suburbs.

But—and this is a very important qualification—he did not increase Romney's total vote in either the South or the Midwest; indeed he fell slightly shy in both regions. Clinton, however, received almost one million fewer votes than Obama in the South and almost three million less than the president in the Midwest. (See tables 1 and 2.) Abdicating any serious effort in smaller industrial towns and cities, she focused almost entirely on major metropolitan counties and media markets in battleground states. (An astonishing 99 percent of campaign ad spending by both sides was targeted on just fourteen states, with Florida, North Carolina, Ohio, and Pennsylvania alone constituting 71 percent of national spending.)[9]

Furthermore, in contrast to Obama, she had no outreach strategy toward evangelicals and her position on late-term abortion, even if misrepresented, alienated untold numbers of Obama Catholics. Likewise, she ignored agriculture secretary Tom Vilsack's urgings to invest campaign resources in rural areas. While Trump was factory-hopping in the hinterlands, her itinerary skipped the entire state of Wisconsin as well as major contested centers such as the Dayton, Ohio, area. The Clinton camp obviously believed that aggressive campaigning in the last weeks by the Obamas and Sanders, reinforced by celebrities such as Springsteen and Beyoncé, would ensure strong turnouts by African Americans and millennials in the urban cores while she harvested votes from irate Republican women in the suburbs.[10]

Table 1
The Regional Vote, 2016 vs 2012 (millions)

10 SOUTHERN STATES (EXCLUDING TX AND FL)

Obama	11.46	Romney	13.8
Clinton	10.6	Trump	13.75

9 MIDWESTERN STATES (INCLUDING PA)

Obama	17.43	Romney	15.78
Clinton	14.51	Trump	15.35

Table 2
Vote Margins For Clinton vs Obama (2012) Compared to Green Party Vote

	CLINTON	OBAMA (2012)	STEIN
Wisconsin	-27,000	+205,000	31,000
Michigan	-12,000	+450,000	51,000
Pennsylvania	-68,000	+288,000	49,000
Margin	*-107,000*	*+943,000*	*131,000*
Ohio	-460,000	+104,000	44,000
Iowa	-148,000	+90,000	11,000
North Carolina	-177,000	-97,000	Write-in only
....			
Florida	-120,000	+83,000	64,000
Minnesota	+44,765	+226,093	36,985
New Hampshire	+2,736	+40,659	6,496
....			
USA (millions)	*64.818*	*62.611*	
Eligible voters	*26.5%*	*30.6%*	

Note: There were 10.7 million more eligible voters in 2016 than in 2012.

Her campaign refused to heed the dangerous signals from the Rust Belt, going "totally silent on the economy and any future plan that would be helpful to people," was veteran pollster and former Clinton adviser Stanley Greenberg's incredulous response. "She no longer ran on change, she ran on continued progress [the

Obama legacy] in a change election. She lost the election in the final two weeks because of avoidable things that could have put them in the lead."[11] Her stupefying inattention to voter unrest in long-Democratic nonmetropolitan counties contrasted with the strategy urged upon Trump by his "pugnacious pollster" Tony Fabrizio. "From the beginning he assumed a lower Black turnout, a surge of white Catholic Democrats who voted for Obama but would move to Trump, and the exodus of older white women, 53 percent of whom ended up voting for Trump. Fabrizio pushed relentlessly to 'expand the map' into Wisconsin and Michigan as well as doubling down on western Pennsylvania."[12] In the event, Clinton's huge popular majorities on the West Coast were worthless currency in the Electoral College while Trump reaped a windfall from his final few weeks of barnstorming the Rust Belt.

Clinton equaled or exceeded Obama's 2012 proportion of the vote only in Massachusetts, Georgia, Texas, Arizona, and California—the latter three, of course, proof of a tremendous Latino mobilization.[13] In three key states, Wisconsin, Michigan, and Florida, an additional factor in her defeat was a smaller, less energized African American vote than in 2012. Her Achilles' heel in Florida, despite massive efforts in the southern half of the state, was the desultory Black turnout in the Tallahassee, Gainesville, and Hillsborough areas, while in Michigan, the smaller vote in Wayne County made her vulnerable to the swing toward Trump in suburban Macomb County, the home of the original "Reagan Democrats."[14] The legacy of welfare reform and super-incarceration had come back to haunt her, especially amongst younger Black urban voters. Furthermore, in Wisconsin and Michigan she failed to rally Sanders's youth support, and in both states Jill Stein's vote ended up larger than Clinton's margin of defeat.

But we should be cautious about dumping all the blame on Clinton and her troubled inner circle. If she had been the principal problem, then local Democrats should have consistently outperformed her. In fact, that seldom happened, and in several states her vote was significantly higher than that of the hometown Democrats. The malaise of the Democrats, it should be clear, permeates every level of the party, including the hopelessly inept Democratic Congressional Campaign Committee. In the Midwest, in particular, the Democrats have largely been running on retreads, nominating such old inventory as former Milwaukee mayor Tom Barrett (who lost to Scott Walker in 2012) and ex-Ohio governor Ted Strickland (slaughtered by Rob Portman in the 2016 Senate race). Writing recently in the *American Prospect*, John Russo portrayed the Ohio party as an entrenched clique of incompetent pols and expensive consultants, mutually addicted to failure, who have failed to create a modern party infrastructure or address demands for change from Sanders's supporters and others.[15]

Meanwhile, the relentless and at times exclusive priority for the gifted team around Obama had always been holding on to the White House, not strengthening sclerotic state parties. East of the Rockies, as a result, Republicans have surpassed their 1920 benchmark in state legislative seats. Twenty-five states are now Republican "trifectas" (control of both chambers and the governorship) versus a mere six for the Democrats. Progressive initiatives by Democratic cities such as Minneapolis (paid leave) and Austin (sanctuary) face the veto of reactionary legislatures.

In addition, as Brookings researchers have recently shown, since 2000 a paradoxical core-periphery dynamic has emerged within the political system. Republicans have increased their national electoral clout yet have steadily lost strength in the economic powerhouse metropolitan counties. "The less-than-500 counties that Hillary Clinton carried nationwide encompassed a massive 64 percent of America's economic activity as measured by total output in 2015. By contrast, the more-than-2,600 counties that Donald Trump won generated just 36 percent of the country's output— just a little more than one-third of the nation's economic activity."[16] Trump voters, the countryside against the cities, have become something like the American version of the Khmer Rouge. Parts of this "other America," to be sure, have always been Stone Age Republican territory, dominated by big farmers, small industrialists, and bankers, and the descendants of the KKK. But the not-sobenign neglect of once staunchly Democratic factory towns and mountain coal country is a reflection both of the marginalization of the former CIO unions within the party and—here the stereotype is accurate—the preempting priorities of Hollywood, Silicon Valley, and Wall Street. Digital America is blue and Analog America, despite being poorer, is red.

Finally, we need to acknowledge the bizarre framework of the contest. In comparative election analysis, the structure of the system is usually assumed to be unchanging between cycles. This was manifestly not the case in 2016. Thanks to the Supreme Court's *Citizens United* (2010) decision, this was the second presidential election with the dark money floodgates wide open, and, in contrast to 2012, the national party apparatuses lost control of the primaries to the shadow parties of Trump and Cruz and, in the case of the Democrats, to the unprecedented grassroots-financed crusade of Sanders. It was also the first election conducted after the gutting of key sections of the Voting Rights Act and the widespread adoption of "voter suppression" strategies by Republican state legislatures. As a result, according to a Brennan Center for Justice report, "14 states had new voting restrictions in effect in 2016, including strict voter ID laws, fewer opportunities for early voting and reductions in the number of polling places."[17] Poll closures were outrageously extensive in Arizona, Texas, Louisiana, and Alabama.

And, as a horrified David Brooks emphasized, this was first "post-truth" election, surreally awash in Trumpian lies, false news manufactured in Macedonia, invading chatbots, "dark posts," dog whistles, conspiracy theories, and a deadly drip of hacked email revelations. Of all the thumbs on the scale, however, including the interventions by Comey and Putin, the most disastrous for the ex-secretary of state was the mainstream media's decision to "balance" reportage by giving equal coverage to her emails and Trump's serial sexual assaults. "Over the course of the 2016 campaign, the three network news shows devoted a total of 35 minutes combined to policy issues—all policy issues. Meanwhile, they devoted 125 minutes to Mrs. Clinton's emails."[18]

The Mythic Blue Wall

Looking ahead to future presidential elections, the Trump strategy points to a red wall that could be bigger and more beautiful than the Democrats' blue one.[19]

Clinton's "blue firewall" cracked in Minnesota, was narrowly breached in Wisconsin, Michigan, and Pennsylvania, and totally collapsed in Ohio (and Iowa, if we consider it a Democrat-leaning state.) Whole swathes of 2012 Obama counties in northwestern Illinois, eastern Iowa, western Wisconsin and Minnesota, and northern Ohio and New York were won by Trump. The "margin shift"—the win or loss percentage of Clinton 2016 versus Obama 2012—was more than 15 points in West Virginia, Iowa, and North Dakota; 9 to 14 points in Maine, Rhode Island, South Dakota, Hawaii, Missouri, Michigan, and Vermont. In southern Wisconsin's former auto belt (Kenosha and Rock counties), where Obama had crushed Romney by huge margins in 2012, the Democratic vote was down 20 percent and the former UAW stronghold of Kenosha went for Trump. Even in New York, Clinton finished seven points behind Obama, thanks to a massive Republican surge in eastern Long Island (Suffolk County) and poor support from blue-collar Democrats in older industrial districts upstate. According to exit polls, she won 51 percent of union households, a poor showing compared to the 60 percent of Obama in 2008 and 2012. Trump beat the union vote of the previous three Republican candidates and in Ohio won a flat-out majority.

This pattern is particularly ironic since Democrats in many of these areas had cast outsized votes for her during the 2008 primaries. Indeed, this had been presumed to be Clinton country. "How could they lose Michigan with 10,000 votes!" groused Stanley Greenberg, a key architect of Bill Clinton's 1992 victory, when he saw the final figures.[20] But one overriding fact determined the outcome: the Republicans have had an aggressive strategy for winning dominance in the Rust Belt, supported by an elaborate infrastructure of state-level think tanks, regional billionaire donors, ready-to-wear legislation from the Koch-funded American Legislative Exchange Council (ALEC), and wizard gerrymanderers from the Republican State Leadership Committee. In contrast, the Democrats, especially those in the industrial but nonmetropolitan counties so common throughout the upper Midwest, have been left to swing in the wind by a national party that offers no serious remedies (the 2009 GM and Chrysler rescues aside) to further decline and communal pauperization.[21]

As readers of David Daley's bestselling *Ratf**ked* know, Karl Rove and his conservative quants had responded to the meltdown of Republican power in 2008 with an audacious scheme for retaking power in Washington through control of decennial redistricting. The Midwest was the bullseye. "There are 18 state legislatures," Rove wrote in the *Wall Street Journal*, "that have four or fewer seats separating the two parties that are important for redistricting. Seven of these are controlled by Republicans and the other 11 are controlled by Democrats, including the lower houses in Ohio, Wisconsin, Indiana and Pennsylvania. Republican strategists are focused on 107 seats in 16 states. Winning these seats would give them control of drawing district lines for nearly 190 congressional seats."[22]

In the event, as Daley shows, chump change (about $30 million) spent on targeted state races in 2010 produced a revolution in party power, with the Republicans winning nearly seven hundred seats and control of key legislatures in Wisconsin, Ohio, and Michigan as well as Florida and North Carolina. Computer-generated redistricting punctually produced a dream map that made Republican control of the House virtually invulnerable until the 2020 Census, despite the demographic forces favoring Democrats. The pièce d'résistance was the gerrymandering of Ohio overseen by John Boehner. "The GOP controlled the redrawing of 132 state legislative and 16 congressional districts. Republican redistricting resulted in a net gain for the GOP state house caucus in 2012 and allowed a twelve-to-four Republican majority to return to the US House of Representatives— despite voters casting only 52 percent of their vote for Republican congressional candidates."[23] (There are worse cases: in North Carolina in 2012 Democrats won a majority of the congressional vote statewide but gained only four out of thirteen House seats.)

Table 3
Republican Lock on Midwestern State Houses
(as of December 2016)

(DEMOCRAT/REPUBLICAN)

	House	Senate	Governor
Minnesota	76/57	33/34	D
Iowa	41/59	20/29	R
Missouri	46/117	8/26	R
Wisconsin	35/64	13/20	R
Michigan	47/63	10/27	R
Illinois	67/51	37/22	R
Indiana	30/70	9/41	R
Ohio	33/66	9/24	R
Pennsylvania	81/122	16/34	D

In the Midwest the 2010 Tea Party victories brought a new generation of feral Republicans to power, many of them groomed by far-right think tanks such as Indiana's Policy Review Foundation (once headed by Mike Pence), Michigan's Mackinac Center, Wisconsin's MacIver Institute and Minnesota's Center of the American Experiment, all of them spoiling for a fight to the death with the region's public-sector unions and progressive big-city governments. Coordinating through the State Policy Network (sixty-five conservative think tanks) and ALEC, they launched campaigns to destroy public-sector bargaining rights, defund unions through right-to-work laws, and privatize public education through vouchers. They focused, in other words, on increasing their structural and legal advantages in ways that Democrats would find difficult, even impossible, to roll back. Unions and students, of course, conducted an epic resistance in Wisconsin but were unable to recall Scott Walker, in large part because of the lackluster character of the Democratic candidate. In Ohio, the unions were more successful and repealed right-to-work by referendum, but in Indiana, Michigan, and West Virginia, Republican majorities rammed through right-to-work and, in Michigan, a Mackinac Center–inspired receivership for Detroit's schools.[24]

The Republican "down ticket" in 2016, from Senate incumbents to state representatives and judges, ironically benefited greatly from Trump's poor backing from the Kochs and other conservative megadonors who switched funding from the presidential race to preserving control of Congress. For the first time, super PACs spent more on the Senate races than on the presidential campaign. Trump, whom the *New York Times* estimated received $2 billion of free publicity from the media, was little affected, but the huge injection of dark money into state races was revolutionary. More than three-quarters of Senate campaign funding came from out-of-state sources in 2016 and "just three groups, One Nation [Adelson], the Koch network's Americans for Prosperity, and the US Chamber of Commerce, account[ed] for 67 percent in dark money spending."[25] The result, according to some political scientists, has been the "nationalization" of state politics. "As a result of the growing connection between presidential and state elections, the once clear divide between state politics and national politics has largely disappeared in most of the country."[26] Thus, for the first time in history, there were no split votes in 2016 between Senate candidates and presidential contenders; the thirty-four states with Senate contests all voted the same party for both offices.

Obama ended his presidency with the Democrats having lost nearly one thousand legislative seats across the country. With all attention now riveted on Congress and the Kremlin West, the media has largely ignored the Republican ALEC-scripted blitzkriegs in the state legislatures they won in 2016. In Iowa, for example, where the Democrats lost control of the senate, the Republicans took little more than three weeks in the new session to decimate public-sector bargaining rights. Similarly, Republican legislators are now targeting Missouri and Kentucky—possibly Ohio again, as well as Pennsylvania and New Hampshire—as the next right-to-work states. In Missouri and New Hampshire, right-to-work amendments recently had been passed by the legislatures but were vetoed by Democratic governors. Both states now have Republican governors and the counter-revolution continues.

Cradles of the CIO

In 1934, a konor predicted not merely the coming of a four-funnelled steamer with Mansren on board but an event which was to become a very important element in the Cargo ideology of northern Dutch New Guinea movements: the miraculous coming of a factory.[27]

The millenarian aspects of the Trump campaign—the magical nativism and promise of a world restored—have received surprisingly little comment, although together with his raving Tourette's syndrome they were perhaps its most striking features. Clinton's promise to competently manage the Obama legacy seemed utterly jejune next to Trump's assurance, more chiliastic than demagogic, that "jobs will return, incomes will rise, and new factories will come rushing back to our shores." Amongst "Trump Democrats," especially those white, working-class Obama voters who flipped Ohio and Pennsylvania, the embrace of Trump took on the desperate overtones of the Papuan cargo cult, its members praying for a magical factory, described in Peter Worsley's classic *The Trumpet Shall Sound*.

If Trump is one part P. T. Barnum and one part Mussolini, he's become another part John Frum: the "mysterious little man [an American sailor?] with bleached hair, high-pitched voice and clad in a coat with shining buttons" whom some Melanesians worship because he supposedly brought "cargo" out of the sky to the island of Tanna during the Second World War.[28] At the end of the day, is the Trumpian field of dreams—Mexicans depart, Chinese surrender, factory jobs return home—that much different from a landing strip hacked out of the jungle?

But perceived anthropological condescension is precisely what drives people in Dubuque, Anderson, and Massena to pick up their pitchforks against "elite liberals" as well as "establishment conservatives." "Deplorables" indeed. The counties in table 4 all have industrial unionism in their DNA; they were the cradles of the Congress of Industrial Organizations (CIO) in the great labor wars of the New Deal. With few exceptions (1972 and 1984), they remained loyally Democratic in rain, sleet, and snow, voting strongly for Obama in 2008. So why, in the face of positive economic indicators and the lowest national unemployment rate in a decade, did these older industrial counties suddenly desert the Democrats and embrace Trump's reindustrialization cargo cult?[29] Fumbling with the odd pieces of the Trump puzzle, the *Economist* decided that "the pitch of economic anxiety motivating Mr. Trump's supporters has been exaggerated."[30] But when analysis goes micro, plentiful reasons for such anxiety emerge. Table 5 itemizes plant closures that occurred *during* the campaign season—striking evidence of a new wave of job flight and deindustrialization. In almost all of these "flipped" counties, a high-profile plant closure or impending move had been on the front page of the local newspaper: embittering reminders that the "Obama boom" was passing them by.

Some examples: Just before Christmas, West Rock Paper Company, the major employer in Coshocton County, closed its doors. In May, GE's century-old locomotive plant in Erie announced that it was transferring hundreds more jobs to its new facility in Fort Worth. The day after the Republican Convention ended in Cleveland, FirstEnergy Solutions announced the closure of its huge generating plant outside of Toledo, "the 238th such plant to close in the United States since 2010." At the same time in Lorain, Republic Steel formally reneged on its promise to reopen and modernize the enormous three-mile-long US Steel plant that had once been the area's largest employer. In August, meanwhile, GE warned of the closing of its light bulb plants in Canton and East Cleveland. Simultaneously, pink slips were being handed out to workers at Commercial Vehicle Group's big stamping plant in Martin's Ferry on the Ohio River (Belmont County). "I think 172 job losses in the community and even the county in an area like ours is devastating," said the local superintendent of schools. "This is another kick in the gut to the valley, with the coal mines closing, the power plant and now this. It's just one piece of bad news after another.[31]

Table 4
"Trump Democrat" Counties
(Table shows percent change in vote for Democrats and Republicans from 2012 to 2016)

State	County (City)	O:2012/C:2016	R:2012/T:2016
CO	Pueblo (Pueblo)	-31%	-11%
IL	Madison (Granite City)	-14%	+16%
IW	Dubuque (Dubuque)	-20%	+10%
MI	Bay (Tri-Cities)	-19	+19
	Macomb (Warren)	-15	+17
	Saginaw (Saginaw-Midland)	-18%	+6%
MN	St. Louis (Duluth)	-21%	+14%
NY	Broome (Binghamton)	-8%	+9
	Niagara (Lockport)	-20%	+22%
OH	Trumbull (Warren)	-29%	+28%
	Mahoning (Youngstown)	-24%	+27%
	Ashtabula (Ashtabula)	-34%	+27%
	Summit (Akron)	-12%	0
	Lorain (Lorain)	-24%	+12%
	Stark (Canton)	-25%	+11%
PA	Beaver (Aliquippa)	-18%	+6%
	Erie (Erie)	-16%	+24%
	Lackawanna (Scranton)	-16%	+39%
	Luzerne (Wilkes-Barre)	-20%	+34%
Quad Cities IL/IA	Scott (Davenport)	-20%	+2%
	Rock Island (Moline)	-8%	+8%
WI	Kenosha (Kenosha)	-20%	+4%
	Rock (Janesville)	-20%	+3%
WV	Kanawha (Charleston)	-13%	+6%

Table 5

Plant Closures during the 2016 Presidential Election Campaign

COUNTY	
Madison	East Alton coal plant + US Steel (2,090 jobs)
Rock Island	Exelon (800 jobs)
Dubuque	FlexSteel + CVG (456 jobs)
Scott	Kraft Heinz (1,000 jobs)
Tri-Cities	Weadock power plant + Dow Midland (750 jobs)
Macomb	Faurecia auto parts (350 jobs)
St. Louis	Caraustar (100 jobs)
Broome	Emerson Electric (60 jobs)
Niagara	Chemours (200 jobs)
Ashtabula	First Energy coal plant + Super K-Mart (300 jobs)
Lorain	Republic Steel (reopening cancelled)
Stark	Hoover + Dover GE (150 jobs)
Summit	Parker Hannifin + Plasti-Kote (200 jobs)
Trumbull	Resco + Alliance Castings + Warren Steel (approx. 1,000 jobs)
Beaver	Allegheny Technologies (600 jobs)
Erie	GE (1,500 jobs)
Mahoning	Exterran (68 jobs)
Lackawanna	BAE (111 jobs)

But what about race? Trump, of course, won the white vote nationally by 21 points (one point more than Romney), and his campaign rallies were Woodstocks for bigots. Yet, as commentators on both the right and the left have emphasized, these flipped counties had with only one exception voted at least once for Obama. (Trump nationally won 10 percent of Obama supporters.) Perhaps a distinction should be made between the true *Sturmtrumpen* who mobbed the rallies and the former Obama voters who joined the cargo cult in protest. As a British journalist, contradicting his own paper's characterization of the white working class as the "engine" of the insurgency, pointed out: "At over a dozen Trump rallies, in almost as many states, over the past year, your correspondent has met lawyers, estate agents, and a horde of middle-class pensioners—and relatively few blue-collar workers."[32]

On the other hand, there is evidence for a regionally generated backlash, long nurtured by Tea Party types, against immigrants and refugees. In part, this may be the result of federal policies that allocate refugees to areas with cheap housing and a low cost of living, where they're often perceived as competitors for remaining service-sector jobs as well as beneficiaries of state support denied to citizens. Erie, where refugees now constitute a tenth of the population and a labor reserve army for the nearby casino industry, is a well-known example. In other Rust Belt areas, such as Reading, Pennsylvania, rapidly growing Mexican communities have been the target of sustained nativist attacks, encouraged by Tea Party and alt-right types. In a recent study of state policies and programs, Ohio was ranked worst in its treatment of undocumented immigrants, a rating that was confirmed when Republicans in the legislature drafted a congratulatory message (HCR 11) to Arizona and Sheriff Joe Arpaio.

A Note on a Forgotten Land

"We're going to put the miners back to work!" Trump declared just minutes into his speech. The crowd roared, Trump smiled, and several miners frantically waved aloft signs that read "Trump digs coal."[33]

Newfoundland, Ordinary, Sideway, and Spanglin are hamlets in Elliot, a typical Appalachian county in eastern Kentucky. Its residents once grew tobacco and corn; now many of them—"fortunate" by local standards—work at the Little Sandy state prison. Elliot's great distinction, however, is its voting record: the last white county in the South to vote Democratic. Indeed, it has been blue in every presidential election since the county was formed in 1869. George McGovern, Walter Mondale, and Michael Dukakis all won here, and in 2008 Obama buried McCain by a two to one margin. In 2012, despite having endorsed gay rights, he nudged past Romney. Last year, however, Elliot finally put out the lights for the Democrats, voting 70 percent for Trump and the old-time religion of the Republican platform.

In all of postwar political history, Appalachia (defined by its regional commission as 428 upland and mountain counties, from Alabama to New York) has had only a single season in the sun. Thanks to bestselling books by a New York socialist, Michael Harrington (author of *The Other America*), and maverick Kentucky lawyer Harry Caudill (*Night Comes to the Cumberlands*), the region briefly became a major focus of the War on Poverty, but then was shunted aside after the inauguration of Nixon. The largest concentration of white poverty in North America, the Southern mountains have been orphaned not just in Washington but also in Frankfort, Nashville, Charlestown, and Raleigh, where coal lobbyists and big-power companies have always dictated legislative priorities. Traditionally, their henchmen were county Democratic machines, and the blue faded from Appalachia only reluctantly at first. Carter won 68 percent of the vote in the region and, in 1996, Clinton won 47 percent. However, as the national Democrats became increasingly identified with "the war on coal," abortion, and gay marriage, local Blue Dogs were euthanized by popular vote.[34] The United Mine Workers (UMW) and Steelworkers, under the best leadership in decades, fought desperately in the 1990s and 2000s for a major political initiative to defend industrial and mining jobs in the region but were turned away at the door by the Democratic Leadership Council and the ascendant New York/California congressional leadership.

Ironically, Clinton this time around did have a plan for the coal counties, although it was buried in the fine print of her website and poorly publicized. She advocated important safeguards for worker health benefits tied to failing coal companies and proposed federal aid to offset the fiscal crisis of the region's schools. Otherwise, her program was conventional boilerplate: tax credits for new investment, boutique programs to encourage local entrepreneurship, and subsidies for the cleanup and conversion of mining land into business sites (Google data centers were mentioned—talk about cargo cults). But there was no major jobs program or public-health initiative to deal with the region's devastating opiate pandemic. It was a mirror image, in other words, of her equally slim offerings to the urban poor. Ultimately the plan made no difference, as the only Clinton promise that everyone remembered was: "We're going to put a lot of coal miners and coal companies out of business." Her only Appalachian victories were a couple of college counties. Trump, meanwhile, hitched a ride with Jesus and recapitulated Romney's vote.

The exception was formerly blue West Virginia where the Democratic wipeout was so enormous that it will probably end up in the *Guinness Book of Records.* Only Wyoming gave Trump a higher percentage of its presidential vote. But even more striking than his 42-point margin of victory was the fact that Clinton received 54,000 fewer votes than were cast earlier for candidates in the Democratic primary—a contest that Sanders won (125,000 votes total) in every single county. The failure to carry primary voters was a stunning index of her unpopularity. Meanwhile, the Mountain Party, West Virginia's *sui generis* affiliate of the Greens, focused on the governor's race (won by billionaire Democrat and self-proclaimed pro-coal populist Jim Justice) and picked up 42,000 votes, an encouraging result. Otherwise the Republicans took over the legislature and con-gressional delegation of this once famous Democratic state for the first time since dinosaurs roamed the earth.

Making sense of West Virginia's nonlinear politics is not always easy, especially since the Democratic Party has largely devolved into a personal election machine and survivalist cult for Joe Man-chin (ex-governor, now senator) and his sidekick, Jim Justice. But one lesson is clear and it probably holds true for most of Appala-chia: a large minority of working people, custodians of a heroic labor history, are ready to support radical alternatives, but only if they simultaneously address the economic and cultural crises of the region. The struggles to maintain traditional kinship networks and community social fabrics in Appalachia or, for that matter, in the embattled Black-majority counties of the former cotton South, should be every bit as important to socialists as defending individual rights to make free reproductive and gender choices. They're usually not.

What Witches Brew

Any future demagogue who attempts to carve a road to power in the United States—for instance through the next depression if one comes—is almost certain to follow Huey's path.[35]

"Huey Long, had he lived," wrote John Gunther in *Inside U.S.A.* (1947), "might very well have brought Fascism to America." Is Trump giving good-ole-boy fascism a second chance?

Like Gunther's Long, he's also "an engaging monster," as well as "a lying demagogue, a prodigious self-seeker, vulgar, loose . . . a master of political abuse." Likewise, he has "made every promise to the underpossessed," appearing "a savior, a disinterested messiah."

But the great Kingfish actually made good on most of his pledges to the plain folk of Louisiana. He did bring them "cargo" in the form of public services and entitlements. He built hospitals and public housing, abolished the poll tax, and made textbooks free. Trump and his billionaire cabinet, on the other hand, are more likely to reduce access to healthcare, increase voter suppression, and privatize public education.[36] "Fascism," if that's our future lot, will not "come in disguised as socialism," as Gunther predicted (and Sinclair Lewis before him), but as a neo-Roman orgy of greed.[37]

This analysis has focused on only one part of the puzzle of the heartland: the old industrial and coal counties, now in decline for two generations. It is hardly a comprehensive account. The regional portrait, for example, might look considerably different if we took the perspective of the larger public-sector and health-industry workforces. Moreover, the story of the Rust Belt is in many ways the old political news; the major novelty of the last election was the politicization of the downward mobility of young college graduates, especially those from working-class and immigrant families. Trumpism, whatever its temporary successes, cannot unify millennials' economic

distress with that of older, white workers because it interposes geriatric white privilege as the touchstone of all of its policies. The Sanders
movement, in contrast, has shown that heartland discontent can be
brought under the canopy of a "democratic socialism" that reignites
New Deal hopes for fundamental economic rights and the civil rights
movement's goals of equality and social justice. The real opportunity for transformational political change ("critical realignment" in
a now archaic vocabulary) belongs to the Sandernistas, but only to
the extent that they remain rebels against the neoliberal Democratic
establishment and support the resistance in the streets.

Trump's election has unleashed a legitimation crisis of the first
order and the majority of Americans who opposed him have only
two credible political rally points: the Sanders movement and the
ex-president and his coterie. While our hopes and energies should
be invested in the first, it would be foolish to underestimate the
second. With Hillary's descent into hell, there is no successor to
Obama. The only world-class political figure left on the American
scene, he will become even more formidable out of office, particularly as his presidency becomes heavily burnished with nostalgia.
(Most will forget that the current debacle, beginning with the rout
of Democrats in 2010, bears the signature of a president who par-
doned Wall Street while deporting 2.5 million immigrants.) Chicago is likely to become the capital of a government in exile with
the Obamas directing efforts to reinvigorate the Democratic Party
and centrist politics without ceding power to the left. (If this dual
power scenario seems fanciful, one should recall the precedent of
Teddy Roosevelt at Sagamore Hill during the Taft years.) Those
who believe that the Progressive Caucus now holds the balance of
power within the Democratic Party may be rudely disenchanted
when Obama again picks up the lance on behalf of the party's elites.

Meanwhile, Trump, augur of fascism or not, seems destined
to be the American Macbeth, sowing brutal chaos throughout the
dark highlands of the Potomac. The political and social war that
is now inevitable in the United States could shape the character
of the rest of the century, especially since it is synchronized with

similar eruptions across the European Union and the collapse of left-populist rule in South America. As Trump's spiritual godfather, Pat Buchanan, recently gloated, "The forces of nationalism and populism have been unleashed all over the West and all over the world. There is no going back."[38] Hair-raising global scenarios are only too easy to imagine. One could envision, for instance, an angry, foundering Trump regime that represses protest and incites late 1960s-like revolts in US cities, while futilely trying to reconcile its contradictory economic policies and promises. The ensuing geo-economic turmoil might prompt Europeans to invite China to take increasing monetary and financial leadership within the Organisation for Economic Co-operation and Development (OECD) bloc. The year 2016, in this scenario, would mark the end of the American Century. Alternately, Beijing might be unwilling or unable to arrest a world downturn or prevent a partial unraveling of transnational production chains. It might pivot from the Pacific toward Eurasia. In that case, 2016 might be remembered as the birthday of deglobalization and a world more recognizably like the 1930s than the 2000s.

CHOOSING OR REFUSING TO TAKE SIDES IN AN ERA OF RIGHT-WING POPULISM

Neil Davidson

Two events during 2016—the UK referendum on membership in the European Union (EU) and the US presidential election—raised the question of whether or not socialists should take sides in situations where there are two alternatives, both opposed, in different ways, to working-class interests. The most obvious answer would be to abstain from the vote, argue against both options, and make the case for a socialist alternative capable of forcing its way onto the ballot in the future. But if one of the existing alternatives represents the politics of the populist hard right, as it did in both these cases, can socialists avoid supporting the other, however unpalatable doing so might be?

Faced with the xenophobia and outright racism, which respectively dominated and constituted the Leave and Donald Trump campaigns, sections of the left in both countries argued that, whatever problems there may be with the EU as an institution or with Hillary Clinton as a candidate, a vote to remain within the former and to elect the latter was "the lesser of two evils." The same argument has already been raised in advance of the 2017 French presidential elections, where the Thatcherite François Fillon of the Republicans has been proclaimed the lesser evil compared to Marine Le Pen of the Front National, just as Jacques Chirac was the lesser evil in the runoff against Le Pen's father, Jean-Marie, in 2002. In some respects, these are more plausible cases than those of the United Kingdom and United States since, unlike Nigel Farage or Trump, the Le Pens are actual fascists.

France is unlikely to be the last place where the left is faced with this type of choice, which indicates the urgency with which the left needs to establish an independent position. Before addressing the concrete question of on what basis we should make such choices, I want to explore the roots and nature of what is usually regarded as "the greater evil": the populist right, in both its fascist and non-fascist variants.[1]

Neoliberalism's Crisis

But first, it is perhaps worth briefly discussing why it has become—temporarily at least—the main alternative to the current orthodoxies of capitalist governance. The economic crash of 2007 was at one and the same time a general crisis of capitalism comparable to those of 1873, 1929, and 1973, and a crisis of a particular form of capitalist organization we have come to know as neoliberalism. But the latter has occurred at a particular phase in its history, that of "social" neoliberalism, which emerged after 1989, first within the EU, then in the administrations of Bill Clinton in the United States (from 1992) and of Tony Blair in the UK (from 1997). Perhaps the greatest ideological success of social neoliberalism was to turn the categories of "left" and "right" to essentially cultural concepts. When everyone—or at least, everyone who mattered—came to accept neoliberal economics, then the only terrain on which debate was permissible was that of identity: the so-called culture wars. So, to be on the left was, for example, to be in favor of gay marriage and migration, and to be on the right was to oppose them: the legitimacy of capitalism was never in doubt on either side.

In reality, what had happened was that right-wing politics—that is, politics openly supportive of the capitalist system—had effectively split in two, or perhaps returned to the classic pre-socialist "conservative" versus "liberal" division of the nineteenth century, with both sides supporting the same economic model, but the latter being more willing to accept rights for what were usually (and in the case of women, inaccurately) referred to as "minorities." To be clear: the problem with the latter position is not, as Mark Lilla and others are arguing, that the Democrats became obsessed with *identity* at the expense of economics, but that their policies did nothing to stop the *oppression* of these groups, in particular their working-class members, since, under the Obama administration in which Hillary Clinton served, women continued to be sexually assaulted with impunity, people of color continued to be incarcerated, and migrants continued to be deported in record numbers.[2]

Two changes have taken place since 2007, both associated with shifts in the position of a faction within the conservative wing of the ruling class—the populist hard right. One is that it has also adopted a politics of identity, in this case a majoritarian identity based on that most pernicious of invented categories, "the white working class," whose interests have supposedly been sacrificed to those of the minority populations. However, perhaps realizing that the plight of unemployed coal miners in Pennsylvania is hard to blame on government handouts supposedly being showered on Black lesbians in North Carolina, it has also adopted another position, which is to—rhetorically at least—abandon many neoliberal shibboleths and argue for protectionism and government investment in infrastructure.

Ironically, it was under Bill Clinton, rather than Reagan or Bush the First, that the United States finally abandoned protectionism, which had been used to protect the steel industry during the 1980s. But this simply added to the case for Democrats having abandoned workers to the ravages of the market. Now, whether Trump is serious about implementing his economic policies is still unclear, and he may not even know himself; but what is perhaps more interesting is not only that a break with neoliberalism is being articulated within the ruling class, but that many of the proposals associated with it would actually be detrimental to US capitalism, which is one of the reasons why so many capitalists were opposed to his candidacy.

Contesting Lesser-Evilism and Right-Wing Populism

One consequence of these changes is that previous arguments against choosing the lesser evil have to be revised, although not, I will argue, the stance itself. The classic discussion is generally thought to be a much-reprinted piece by Hal Draper, first published in 1967.[3] The context was the presidential election of the following year, in which it was expected that the incumbent, Lyndon Johnson, would stand for the Democrats against an as yet unknown Republican candidate. As it turned out, Johnson refused to stand and Hubert Humphrey ultimately won the Democratic nomination, only to lose the presidency to Richard Nixon. Johnson had, of course, been the lesser evil against Barry Goldwater in 1964, although, as Draper pointed out, the former subsequently unleashed far greater violence against the Vietnamese than the latter had ever contemplated—and was able to get away with it precisely because he knew that most of the left were paralyzed by their fear of the greater evil. But, although Draper was primarily concerned with the United States, he did examine the most extreme example possible in order to demonstrate where the lesser-evil argument could lead: the rise of Nazism in Germany.

In the presidential elections of March and April 1932, both the Social Democratic Party and Centre Party had refused to stand their own candidates, but called on their members and supporters to vote for the incumbent, the independent but deeply conservative candidate Paul von Hindenburg, in an attempt to block the greater evil represented by Adolf Hitler. Once reelected with the help of the left, Hindenburg appointed Hitler as chancellor, in the misplaced expectation that he would be constrained by the responsibilities of office.

Draper rather foreshortens the actual process, as Hitler was not appointed immediately, but the following January, on the grounds that the Nazis were the largest political party in the Reichstag. His central point, however, remains valid: support the lesser evil and you might well end up getting the greater evil too. Draper was careful to point out the extremity of the situation in Germany during the early 1930s, both in relation to the extent of the crisis and the nature of the Nazi program, but argued that if the lesser evil argument was wrong in these conditions, it was far more so in the relatively stable context of the USA in the late 1960s.

Draper made two general points. First, the left has to create its own political alternative, or it will endlessly be faced with choices ultimately determined by defenders of capitalism. Second, even though serious differences remained between parties and candidates—such as had also existed between Hindenburg and Hitler—these were becoming less significant in practice: the increasing centrality of state intervention, ownership, and control after the crisis of 1929 meant that all political formations (other than those committed to the overthrow of capitalism) were effectively forced to follow the same core policies, whatever their beliefs or electoral rhetoric. The retreat of state capitalism in the West began after the return of economic crisis in 1973, but Draper's argument was still relevant as the subsequent neoliberal era involved as great a convergence around economic policy as there had been between 1929 and 1973, albeit in the opposite direction.

But, as I have suggested, since the onset of a further crisis in 2007, this agreement has begun to break down. In other words, anyone wanting to oppose arguments for supporting the lesser evil can no longer simply argue that supporting one alternative rather than another will lead to the same result: it would scarcely be credible to argue that it makes no difference whether the UK is in or out of the EU, or to claim that Clinton would have pursued the same foreign policy as Trump. But before turning to the alternative posed by the populist hard right, we need to understand the nature of political leadership under capitalism, which it seeks to command.

The Political Incapacities
of the Capitalist Ruling Class

Under all precapitalist modes of production, exploitation took place visibly through the extraction of a literal surplus from the direct producers by the threat or reality of violence: economics and politics were "fused" in the power of the feudal lord or the tributary state. Under the capitalist mode of production, exploitation takes place invisibly in the process of production itself through the creation of surplus value over and above that required in reproducing the labor force. The late Ellen Wood identified a resulting "division of labor in which the two moments of capitalist exploitation—appropriation and coercion—are allocated separately to a 'private' appropriating class and a specialized 'public' coercive institution, the state: on the one hand, the 'relatively autonomous' state has a monopoly of coercive force; on the other hand, that force sustains a private 'economic' power which invests capitalist property with an authority to organize production itself." Furthermore, unlike previous exploiting classes, capitalists exercise economic power without "the obligation to perform social, public functions": "Capitalism is a system marked by the complete separation of private appropriation from public duties; and this means the development of a new sphere of power devoted completely to private rather than social purposes."[4]

The implications of this division for capitalists as a ruling class were noted by earliest social theorists to concern themselves with the emergent system. Since Adam Smith is—quite unfairly—treated as the patron saint of neoliberalism it may be worth reminding ourselves of his actual views on capitalists and the narrowness of their interests: "As their thoughts ... are commonly exercised rather about the interest of their own particular branch of business, than about that of the society, their judgment, even when given with the greatest candor (which it has not been upon every occasion) is much more to be depended upon with regard to the former of those two objects than with regard to the latter."[5] For the purposes of our discussion, the interest in this passage lies not in Smith's still refreshingly candid views about the capacity of business interests for deception and oppression, but their inability to see beyond their own immediate interests. This was one of the reasons why he also wrote (thinking of the East India Company): "The government of an exclusive company of merchants is, perhaps, the worst of all governments for any country whatsoever."[6]

Nearly a century later, in the 1860s, Smith's greatest successor, Karl Marx, was able to point in *Capital* to the British Factory Acts as an example of how the state had to intervene to regulate the activities of capital in the face of initial opposition from the capitalists themselves: "It is evident that the British Parliament, which no one will reproach with being excessively endowed with genius, has been led by experience to the conclusion that a simple compulsory law is sufficient to enact away all the so-called impediments opposed by the nature of the process to the restriction and regulation of the working-day."[7] Reflecting on the entire legislative episode, Marx noted: "But for all that, capital never becomes reconciled to such changes—and this is admitted over and over again by its own representatives—except 'under the pressure of a General Act of Parliament' for the compulsory regulation of the hours of labor."[8]

The thesis concerning bourgeois incapacity was restricted not only to critics like Marx, but to supporters of capitalism and even of fascism. Carl Schmitt, for example, complained after the First World War that, unlike working-class ideologues, members of the bourgeoisie no longer understood the friend/enemy distinction, which was central to his concept of "the political"; the spirit of Hegel, he thought, had moved from Berlin to Moscow.[9] Joseph Schumpeter argued a more general case during World War II. Yielding to no one in his admiration for the heroic entrepreneur, he nevertheless also noted that, with the possible exception of the United States, "the bourgeois class is ill-equipped to face the problems, both domestic and international, that normally have to be faced by a country of any importance"; the bourgeoisie needs "protection by some nonbourgeois group"; ultimately, "it needs a master."[10] Without the kind of constraints provided by this precapitalist framework, the more sober instincts of the bourgeois would be overcome by the impulse towards what Schumpeter called "creative destruction."

The delegation of power to the state therefore exists because of what Draper calls "the political inaptitude of the capitalist class" compared to other ruling classes in history. It is not only that feudal lords combine an economic and political role while capitalists perform only the former; it is also that the necessity for capitalists to devote their time to the process of accumulation and their own multiple internal divisions militates against their functioning directly as a governing class.[11] More broadly, Bernard Porter notes that capitalists "tend to be hostile to 'government' generally, which they see mainly as a restraint on enterprise and, on a personal level, don't find 'ruling' half so worthwhile or satisfactory as making money."[12] This arrangement is quite compatible with the exercise of bourgeois hegemony over society as a whole, although even in this respect, some sections of the bourgeoisie tend to play a more significant role than others; but politically, as Fred Block has written, "the [capitalist] ruling class does not rule."[13]

As a result, two other forces have tended to rule jointly in place of the capitalists themselves: politicians and state managers, in other words, the senior component of the permanent state bureaucracy. In both cases the very distance of the groups involved from direct membership of the capitalist class allowed them to make assessments of what was required by the system as a whole. Politicians need not belong to the same class as the capitalists: indeed, it was landed aristocracies who played this role for much of modern European history down to 1945. "A plainly bourgeois society—nineteenth-century Britain—could, without serious problems, be governed by hereditary peers," noted Eric Hobsbawm.[14] Social democracy—originally a working-class political tendency at least nominally committed to overturning capitalism—has intermittently done so afterwards, and similar patterns can be found in most other Western nation-states.

Throughout the long boom after World War II, the capitalist class had called to order social democratic politicians when their policies were perceived, however unreasonably, as being too concerned with defending the interests of their supporters. Their normal methods for disciplining disobedient politicians involved currency speculation, withholding investment, and moving production—or at least threatening to do so, which was often sufficient to achieve the desired effect. These police actions by capital were often aided by state managers who tended to be more conscious of what capital would find acceptable or permissible than mere elected representatives of the people.

But economic or bureaucratic resistance to government agendas is a blunt instrument, capable of blocking or reversing one set of policies and making others more likely, not of bringing about a complete reorientation in policy terms. Capitalist states are sets of permanent institutions run by unelected officials who act in the interests of capital more or less effectively; parliamentary government is a temporary regime consisting of elected politicians who act in the interests of capital, more or less willingly. But, in times of crisis, capital requires politicians who will decide on a particular strategy and fight for it with absolute conviction, if necessary against individual members of the capitalist class themselves.

During the 1930s, Antonio Gramsci discussed this type of ruling class response to crisis as "an organic and normal phenomenon": "It represents the fusion of an entire social class under a single leadership, which alone is held to be capable of solving an overriding problem of its existence and of fending off a mortal danger."[15] Gramsci was thinking of Italian fascism, but a similar shift took place during what I call the "vanguard" phase of neoliberalism under Thatcher and Reagan. It would be quite wrong, however, to imagine that new strategic initiatives are necessarily beneficial to the operation of capitalism.

Contrary to extreme functionalist or economic determinist positions, representatives of the dominant classes are not infallible or all-knowing. As Gramsci once noted, we have to allow for the possibility of error, but "error" is not reducible to a "mistake": "The principle of 'error' is a complex one: one may be dealing with an individual impulse based on mistaken calculations or equally it may be a manifestation of the attempts of specific groups or sects to take over hegemony within the directive grouping, attempts which may well be unsuccessful."[16]

In one sense, however, neoliberalism has been *too* successful. For it has weakened, to varying degrees, the capacity of capitalist states to act in the interest of their national capital as a whole. The relationship between neoliberal regimes and capital has, since the 1970s, prevented states from acting effectively in the collective, long-term interest of capitalism and leading instead to a situation where, according to Robert Skidelsky, "ideology destroys sane economics."[17] It is true that neoliberal regimes have increasingly abandoned any attempt to arrive at an overarching understanding of what the conditions for growth might be, other than the supposed need for lowering taxation and regulation and raising labor flexibility.

Apart from these, the interests of the total national capital are seen as an arithmetical aggregate of the interests of individual businesses, some of which, to be sure, have rather more influence with governments than others. These developments have led to incomprehension among remaining Keynesians of the liberal left.[18] But their assessments are correct in noting that, insofar as there is a "strategic view," it involves avoiding any policies that might incur corporate displeasure, however minor the inconveniences they might involve for the corporations, which of course includes regulation.

The weakening of the labor movement and consequent rightward shift by social democracy may therefore ultimately prove self-destructive for capital since, as we have seen, one of the inadvertent roles that it historically played was to save capitalism from itself, not least by achieving reforms in relation to education, health, and welfare. These benefited workers, of course, but also ensured that the reproduction of the workforce and the conditions for capital accumulation more generally took place. But with the weakening of trade union power and the capitulation of social democracy to neoliberalism, there is currently no social force capable of either playing this "reformist" role directly or by pressurizing nonsocial democratic state managers into playing it.

That leaves the state apparatus itself, but the necessary distance between the state and capital (or between state managers and capitalists), to which I earlier alluded, has been minimized. Any longer-term strategy in the overall interests of capital would have to address the dysfunctionality of the financial system, the refusal of firms to invest in productive capacity, and low levels of tax intake attendant on a fiscal system massively skewed towards the wealthy. But state managers are no longer prepared to do this and neither are most politicians—with the exception of one tendency: right-wing populism.

Varieties of Right-Wing Populism

Given the hysteria about Trump's supposed incipient fascism, it is important to begin by distinguishing between fascist and non-fascist variants of the hard right. All wings are united by two characteristics. One is a base of membership and support in one or more fraction of the middle class (i.e., the petty bourgeoisie, traditional middle-class professionals, or the technical-managerial new middle class)—although as we shall see, this does not mean that they necessarily lack working-class support. The other is an attitude of extreme social conservatism, always in relation to race and nation, sometimes in relation to gender and sexual orientation: far-right politicians in the Netherlands, for example, have rhetorically invoked the relative freedoms of women or gays in the West as way of denouncing the supposedly oppressive beliefs of Muslims. The political goal is always to push popular attitudes and legal rights back to a time before the homogeneity of "the people" was polluted by immigration, whenever this Golden Age of racial or cultural purity is deemed to have existed, which is usually at some undetermined period before World War II.

There are nevertheless large differences between these two types of organization. As Jan-Werner Müller has pointed out, "National Socialism and Italian Fascism need to be understood as populist movements—even though, I hasten to add, they were not just populist movements but also exhibited traits that are not inevitable elements of populism as such: racism, a glorification of violence, and a radical 'leadership principle.'"[19] More specifically, Michael Mann argues that non-fascist far-right parties are distinguished from fascism by three characteristics: 1) they are electoral and seek to attain office through the democratic means at local, national, and European levels; 2) they do not worship the state and, while they seek to use the state for welfare purposes for their client groups, some (e.g., the Austrian Freedom Party or the Tea Party) have embraced neoliberal small-state rhetoric; 3) they do not seek to "transcend" class: "These three ambiguities and weaknesses of principle and policy make for instability, as either extremists or moderates seek to enforce a more consistent line that then either results in splits and expulsions, such as the makeover of the Italian MSI and the disintegration of the German Republikaner in the mid-1990s."[20]

The first of these distinctions, adherence to bourgeois democracy, is crucial, since it indicates the fundamental distinction between the fascist and non-fascist far right: the latter, as Peter Mair notes, "do not claim to challenge the democratic regime as such."[21] Activists and commentators often draw an absolute distinction between fascism and other forms of right-wing politics, based on the way the former rely on paramilitary organization and violence as part of their strategy for attaining power. In that sense, Golden Dawn in Greece is a classic fascist formation in a way that the Northern League in Italy is not. The distinction is important, not least in determining the tactics of their opponents, but fascism is not defined simply by its recourse to extraparliamentary or illegal activity. Here, Trotsky's analysis remains relevant: "When a state turns fascist . . . it means, primarily and above all, that the workers' organizations are annihilated; that the proletariat is reduced to an amorphous state; and that a system of administration is created which penetrates deeply into the masses and which serves to frustrate the independent crystallization of the proletariat. Therein precisely is the gist of fascism."[22]

Fascism, then, is revolutionary, and the non-fascist far right is not; but what does *revolutionary* mean in this context? Many Marxists are reluctant to use this term in relation to any modern political movement not of the left, with the possible exception of nationalisms in the Global South. But if we consider fascist seizures of power as political revolutions—in other words, as those which change the nature and personnel of the regime without changing the mode of production, then there is no reason why the term should not be applicable.[23]

The second major difference, which flows directly from the first, is their respective attitudes to society, which they are trying to build. As Roger Griffin points out, the "revolution from the right" in both fascist Italy and Nazi Germany claimed to be using the state to socially engineer a "new man and woman" with "new values." This is a project of *transformation*. The non-fascist far right, however, insists that the people are *already* the repositories of homogeneity and virtue: "By contrast, the enemies of the people—the elites and 'others'—are neither homogeneous nor virtuous. Rather, they are accused of conspiring together against the people, who are depicted as being under siege from above by the elites and from below by a range of dangerous others."[24] The purpose of the non-fascist far-right is to return the people to their formerly happy condition before these twin pressures began to be applied: "This is not a Utopia, but a prosperous and happy place which is held to have actually existed in the past, but which has been lost in the present era due to the enemies of the people."[25] This is a project of *restoration*.

The revival of the far right as a serious electoral force is based on the apparent solutions it offers to what are now two successive waves of crisis, which have left the working class in the West increasingly fragmented and disorganized, and susceptible to appeals to blood and nation as the only viable form of collectivism still available. This is particularly true in a context where the systemic alternative to capitalism—however false it was—had apparently collapsed in 1989–91. The political implications are ominous. The increasing interchangeability of political parties gives the far right an opening to appeal to voters by positioning themselves as outside the consensus in ways that speak to their justifiable feelings of rage.[26]

The potential problem for the stability of the capitalist system is, however, less the possibility of far-right parties themselves coming to power with a program destructive to capitalist needs than their influence over the mainstream parties of the right, when the beliefs of their supporters may inadvertently cause difficulty for the accumulation process—as in the impending withdrawal from the EU in the case of the United Kingdom or, potentially at least, a halt to migration from Mexico and Central America and the mass deportation of all undocumented immigrants at the behest of the Trump presidency in the case of the United States. Here we see emerging a symbiotic relationship between one increasingly inadequate regime response to the problems *of* capital accumulation and another increasingly extreme response to the most irrational desires and prejudices produced *by* capital accumulation. Again, this is not a new problem for capital.

There is a problem with some left analyses of the hard right and its far-right component in particular, which is the assumption that it represents the "real" face of capitalism unmasked ("the naked dictatorship of monopoly capital" and so forth). In fact, in the developed world at least, it is only in very rare situations of dire extremity—and usually after facing the kind of threat from the labor movement that has unfortunately been absent for several decades—that capital has ever relied on the far right to solve its problems. Right-wing social movements can relate to the accumulation strategies of capital in three ways: 1) they are directly supportive; 2) they are compatible with and/or indirectly supportive through strengthening ideological positions that are associated with capitalist rule, but that may not be essential to it; or 3) they are indirectly and possibly unintentionally destabilizing.

Until recently, at any rate, examples of type 1 have been very rare indeed, since, as I have argued above, capitalists prefer to use corporate pressure rather than mass movements to achieve their political goals. Examples of type 2 are the most frequent, but, as I will argue below, we are currently seeing, and are likely to see more, examples of type 3, which raises the question: What is the relationship between the far-right politics and capitalism? What if a fascist or far-right movement came to power that implemented policies against the needs of capital—not because they were "anticapitalist" in the way that the Strasserite wing of the Nazi Party were (falsely) supposed to be, but simply because their interests lay elsewhere?

The Nazi Regime performed two services for German capital: crushing an already weakened working class and launching an imperial expansionist drive to conquer new territory. But while racism and anti-Semitism were important for the Nazis, notes Ulrich Herbert, they were not for German national capitals:

> Any attempt to reduce the Nazi policy of mass annihilation solely or largely to underlying economic, "rational" interests, however, fails to recognize that, in the eyes of the Nazis, and in particular the advocates of systematic racism among them, the mass extermination of their ideological enemies was itself a "rational" political goal. It was supported by reference to social, economic, geopolitical, historical and medical arguments, as well as notions of "racial hygiene" and "internal security." Racism was not a "mistaken belief" serving to conceal the true interests of the regime, which were essentially economic. It was the fixed point of the whole system.[27]

It is therefore true, as Alex Callinicos points out, that "the extermination of the Jews cannot be explained in economic terms." He sees the connection between the Holocaust and German capitalism as an example of an interpenetration of interests, in this case between "German big business" and "a movement whose racist and pseudo-revolutionary ideology drove it towards the Holocaust."[28] The position that Callinicos is articulating here was first expressed by Peter Sedgwick in 1970: "German capitalism did not need Auschwitz; but it needed the Nazis, who needed Auschwitz."[29] But where did the Nazi "racist and pseudo-revolutionary ideology" come from in the first place? Callinicos only sees a connection with capitalism as arising from the immediate needs of the economy at a time of crisis; but the ideological formation of the Nazi worldview took place over a much longer period, which saw the combination of a series of determinations arising from the contradictions of German and European capitalism, and including the authoritarian character of a subordinate middle-class that had never successfully developed its own political identity; extreme right-wing nationalism first formed in response to the French Revolution, racism in its anti-Semitic form, disappointed imperialism, a taste for violence acquired in the trenches, and so on.[30]

Adapting Sedgwick then, we might say that German capitalism didn't need the Holocaust, but the long-term development of German capitalism produced, through a series of mediations, the ideology of Nazism, which contained the possibility of a Holocaust, and when German capitalists turned to the Nazis in its moment of crisis, they were given the opportunity to realize that possibility, however irrelevant and outright damaging it was to German capital's more overarching imperial project. In other words, the barbaric ideology of Nazism and the socioeconomic crisis of Germany (to which the Nazis provided one solution) were already connected as different moments in the mediated totality of capitalism.

But if the Holocaust was a barbaric irrelevance—except incidentally—for German capital, the Nazi regime also presents us with examples of policies that were instrumentally irrational from the perspective of the capitalist state. As Detlev Peukert writes: "To see fascism as an effective answer to the weakness of the bourgeois democratic state, i.e., as a functional solution to the crisis in the interests of capital, is to be taken in by the self-image of National Socialism created by its own propaganda." For one thing, it led to the creation of a deeply fragmented and incoherent institution:

> The equipping of state bodies with economic functions, and of business enterprises with quasi-state powers, led not to a more effective and rationally functioning "state monopoly capitalism," but to a welter of jurisdictions and responsibilities that could be held in check only by short-term projects and campaigns. The splintered state and semi-state managerial bodies adopted the principle of competition. The "nationalization" of society by Nazism was followed by the "privatization" of the state. This paradox meant that, on the one hand, there were huge concentrations

of power as a result of internal and external Blitzkrieg campaigns, while, on the other hand, inefficiency, lack of planning, falling productivity and general decline prevailed.[31]

This had the most serious implications in relation to German war-making. Götz Aly claims that the plundering of conquered territories and externalization of monetary inflation undertaken by the Nazis as World War II progressed served to bind the German masses to the regime by raising their living standards.[32] The thesis is massively exaggerated and ignores such opposition and resistance that did take place.[33] Nevertheless, it inadvertently identifies a central problem for the regime: the provision of material resources for German industry and provisions for the German population would have been impossible without territorial expansion through war; yet this was precisely what the nature of the regime undermined. As Tim Mason noted, "The racial-ethical utopia . . . was taken so seriously by the political leadership, in particular by Hitler and by the SS, that in decisive questions even the urgent material needs of the system were sacrificed to it."[34]

Germany had higher rates of female participation in the workforce than either Britain or the United States at the beginning of the war, although many of these jobs were in roles considered suitable for women and which would not be detrimental to their roles as wives and mothers.[35] Yet, despite a desperate shortage of labor, Hitler resisted female conscription until after German defeat at the battle of Stalingrad, apparently for ideological concerns over a potential decline in the birth rate (and hence to the strength of the "Aryan" race) and the threat to female morals; but even then his resistance was applied halfheartedly and was widely evaded.[36]

Thus, there can be situations where there is a genuine "non-identity of interest" between capitalists and what are—from their point of view—the irrational demands made by the social base of the political party that they prefer to have custody of the state. This may appear to be sheer stupidity, but as Theodor Adorno once pointed out, specifically in relation to the Nazi regime, "Stupidity is not a natural quality, but one socially produced and reinforced."

Hitler failed to invade the United Kingdom when he had the chance and invaded the Soviet Union when he did not need to:

> The German ruling clique drove towards war because they were excluded from a position of imperial power. But in their exclusion lay the reason for the blind and clumsy provincialism that made Hitler's and Ribbentropp's policies uncompetitive and their war a gamble.... Germany's industrial backwardness forced its politicians—anxious to regain lost ground and, as have-nots, specially qualified for the role—to fall back on their immediate, narrow experience, that of the political façade. They saw nothing in front of them except cheering assemblies and frightened negotiators: this blocked their view of the objective power of a greater mass of capital.[37]

The contemporary relevance of this experience is limited: The working class is not currently combative enough to inspire fear in the bourgeoisie, and the states in which the fascist far right is large enough even to conceive of achieving power, like Greece or Hungary, are not imperialist powers capable of attempting continental domination in the way that Germany or even Italy was capable of doing. The point is that, in the contemporary situation, all that may remain are those aspects of the far-right program that are irrational for capital, particularly in its current neoliberal manifestation.

The Appeal of the Populist Right

Fascist movements cannot base themselves on working-class organizations, since one of their defining characteristics is to seek the destruction of such movements. This is why a movement like Ulster Loyalism in Northern Ireland, based as it was on the skilled Protestant working class, cannot be described as fascist, however reactionary and divisive it may otherwise have been. But if fascist movements are incompatible with working-class organizations, they can and do draw support from individual members of the working class, as can the far right more generally. This is the real threat posed by Trump in the United States and the UK Independence Party (UKIP) in the United Kingdom.

Chip Berlet and Matthew Lyons observe that, in the context of the United States, there are "two versions of secular right-wing populism," each drawing on a different class base: "one centered around 'get the government off my back' economic libertarianism coupled with a rejection of mainstream political parties (more attractive to the upper-middle class and small entrepreneurs); the other based on xenophobia and ethnocentric nationalism (more attractive to the lower-middle class and wage workers)."[38] As the reference to "wage-workers" in relation to the second version suggests, the reactionary role played by sections of the middle classes does not exhaust the social basis of right-wing social movements. Since the majority of the population are exploited and oppressed, such movements must draw at least some support from their ranks.

Unfortunately, the spectacle of the working class, or the oppressed more generally, mobilizing against their own interests alongside members of other social classes has produced a number of inadequate responses from socialists. One is the claim that working-class demands or actions, which might appear reactionary, actually contain a rational core that renders them defensible by the left: in relation to migration this is sometimes expressed as the need for socialists to pay heed to the "genuine concerns" of the working class, as if the sincerity of the belief rendered it valid. The other inadequate response is the argument that, even if working-class people participate in them, right-wing movements are illegitimate because they are funded or led by wealthy corporations or individuals.

This argument inverts the classic conservative theme that popular unrest against the established order is never, as it were, natural, but always orchestrated by external forces ("outside agitators"), inventing or, at most, manipulating grievances in order to further their own ends.[39] Some of the people who supported Trump may well be morally wrong and politically misguided, but it is patronizing—and above all politically useless—to pretend that they are simply being manipulated by elite puppet masters. Sara Diamond is therefore correct that left critics of the US Christian right are wrong to adopt what she calls "a view of conspiracies by small, right-wing cliques to stage-manage what was truly a mass move-ment." She is also right to emphasize the complexity of right-wing populism towards "existing power structures," being "partially *op-positional* and partially . . . *system supportive.*"[40]

Why, then, might working-class people be predisposed to re-spond positively to right-wing arguments? There are both general reasons true at all periods in the history of capitalism and specific reasons relevant to the present neoliberal conjuncture. Marxists, above all Gramsci, have shown that most members of the subor-dinate classes have highly contradictory forms of consciousness.[41] Nevertheless, the capitalist system could not survive unless it was accepted at some level, most of the time, by the majority of the people who live under it. The implications of this are darker than is sometimes supposed. A characteristic form of contradictory con-sciousness involves a reformist inability to conceive of anything beyond capitalism, while opposing specific effects of the system.

But the alternatives are not restricted to active rejection at one extreme and passive acceptance at the other. There can also be *ac-tive* support, the internalization of capitalist values associated with the system to the point where they can lead to action. Marxists and other anticapitalist radicals frequently point out that, rather than men benefiting from the oppression of women, whites from the oppression of Blacks, or straights from the oppression of LGBTQ people, it is capitalism and the bourgeoisie that do so. This is a use-ful corrective to the argument, common in many left-wing move-ments, that each form of oppression is separate from the others and that none has any necessary connection to the capitalist system.

Nevertheless, it fails to take seriously the distinction made by Lukács between "what men *in fact* thought, felt and wanted at any point in the class structure" and "the thoughts and feelings which men would have in a particular situation if they were *able* to assess both it and the interests arising from it in their impact on immedi-ate action and on the whole structure of society."[42] For we cannot assume that members of the working class are not only capable of having, but actually *have* the thoughts and feelings "appropriate to their objective situation." If the workers do not attain this level of consciousness, a significant minority take positions supportive of, for example, racial oppression, which may not have benefited them compared with the benefits they would have received by struggling for racial equality, let alone full social equality. Without some degree of class consciousness, however, they need not ever consider this alternative: in the immediate context of their situation, a stance that is detrimental to working-class interests as a whole may not make sense to particular individual members of the working class.

The victories of neoliberalism have left the working class in the West increasingly fragmented and disorganized, and, for some workers, appeals to blood and nation appear as the only viable form of collectivity still available, particularly in a context where any systemic alternative to capitalism—however false it may have been— had apparently collapsed in 1989–91. Dismissing their views on grounds of irrationality is simply an evasion. As Berlet and Lyons write: "Right-wing populist claims are no more and no less irrational than conventional claims that presidential elections express the will of the people, that economic health can be measured by the profits of multimillion dollar corporations, or that US military interventions in Haiti or Somalia or Kosovo or wherever are designed to promote democracy and human rights."[43] Yet these beliefs, which are accepted by many more people than those who believe in, say, the literal truth of the Book of Genesis, are not treated as signs of insanity. The issue, as Berlet has argued elsewhere, is not "personal pathology" but collective "desperation."[44]

The increasing interchangeability of mainstream political parties, including those on the social democratic left, gives the far right an opening to voters by positioning themselves as outside the consensus in relation to social policy.[45] Michael Kimmel points out that, although it would be absurd to claim that "women or gay people or people of color *are* being treated equally," it is true that "we have never been *more* equal than we are today"; but "at the same time . . . economically we are more *unequal* than we have been in about a century":

So it's easy to think these phenomena are related—that the greater class inequality is somehow attendant upon, even caused by, greater social equality. Perhaps we can be convinced that the reason for the dramatic skewing of our country's riches is somehow that these newly arrived groups are siphoning off the very benefits that were supposed to be trickling down to middle- and lower-middle-class white men.[46]

Kimmel follows the characteristic, everyday discourse in the United States, in which working-class people are described as, or contained within the categories of, "middle- and lower-middle-class," but his conclusion is apt: "To believe that greater social equality is the cause of your economic misery requires a significant amount of manipulation, perhaps the greatest bait and switch that has ever been perpetuated against middle- and lower-middle-class Americans."[47]

A majority of the people involved in right-wing social movements do so because of underlying economic concerns; the more relevant question is perhaps whether, in the absence of any left-wing solution to those concerns, they continue to demand the implementation of their social program as a condition of support for politicians who claim to represent them. In these circumstances, a deeper problem for the stability of the capitalist system than the possibility of far-right parties themselves coming to power with a program destructive to capitalist needs might be their influence over the mainstream parties of the right, when the beliefs of their supporters may inadvertently cause difficulty for the accumulation process. As Müller writes, from the perspective of the liberal left:

It's hard to deny that some policies justified with reference to "the people" really can turn out to have been irresponsible: those deciding on such policies did not think hard enough; they failed to gather all the relevant evidence; or, most plausibly, their knowledge of the likely long-term consequences should have made them refrain from policies with only short-term electoral benefits to themselves. One does not have to be a neoliberal technocrat to judge some policies as plainly irrational.[48]

The clearest examples of this type of irrationality are to be found in the Anglo-Saxon heartlands of neoliberalism: the United States and Britain. Take an important area of Republican Party support. Since the late Sixties, Republicans have been increasingly reliant on communities of fundamentalist Christian believers, whose activism allows them to be mobilized for voting purposes. The problem, and not only for the Republicans, is not only that the extremism of fundamentalist Christianity may alienate the electoral "middle ground" on which the result of American elections increasingly depends, but that politicians are constrained from undertaking policies that may be necessary for American capitalism. Unwanted outcomes for capital need not be the product of a coherent religious worldview, simply one that no longer believes anything produced outside its own experience—or the way in which that experience is interpreted by their trusted sources of information.

But it is not only religious belief that can cause difficulties for US capital; so too can overt anti-migrant racism. One concrete example of this is the Tea Party–inspired Beason-Hammon Alabama Taxpayer and Citizen Protection Act—HB56, as it is usually known—which was passed by the state legislature in June 2011, making it illegal not to carry immigration papers and preventing anyone without documents from receiving any provisions from the state, including water supply. The law was intended to prevent and reverse immigration by undocumented immigrants, but the effect was to cause a mass departure from the many of the agricultural businesses that relied on these workers to form the bulk of their labor force: "In the north of the state, the pungent smell of rotting tomatoes hangs in the air across huge tranches of land that have been virtually abandoned by workers who, through fear or anger, are no longer turning up to gather the harvest."[49] But the effects went deeper. Before the laws introduced it was estimated that 4.2 percent of the workforce, or ninety-five thousand people, were undocumented but paying $130.3 million in state and local taxes. Their departure from the state or withdrawal to the underground economy threatened to reduce the size of the local economy by $40 million. Moreover, employers had to spend more money on screening prospective employees, on HR staff to check paperwork, and on insuring for potential legal liabilities from inadvertent breaches of the law.[50]

These developments are *not* equivalent to the type of policies with which social democracy occasionally (and decreasingly) attempts to ameliorate the excesses of capitalism. On the one hand, social democratic reforms are usually intended to enable the system as a whole to function more effectively for capitalists and more equitably for the majority, however irreconcilable these aims may be. But far-right reforms of the type just discussed are not even intended to work in the interests of capitalists, nor do they: they really embody irrational racist beliefs that take precedence over all else.

Independent Class Politics in a New Era

I have tried here to set out a general argument about the nature of the populist hard right and, in particular, to show that it plays a contradictory role: always opposed to the actual interests of the working class, but sometimes also undermining—albeit unintentionally—the interests of capital. What does it mean in relation to the two episodes with which I began: the UK vote to leave the EU and the election of Trump? These required different responses: a choice in one and a refusal to choose in the other, despite the presence of the populist hard right in both.

In one, socialists were faced with a particular outcome, UK withdrawal from the EU, which was indeterminate in its effects (there are both left- and right-wing reasons for leaving) and in which the pro-Leave sections of the bourgeoisie were (in Gramsci's terms) "in error" over what it meant for British capital. In the other, socialists were being asked to support a party (the Democrats) that had engineered the exclusion of the only genuine left-winger from the ballot and a particular candidate (Clinton) standing on a platform of maintaining the very neoliberal policies that the left is opposed. This is the difference between a situation in which socialists can at least attempt to shape events and one in which they are effectively their prisoners. The key, as always, is being able to tell which is which.

FROM HOPE TO DESPAIR

How the Obama Years Gave Us Trump

Lance Selfa

The Trump presidency dawned with the opposition Democratic Party finding itself at its lowest ebb since the 1920s. The Democrats lost the executive branch, remained minorities in both houses of Congress, and stood to·see the Republicans lock in another generation of control of the Supreme Court and US judiciary. At the state level, Republicans controlled sixty-eight of the ninety-nine state legislative bodies and held thirty-three of fifty governorships, and the Democrats held more than one thousand fewer state legislative seats than they controlled in 2009.[1] Republican dominance at the state level brought a counterrevolution against labor rights, women's rights, and voting rights.

Of course, it wasn't supposed to be like this. In 2006 and 2008, two "wave" elections swept Democrats to power. In 2008, with the US and world economies melting down, with neoliberal dogma discredited ("We're all socialists, now!" proclaimed *Newsweek*), and with George W. Bush departing office as the most unpopular president since Jimmy Carter, a new Democratic era seemed to be dawning. The conservative pundit and former Bush speech writer David Frum voiced conservative dread:

The stage has been set for the boldest and most dramatic re-direction of US politics since Reagan's first year in office. Of course, there are no guarantees in politics. An inept president could bungle his or her chances. Unexpected events could intrude: a nuclear test in Iran, a major terrorist attack on US soil or some attention-grabbing political scandal. But given moderate luck and skill, the next president could join Reagan, Lyndon Johnson and Franklin Roosevelt as one of the grand reshapers of politics and government.[2]

Barack Obama's 2008 election certainly marked a historic high point in history—the election of an African American president in a country that was founded and sustained for most of its history on slavery. A sense of hope and optimism pervaded the multiracial crowd of hundreds of thousands who rallied in celebration of Obama's win in 2008 in Chicago's Grant Park.

And yet, eight years later, Obama's secretary of state and one of the world's most influential politicians lost the Electoral College to an admitted sexual predator, bigot, and buffoon whom Obama had insisted the American people would never support.

"Change" Many Believed In

Obama assumed power at a time when the US economy was in free fall in the worst recession since the Great Depression of the 1930s. On the eve of President Barack Obama's inauguration in January 2009, Obama's popularity reached 80 percent, and large numbers of Americans had high expectations of the incoming administration. A *USA Today* poll showed that seven of ten people believed the country would be better off after Obama's first term.

After two straight national elections in which the Republicans took a beating, the largest Democratic majority since the 1970s looked set to shift American mainstream politics away from three decades of conservative domination. The American right looked small, irrelevant to the concerns of most Americans, and appeared ready to spend years in the political "wilderness." Two years later, the formerly discredited and out-of-touch Republican Party scored a historic landslide in the 2010 midterm election. In the largest congressional midterm shift since 1938, the Republicans captured sixty-three seats, ending the four-year Democratic majority in the House of Representatives.

Much liberal commentary portrayed Obama as a good and decent president who tried to accomplish big goals against unscrupulous opponents who used every dirty trick they could—including promoting the racist myth that Obama wasn't born in the United States—to undercut him at every turn. Obama himself often compared implementing change in Washington to "turning an ocean liner." It was as if Obama, the most powerful man in the world for eight years, was a helpless bystander to historical events.

That's why any evaluation of "the Obama years" has to focus on the first two years of his term, when Obama held huge Democratic majorities in the Congress and a mandate to enact big changes in an atmosphere of national crisis. The "Great Recession," which most acknowledged stemmed from the bursting of a Wall Street–engineered credit bubble, dominated every aspect of politics and popular consciousness through most of Obama's term. The administration would rise or fall on how it dealt with the economic crisis.

But Obama was dedicated to the pro-business neoliberal agenda that has dominated Democratic Party circles since the Clinton administration of the 1990s. Millions voted for Obama hoping for a decisive shift in Washington politics and policy. But Obama and his elite backers were more interested in restoring the capital to its pre-2008 "business as usual." The gap between expectation and reality sapped Obama of mass support.

The economic rescue bill Obama pushed through the Congress early in his term came in at less than $800 billion, which was about half the size that many independent economists estimated it should have been. To win more "bipartisan" support, the administration limited the amount of money allocated to jobs creation and explicitly ruled out direct government jobs programs modeled on the 1930s-era Works Progress Administration. It dedicated far too much of the stimulus, upwards of 40 percent of the total, to a variety of tax cuts and credits to individuals and business that were useless in creating jobs. These concessions won the votes of three Republican senators and no Republicans in the House, but they further limited the bill's impact.

When the administration pushed for the stimulus bill, it released studies claiming that the stimulus package would push the unemployment rate down to 7 percent by 2010. In reality, the unemployment rate increased to over 10 percent. The stimulus bill may have helped avert a plunge into depression, but it failed to reduce unemployment in any noticeable way.

The administration cost itself greater damage when it became associated in the public's mind with coddling Wall Street. Following a March 2009 meeting at the White House between Obama, Treasury Secretary Timothy Geithner, and the CEOs of the largest thirteen banks in the United States, the president reassured the bankers that he had no intention of forcing a change in the way Wall Street did business. Journalist Ron Suskind quoted one of the CEOs who attended: "The sense of everyone after the big meeting was relief. . . . The president had us at a moment of real vulnerability. At that point, he could have ordered us to do just about anything, and we would have rolled over. But he didn't—he mostly wanted to help us out, to quell the mob."[3]

No wonder more and more Americans came to see the Obama administration as a bankers' administration—in the same way that they viewed the Bush-Cheney regime as an "oil and gas" administration. A September 2009 Economic Policy Institute poll asked a national sample of registered voters to say who they thought had "been helped a lot or some" from the policies that the administration had enacted. The result: 13 percent said the "average working person," 64 percent identified "large banks," and 54 percent said "Wall Street investment companies."[4]

The sense of restoring the status quo pervaded much of Obama's response to the crisis the Bush administration left behind. With the economy teetering on the brink, Obama continued to implement the Bush administration's Wall Street bailouts and reap-pointed Bush's Federal Reserve chairman, Ben Bernanke. With the United States bogged down in two failed wars in Iraq and Afghan-istan, Obama reappointed Bush's defense secretary, Robert Gates, to run the Pentagon.

Using only executive action, Obama could have unwound the Bush administration bailouts for the Wall Street bankers and pressed bankruptcy judges to reduce or wipe out the mortgage holders' debt. At the very least, he could have refused to allow executives from the insurance giant AIG to collect their multimillion-dollar bonuses from the taxpayers' dime. Yet he did none of these things. In fact, billions appropriated to help homeowners avoid foreclosure remained unspent. And after using the excuse of the "sanctity of contracts" to justify allowing the AIG bonuses, the Obama admin-istration enacted a bailout of the auto industry that tore up union contracts and imposed two-tiered wage structures.

And what of Obama's signature healthcare reform that Repub-licans have promised to repeal since the day it passed? This was indeed a "heavy lift" and did result in some significant reforms to health insurance that benefited working people. But in its origin, the Affordable Care Act (ACA) was modeled on healthcare reforms that the conservative Heritage Foundation promoted and that Re-publican governor Mitt Romney—Obama's presidential opponent in 2012—implemented in Massachusetts.

Supporters of genuine healthcare reform knew that the "com-promise" bill was a huge gift to the insurance industry. At the same time, they felt that Democrats got far less than they could or should have, in large part because they didn't even try.[5] In fact, the Obama administration worked with lobbyists from the insur-ance, hospital, and pharmaceutical industries to craft a bill that would be sufficiently pro-corporate to keep them from opposing it. Healthcare advocates pressed for a public insurance component to Obamacare, but Obama batted them away. As journalist Glenn Greenwald pointed out at the time, Obama's support for the "pub-lic option" was always more rhetorical than real: "The evidence was overwhelming from the start that the White House was not only indifferent, but opposed, to the provisions most important to progressives. The administration is getting the bill which they, more or less, wanted from the start—the one that is a huge boon to the health insurance and pharmaceutical industry."[6]

Several years later, the ACA has reshaped the healthcare industry along neoliberal lines, but it has still never managed to win the popular support that Obama thought it would. That's because it retains the role of the private insurance industry, which has continued to shift costs to individuals, while still leaving millions uninsured. Opinion polls have consistently shown that a substantial number of people who say they oppose Obamacare do so because they think it doesn't go far enough. Because Obamacare never reached the level of popularity of programs such as Medicare or Social Security, Republicans were confident they could repeal it without much consequence.[7]

Austerian-in-Chief

After the GOP took the House in 2010 and until it took the Senate in 2014, the Obama administration helped drive an austerity agenda that further cut into working-class living standards. In 2010, the administration and the Democratically dominated Congress agreed to extend the Bush administration's tax cuts for the rich for two more years. And in 2012, when the tax cuts were set to expire, Obama agreed to allow most of them to remain.

In 2011, the Tea Party–addled Republicans in the House threatened to plunge the United States government into default to force through huge cuts in government spending. Instead of calling their bluff, Obama agreed to cutting $1.5 trillion in federal spending over the next decade. In fact, the GOP had to rely on Democratic votes to pass the deal that lifted the debt ceiling. Noting this, Greenwald commented:

> Therein lies one of the most enduring attributes of Obama's legacy: in many crucial areas, he has done more to subvert and weaken the left's political agenda than a GOP president could have

dreamed of achieving. So potent, so overarching, are tribal loy-
alties in American politics that partisans will support, or at least
tolerate, any and all policies their party's leader endorses—even
if those policies are ones they long claimed to loathe.[8]

During the negotiations over the 2011 government shutdown,
Obama offered the Republicans unprecedented cuts to Social Security and Medicare. Feeling perhaps that Obama was on his way
to becoming a one-term president, the GOP rejected him. But like
the spurned yet determined suitor, an Obama reelected in 2012 was
back to courting the GOP for a "grand bargain." Only belatedly
did he give up, but he had wasted years legitimizing GOP talking
points about the need for working people to accept more austerity.

Ironically, Obama only won reelection by adopting a pose as
"fighter for the middle class" against the plutocrat Romney. Working-class voters of all races were willing to give Obama another
chance, especially since—picking up on the sense of class inequality that the 2011 Occupy movement had highlighted—his reelection stump speech foregrounded inequality as "the challenge of our
times." *Rolling Stone's* Matt Taibbi was more than a little skeptical:

> Hearing Obama talk about jobs and shared prosperity . . . remind-
> ed me that we are back in campaign mode, and Barack Obama has
> started doing again what he does best—play the part of a progres-
> sive. He's good at it. It sounds like he has a natural affinity for union
> workers and ordinary people when he makes these speeches. But
> his policies are crafted by representatives of corporate/financial
> America, who happen to entirely make up his inner circle.[9]

The "Lame Duck" President

After the GOP took the Senate in 2014, Obama was mostly a lame
duck. His main initiatives came in foreign affairs, such as concluding
an opening to Cuba and the Iran nuclear deal. The most progressive
recent change in US law and cultural norms—the Supreme Court's
legalization of marriage equality in 2015—resulted from grassroots
pressure. Obama officially opposed the demand until 2012.

Though official indicators show improvements in the economy, Obama left office with a majority of the US population enduring lower living standards than when he moved into the White House. In real terms, median household income did not make it back to 2007 levels and is far away from its all-time high of 1999 levels. And, perhaps more significantly, given how the 2016 election turned out, the maldistribution of economic gains in the recovery has meant that people in rural areas suffered a 2 percent decline in median income in 2015.[10]

In assessing the Obama years, much more could be written. For example, about how the president became the "deporter in chief." Or how his administration transformed the Bush administration's civil-liberties-shredding "war on terror" policies into accepted parts of the bipartisan consensus. Or how his administration abetted a coup in Honduras, or sold record amounts of arms to Saudi Arabia and Israel. Or how he let the union-supporting Employee Free Choice Act die in Congress, or refused to comment when the right-wing state government in Wisconsin gutted public sector unions in 2011. Or how his administration tried to steer clear of speaking out on race, except when Obama was lecturing Black audiences about the need for "personal responsibility." Or how, after signing an executive order directing the closure of the Guantánamo Bay prison camp on his first day in office, the camp remained open as he "passed the baton" to Trump.[11]

Each of those Obama administration actions (or inactions) eroded support from key Democratic constituency groups. In the end, the Republicans didn't so much win the 2016 elections as Democrats lost it.[12] Years of empty rhetoric about "fighting for working families" finally caught up to the Democratic establishment. For the establishment, Vermont senator Bernie Sanders's strong challenge to Clinton in the 2016 Democratic primaries should have been the proverbial "canary in the coal mine." Yet, its contempt for Sanders, for the issues he raised, and for his supporters blinded them to the disaster that loomed in November.

Given how the miserable election ended up, it's difficult to remember that Trump wasn't the only candidate who turned out thousands to huge rallies. In fact, when Sanders packed in more than ten thousand people to an arena in Madison, Wisconsin, in June, 2015, it was the biggest rally for any candidate during the primary season. Thousands responded to his indictment of the "billionaire class" and eagerly sought to join up with his "political revolution." Yet the Democratic Party establishment succeeded in pushing the Sanders campaign out of contention.

To the Democrat leadership, the Sanders campaign was supposed to perform a service of energizing people that Clinton couldn't. He'd have his chance on the public stage, and then would move into the wings in favor of Clinton. The revelations from hacked Democratic National Committee emails, released by WikiLeaks, demonstrated that the supposedly "neutral" DNC wired the process in favor of Clinton from the start. In fact, those revelations were so damning that they forced DNC chair Debbie Wasserman Schultz to resign during the Democratic convention in July. By then, the deed was done, and Clinton was assured the nomination.

Moreover, the chatter between Clinton advisers revealed in the WikiLeaks email drops showed them planning right-wing smears against Sanders. One of her advisers even likened Democratic-base supporters of Sanders's signature call for a fifteen-dollars-per-hour minimum wage to the "Red Army."[13] Finally, WikiLeaks demonstrated that all of the criticisms that Sanders leveled against Clinton during the primaries—that she was in the pocket of the Wall Street banks, that her Democratic primary opposition to the Keystone XL pipeline was opportunistic, and that party primaries were rigged against him, among others—were more correct than he even knew.[14]

And yet, by the time all these revelations saw light—and long after they were useful as fodder in the Clinton-Sanders election contest—they disappeared from the national political conversation. Of course, the media obsession with "horse-race coverage" of the Trump-Clinton contest partially explained this. But a more pertinent—and important—explanation was found in the fact that Sanders himself refused to make them an issue.

"The job of the progressive movement now is to look forward, not backward," Sanders said in a statement to NBC News. "No matter what Secretary Clinton may have said years ago, behind closed doors, what's important today is that millions of people stand up and demand that the Democratic Party implement the most progressive platform in the history of our country."

From "Political Revolution" to Lesser Evilism

During the Democratic primaries, Sanders gained support with segments of the "rising American electorate" for one main reason: he spoke directly to the realities of class inequality in the United States and raised the expectations of his supporters that something could be done about it.[15] His appeals and policy positions fell under his call for a "political revolution." This slogan was both savvy and telling: Savvy in that it appealed to millions whom the political system had abandoned, and for whom the idea of a radical shakeup (or "revolution") didn't sound so bad. Telling because the actual content of Sanders's "political revolution" amounted to reforming the Democratic Party, encouraging "progressives" to run for office as Democrats, and campaign finance reform to check the influence of "millionaires and billionaires" on the US electoral and government system.

Even though Sanders advocated policy positions that are radical when compared to today's neoliberalized and corrupted conventional wisdom, his campaign was actually quite conventional. It was, as were Jesse Jackson's Rainbow Coalition campaigns of the 1980s before it, an electoral campaign waged inside one of the two main political parties of American capitalism. Campaign "insider" reports emerging near the end of the primary season noted that Sanders's top command chose to spend much of its prodigious fundraising haul on expensive, old-school television ads rather than grassroots field organizing.[16] If the Sanders campaign wasn't willing (or able) to organize a "grassroots army" during its primary campaign, it's unlikely that it will leave much of an infrastructure of activists behind.

Subsequent developments seemed to bear this out. When Sanders announced his continuing vehicle, Our Revolution, in

August 2016, four key staffers quit in protest.[17] They objected to Sanders's choice of Jeff Weaver, his longtime campaign manager, as director of the organization. They also opposed the group's tax status as a nonprofit that can accept large anonymous contributions. To them, this indicated that Our Revolution would be just another Democratic Party super PAC accepting unlimited and anonymous donations and funneling them into Democratic Party electoral campaigns rather than into grassroots organizing.

The announcement of Our Revolution followed a few weeks after Sanders rendered his greatest service to the Democratic Party. In the midst of its Philadelphia convention, when the first WikiLeaks revelations were exposing the DNC's blatant favoritism toward Clinton, Sanders moved to quell a revolt of a minority of his pledged delegates on the convention floor. Some Sanders delegates chanted "no war" during a speech by former CIA director Leon Panetta, and a few hundred walked out of the convention. But Sanders stepped into his long-established role. Not only did he endorse Clinton, he actually moved to throw all of his delegates behind her nomination. This allowed Democratic leaders to tout unprecedented party unity, and saved Clinton the embarrassment of seeing how Sanders delegates really felt about her during the convention roll-call vote. Sanders, having performed these "sheepdog" duties, received fulsome praise from Clintonite operatives who had, only a few months earlier, been calling Sanders and his supporters racist, sexist, "privileged," and the like.[18]

Television coverage of Sanders's Clinton endorsement speech zoomed in on groups of young Sanders delegates shouting or weeping as Sanders threw his support behind someone he had rightly criticized as one of the worst representatives of the corrupt bipartisan Washington establishment. And while one could sympathize with the sense of betrayal some young Sandernistas may have felt, Sanders and his closest advisers were hardly babes in the woods. They knew what they were getting into, and they knew what would be expected of them.

After the Democratic convention, Sanders served as a Clinton surrogate, one of whose main tasks was to dissuade his supporters from supporting the Green Party's Jill Stein for president. "When we're talking about president of the United States, in my own personal view, this is not the time for a protest vote," Sanders told the *Washington Post*. "This is [the] time to elect Hillary Clinton and then work after the election to mobilize millions of people to make sure she can be the most progressive president she can be."[19]

In the long history of "insurgent" campaigns inside the Democratic Party—Eugene McCarthy's run against LBJ in 1968, Jesse Jackson's "Rainbow Coalition" runs in the 1980s, or Dennis Kucinich's antiwar campaigns in the George W. Bush years—the challenger may win "hearts and minds" of the most committed Democratic partisans. But, in the end, they become loyal soldiers in helping to herd their supporters behind the establishment choice. As it was in the past, so it was in 2016. Only this time, the "insurgent" was a self-described socialist and (formerly) political independent who animated millions—only to deliver them over to the candidate social democratic scholar Adolph Reed Jr. dubbed a "lying, neoliberal warmonger."[20] Tragically, Sanders not only campaigned for Clinton but also promoted her as the standard-bearer of his platform.

Far from helping to popularize "progressive" issues in the general election, Sanders's work to elect Clinton helped her to marginalize any commitments to them. For most of the general election campaign, Clinton tailored her appeals to "moderate" Republicans repelled by Trump's vulgarity and worried that Trump's election would damage the US image overseas. Needless to say, a strategy of wooing suburban Republicans didn't foreground issues of class and racial inequality in the United States. So Sanders tagged along to assure Democratic "base" voters that Clinton really was committed to implementing "the most progressive Democratic platform in history." Yet, Clinton hardly mentioned the platform or any issue besides Trump's "fitness" to serve as president.[21] And she still managed to lose to the weakest major party candidate in a generation.

The Price of Defending "Hollow Tenets"

Assuming power in 2009 as the economic crisis hit with full ferocity, the Democrats were destined to face a difficult situation. But they also had an opportunity because they were thrust into a position to reorder American politics in the face of obvious crises. As Aziz Rana explained the conjuncture:

> At a moment when the country faced convulsive social crises, and more and more of [Obama's] supporters called for a fundamental reconstruction of American institutions, Obama marshaled his personal story and oratorical gifts to defend hollow tenets: the righteousness of American primacy, the legitimacy of global market liberalism, the need for incremental reform, the danger of large-scale structural overhaul. The consequence—intensified by a virulent right—was that fundamental problems continued to fester and became harder to ignore: mass incarceration and structural racism, dramatic class disparities in power and opportunity, interventionism abroad, and national-security abuses at home.[22]

The price of Obama's defense of these, in Rana's words, "hollow tenets" and the Democrats' "suspicion of politics formed through mass democratic mobilization" was demoralization and despair that led eventually to the Trump disaster.

An honest assessment of the Obama years would also note the myriad ways—from championing austerity politics, to education privatization, to building a machine that deported more than two million undocumented immigrants—paved the way for Trump's policies. Obama and the Democratic Party—the so-called party of the people—managed to position themselves as the chief defenders of a status quo that had led millions of Americans to despair. However cynically, the GOP managed to channel public outrage with that status quo into two "wave" midterm elections and an improbable presidential victory in 2016.

In the summer of 2009, when liberal commentators were waxing on about the potential of Obama to become another transformative president in the mold of Franklin Roosevelt, the writer Kevin Baker aired the unorthodox view that Obama was more comparable to Herbert Hoover, the Republican Roosevelt defeated in 1932.

Much like Hoover, "Barack Obama is a man attempting to realize a stirring new vision of his society without cutting himself free from the dogmas of the past—without accepting the inevitable conflict. Like Hoover, he is bound to fail." Obama's penchant to reach for compromise and "bipartisanship" was exactly the opposite of what the dire situation he inherited required—and what the American populace was ready for. Obama's first term, Baker wrote, offered "one of those rare moments in history when the radical becomes pragmatic, when deliberation and compromise foster disaster."[23] In the wake of the election of Trump, Baker's analysis looks more prescient than ever.

BLACK POLITICS IN THE TRUMP ERA

Keeanga-Yamahtta Taylor

Not so long ago, when Barack Obama became president of the United States, the national conversation in the country was whether or not the United States was going to become a postracial society. Indeed, in December 2008, *Forbes* magazine ran an overexuberant editorial that claimed, "Racism in America is over."

Nearly eight and a half years later, we could not be further from that conversation. Not only is racism not over in the United States, but an unabashed racist sits at the country's helm. Donald Trump ran a campaign fueled on racism, anti-Muslim bigotry, sexism, and rabid nationalism. It is not hyperbole to say that white supremacy sits at the heart of the American government. Not only did Donald Trump choose as his chief strategist Steve Bannon, the former editor of the race-baiting, hate-mongering Breitbart News, which Bannon bragged was a platform for the so-called "alt-right"—simply a new name for the old term *white supremacists*—but there is also Stephen Miller, the architect of the first Muslim travel ban, who was a protégé of white supremacist Richard Spencer when they were both students at Duke University. As a candidate, Trump received the enthusiastic endorsement of white racists like David Duke and the Ku Klux Klan. Indeed, Trump's entire posture as a "law and order" candidate developed in response to the growth of the Black Lives Matter movement. Some of his supporters have referred to the Black Lives Matter movement and affiliated organizations as "terrorists."

With the election of Donald Trump, not only have the campaign promises of a bigot and sexual predator been brought to life, but Trump's rise has also imbued the confidence of white supremacists and other racists who have had to operate at the margins of our society. They have been emboldened to come out into the open, spewing racism and instigating violence against nonwhite people. The growth of anti-Muslim organizations has tripled since Trump began his campaign for president in 2015 and continued to rise in the opening months of his presidency. Hate crimes and violence have occurred across the country, from the desecration of Jewish cemeteries to the burning of mosques and violent attacks on immigrants. When Srinivas Kuchibhotla, an Indian immigrant living in Kansas, was shot and murdered by a white racist, the shooter initially asked, "What visa are you here on?" before yelling "Get out of my country!" Donald Trump's election has unleashed the beasts of racism and reaction.

Despite the so-called populist rhetoric of Trump during the campaign and his fake concern for the plight of "working-class white people," his cabinet choices—an array of billionaires, campaign donors, and wholly unqualified individuals—betray an agenda intended to gut the living standards of ordinary and working-class people across this country, while continuing to line the pockets of the rich.

The already anemic and fragile remnants of social welfare and public services, intended to protect the general public from the ravages of the free market status quo, will be further shredded. Trump has put a fox in every henhouse with regards to the individuals he has chosen to lead the Environmental Protection Agency, the Department of Justice, the Department of Housing and Urban Development, and the Department of Education, to name only the most egregious examples. These individuals question the very necessity of the agencies they have been tasked with overseeing—creating a recipe for either inaction or ineptitude. This unbridled effort to "deconstruct the administrative state," as Steve Bannon has termed it, will have a disproportionate impact on the lives of Black people who disproportionately rely on public services and regulations. This is where the real harm of a Trump administration can be measured. It is not just his racist and dangerous rhetoric, but this threat to further weaken public institutions by starving them of desperately needed human and financial resources. It will also continue the perilous slide of the Black middle class, many of whom rely on government jobs for employment. The promises to "shrink" government will mean a rise in unemployment for Black women, for example.

Perhaps the greatest threat associated with gutting federal agencies, however, is the impact on the quality of life for African Americans. For example, the threats to dismantle and defund the Environmental Protection Agency (EPA) will be devastating for Black families who are overexposed to hazardous and toxic living environments. Environmental racism created the conditions for the lead-poisoned water of Flint, Michigan, and the lead-infested housing across Baltimore. In real terms, this means that Black children are twice as likely to have asthma as white children. It means that nearly half of Latino-majority communities live in counties that do not meet EPA air quality standards. Trump's planned budget cuts to the EPA will wipe out the organization's already flawed and insufficient plans to protect communities at risk of environmental poisoning.

The same story could be relayed about the attacks on public education. In the major metropolitan areas across this country, Black and brown children disproportionately rely on public schools as their source of education. All of the efforts to redistribute public dollars from public schools into charter schools and vouchers for private schools will come at the expense of public schools, where the majority of the students, nationally, are Black and brown.

All of these attacks on public institutions are what fuel the righteous fear and revulsion of Trump. They also animate the urgency of the budding movement of resistance to the dangerous administration. But the horrors and challenges presented by the Trump administration should not obscure the very important discussion of how the administration came into power. Our understanding of how we came to this moment in history impacts and guides what we do next. This also means locating that which connects the Trump administration to the past while allowing for what sets his administration apart.

After all, if we assign Trump and his band of rogues, racists, and reactionaries an exceptional or unprecedented place in American history, then we cannot even make sense of the most recent past. Plainly stated, if things were so great before Trump, why did Ferguson, Missouri, erupt in the summer of 2014; why did Baltimore explode eight months later; why, indeed, did a movement called Black Lives Matter arise during a time of the greatest concentration of Black political power in American history?

You cannot, in fact, understand the emergence of Trump without taking account of this recent history and the failure of the liberal establishment to provide a real alternative to the reactionary populism and isolationism of Trump. As wholly opposite in demeanor, aptitude, and temperament as Barack Obama and Donald Trump are, we cannot actually understand the rise of Trump without taking account of the failure of Obama to deliver on his promises of hope and change.

The multiple media narratives locating Trump's rise solely in his ability to connect with the dispossessed white working class is incomplete at best and disingenuous and exaggerated at worst— the most unfortunate example of this being Van Jones's suggestion that the election results were proof of a "whitelash," or the idea that white voters voted for Trump as revenge for the role African Americans played in the election of Barack Obama. The first problem with this narrative, aside from the fact that tens of millions of white people voted for Obama twice, is that it promotes a mistaken story that African Americans somehow have benefited from the presidency of Barack Obama, and that those supposed benefits have come at the expense of ordinary white people. The genuine fear and disgust of Trump has contributed to intense revisionism and mythology of Barack Obama's record as president. While we can all recognize the power of symbolism and even subscribe to the notion that there was meaning in the election of an African American to the highest office in a nation born and built on the backs of enslaved Black labor, we should not let that acknowledgment cloud our ability to think clearly and tell the truth.

Obama's presidency was not a gift to African Americans; instead, it represented the painful continuity of racism, discrimination, and inequality that has always been at the center of Black life in America. Eight years later, Black unemployment remains twice the rate of whites; eight years later, 38 percent of Black children continue to live below the official poverty line; eight years later, a shocking 55 percent of Black workers—mostly Black women— make under fifteen dollars an hour. It was precisely the inability of the Obama administration to improve the conditions of ordinary Black people that gave rise to the Black Lives Matter movement.

Trump's rise is a story about who did not vote more than who did vote. Trump won with fewer voters than Republican candidate Mitt Romney had in 2012. The 2016 presidential election was about the tens of millions of Americans who did not bother to vote at all. There are 238 million eligible voters in the United States and of that number, only 60 million voted for Trump—and, even among that number, 17 percent of people who voted for him said he was unfit to be president. This doesn't mean that racism was not a key and effective part of Trump's electoral strategy. It clearly was. But we must also look more deeply into what could motivate millions of people to sit out the election in the first place. The media and the political establishment often describe the decision not to vote as apathy. It is an easy description that requires little analysis of what problems exist within our two-party system that create so little confidence and so much indifference, even when it appears that so much is at stake.

It is precisely the lack of real choices that underlines the problem. American voters are regularly told to "hold their noses" when voting, or we describe our vote as the choice between "a lesser of two evils." But within the narrow space of choosing between one party of millionaires over another party of millionaires, the key questions facing ordinary people in this country go unanswered. In the narrow choices constrained between the Democrats and the Republicans, what go unanswered are the questions of who will stop police brutality; who will stop the Immigration and Customs Enforcement (ICE) raids in immigrant communities; who will stop the wars and occupations that feed the racism and bigotry of Islamaphobia; who will be for free education, universal healthcare, and an actual living wage—it all goes unanswered.

We typically expect this kind of callous indifference to the everyday questions of life from the Republican Party, but what about the Democrats, the party that presents itself as representing the interests of ordinary people?

Since the shock of the election, the Democratic Party has blamed its losses on Fox News, the FBI and Clinton's emails, Trump's race-baiting, bad campaign messaging, and the Russians. We cannot say with any certainty that none of these issues factored into the outcome of the election, but what can be said is that the Democratic Party's singular obsession with these other factors has allowed it to ignore the deep and profound political crisis within the party. There is absolutely no reckoning with how this party that purports to be a "party of the people" consistently fails to deliver actual change for the ordinary people it claims to represent.

For example, the presidency of Barack Obama is deemed a success simply because of the absence of any real scandal that marred his presidency. This measure of "success" for the Obama administration is a lesson in how the performance and appearance of "civility" often passes as political accomplishment or legitimacy in this country. While Obama could be complimented for his good manners and wholesome disposition, we can understand the election results in part because of the former president's inability to challenge the political and economic status quo for millions of people. For the political and economic elite, including the leadership of the Democratic Party, the absence of scandal or catastrophe registered as success. This was not like the administration of George W. Bush that took the country into an illegal and immoral war with Iraq. This was not the Bush administration's collective shrug in the face of the catastrophe of Hurricane Katrina in 2005. This was not Bush crashing the American economy in 2007 and 2008.

But for millions of people in this country, it is the status quo that is increasingly intolerable. It gnaws away at the millions of tiny threads that ordinary people are barely hanging onto in their daily struggles to make ends meet. For those who pine for the good old days of Obama or who wistfully long for what could have been with Hillary Clinton as president, it is only because the unspectacular and unglamorous struggles of ordinary people in their daily lives have been rendered invisible. We live in a celebrity culture that glorifies the rich and the famous while ignoring the quotidian and mundane struggles of ordinary people. Imagine if we had a press, a popular culture, or political class that was curious about the lives of working-class people. If we did, what would they find? What is the status quo?

The status quo can be found in the continuing crisis of opioid and narcotic addiction in the country. There are two million people addicted to opioids in the United States, a disproportionate number of whom are white. Half of those people are addicted to heroin. From 2009 to 2014, almost half a million people died from opioid overdoses—a fourfold increase since 1999. In March, in a town in Ohio, a cold-storage trailer was needed to hold dead bodies from suicides and drug overdoses caused by opioid abuse because the morgue was already full from heroin overdoses. In this state, which Trump won, there has been a 775 percent increase in opioid-related deaths in the last thirteen years.

The status quo can be found in the briefly reported story about the reported decline in life expectancy for working-class white women. It is unprecedented for life expectancy to reverse in a so-called first-world country. In the United States' peer countries, life expectancy is actually growing. Why is life expectancy for working-class white women in decline? Drug overdose, suicide, and alcohol abuse.

Indeed, a recent study has found that the life spans of working-class whites and working-class Blacks are merging as working-class and poor whites more generally are dying from suicide and alcohol abuse. The United States is projected to have a life-expectancy rate on par with Mexico and Croatia by the year 2030.

The status quo over the last several years is found in the quiet deportation and removal of 2.5 million undocumented people during the tenure of Barack Obama. In 2012 alone, more than 400,000 undocumented individuals—women, children, men, families—were detained, held in private detention centers with few rights recognized by their captors, until they were forcibly returned to the countries they had fled. We can all look in horror at the indiscriminate way that Trump has empowered ICE agents to swoop into immigrant communities and round people up, but we must acknowledge that Obama's administration greased the wheels to this machinery of injustice long ago.

The status quo in Chicago has been the rise in shootings and murders in the city's working-class Black neighborhoods. In 2016, there were 4,379 people shot and 797 people killed in the city. The overwhelming majority of both groups were African American. The news media offers nonsensical explanations for the violence, including gang retaliation and revenge, but its nonsense is matched by the nonsense offered by elected officials that blames the absence of role models and poor parenting. What is almost never offered, as at least part of the answer, is how Chicago has the highest Black unemployment rate of the nation's five largest cities, at 25 percent; that nearly half of Black men aged twenty to twenty-four in Chicago are neither in school nor employed; or that Chicago has the third-highest poverty rate of large cities, and that it is the most segregated city in the United States.

Finally, there is the status quo of the "shrinking middle class." In the 1970s, 61 percent of Americans fell into that vague but stable category of "middle class." Today that number has fallen to 50 percent. It is driven by the growing wealth inequality that exists in the country. In the last year alone, the "1 percent" saw their income rise by 7 percent, and the "0.1 percent" saw their income rise by 9 percent. In general, the richest 20 percent of households in the United States own 84 percent of the wealth in the country, while the bottom 40 percent own less than 1 percent. The media would have us believe that this is a story primarily about the Rust Belt and disgruntled white workers. In fact, it is also a story about the 240,000 Black homeowners who lost their homes to foreclosure in the last eight years. It is about urban school closures and the decimation of employment for Black educators. Thousands of Black teachers have been fired in the last decade, as school districts retract in size and opt to hire cheaper and whiter replacements for charters that are being used to replace public education.

Eight years later, when we put these conditions of the status quo together, they tell a complete story of deprivation and desperation that exists all over this country. They tell the story of the millions of people left behind. This is the status quo. This is life in the United States without some spectacular catastrophe. This is the so-called lesser evil.

It is the inability of this political and economic system to change this dynamic, and thus deliver actual changes for the better in people's lives, that lead so many people to ignore elections. When people believed that electing Obama would transform the country and their lives, they voted in historic numbers. With big expectations and big hope vested in Obama came even bigger disappointment when he failed to deliver. It is also true that the Republicans were obstinate, recalcitrant, racist, and opposed to giving Obama an inch as president. It speaks to the complete dysfunction of our political system. But it is not only the obstinacy of the Republicans that was the problem. The narrow and limited vision of Obama's political agenda and the Democratic Party in general is what drives the apathy surrounding the party.

Hillary Clinton also ignored the everyday conditions experienced by ordinary people. She ran a campaign where her main slogan was "America is already great." She ran a campaign focused on the abhorrent behavior of Trump, instead of articulating how the Democratic Party could actually transform the hardship experienced by millions of people. Clinton promised to be the third term of Obama, failing to realize that for millions of voters, two terms was enough.

It is easy to understand why Clinton stuck to this message. The Democratic Party is committed to the economic status quo represented by free-market capitalism. It is free-market capitalism's champion. The Democratic Party has also championed the political ethos of what some refer to as "neoliberalism," or the idea that the market is the best way to deliver public services and that competition is what drives efficiency. But if the market is predicated on the idea that there are winners and losers then this, of course, is a terrible way to run a government. It is a terrible way to deliver education, water, housing, food, healthcare, justice, and other vital necessities that any civilization is dependent upon. When this is the root of your political commitment, as I would argue it is for the Democratic Party, then it necessarily limits the range of political change you can advance.

It was impossible for Clinton to argue that her party would deliver change and break the grip of a political order that privileges the rich and powerful, when the Democrats have been in power for the last eight years supporting policies that have maintained the division between the 1 percent and the 99 percent. In other words, we cannot understand the rise of Trump and Trumpism by only looking at what he and the Republicans have done; we must also understand it in terms of what the American center-left party—the Democrats—have not done.

Bernie Sanders recognized this. He ran a campaign in the primaries that tapped into the realization that for most ordinary people, things are getting worse. He recognized it is the responsibility of government to alleviate deprivation through provision. And, with no money, almost no name recognition, and with the entire Democratic Party establishment trained against him, he nearly won the party's nomination for president. If you want to understand the depth of suffering in this country, know that thirteen million people cast their vote for an open socialist here. You need some appreciation of American history to grasp the unprecedented aspect of this. In the 1950s, during the Cold War, the United States was the epicenter of the Red Scare and the witch hunts of Communists. In a moment of macabre illustration, in 1953, the United States executed Ethel and Julius Rosenberg under the pretext of their being Russian spies. It did not hurt if people believed that they were executed because of their membership in the Communist Party. The insurgent campaign of Sanders can be read as an indictment of an economic system that has failed repeatedly to deliver a better way for most people in this country. During the Democratic Party primaries, 44 percent of Black voters aged eighteen to thirty voted for Sanders, compared with the 32 percent of young, Black voters who voted for Clinton—even as the news media, led by the Clinton campaign, continued to refer to Black voters as a "firewall" for Clinton. And today, among nonwhite voters, Sanders has a 72 percent approval rating, which is higher than his 52 percent approval rating among whites. And yet, the leadership of the Democratic Party continues to ignore Sanders's political agenda of massive economic redistribution, because the party has spent a generation trying to distance itself from the reputation that it is the party of social welfare and "big government."

While the Democratic Party continues to insist that it is a party of the mainstream, a growing number of polls indicate that large majorities of Americans actually want a party of "big government." There is massive discontent and bitterness in the United States, but it has no political home. Consider the following poll results: 58 percent of Americans think Obamacare should be replaced with federally funded healthcare for all; most Americans support raising the minimum wage; 61 percent support a minimum wage of at least ten dollars per hour; 59 percent support a minimum wage of twelve dollars per hour; 48 percent support fifteen dollars per hour, a proposal that has been demonized by Dems and Republicans alike; 61 percent of Americans say the rich pay too little in taxes, up from 52 percent a year ago; 69 percent of Americans believe that providing affordable housing is important; 63 pecent of Americans say money and wealth distribution is unfair; 53 percent of whites think the country still has work to do for Blacks to achieve equal rights with whites; 50 percent of whites say Blacks are treated less fairly by the police than whites; 64 percent of white Democrats support Black Lives Matter, 29 percent of whom say they "strongly support" the movement. Even 20 percent of Republicans think the movement will help achieve racial equality in the United States.

The Sanders phenomenon was not an accident, but he tapped into the sentiment reflected in these poll results.

None of this is to imply or say that it is inconsequential that Trump is now president. He is dangerous. But he is also hobbled by reality. Even though he was adept at identifying and exploiting the fears and anxieties of millions of white Americans and handfuls of other people who also voted for him, he cannot deliver on his promise to make America great again. It's a promise based on a foundation of lies that misidentify the problems afflicting the United States. Trump and his white supremacist advisers say that the United States is suffering from an influx of immigrants, "radical Islamic terrorism," crime, and violence. Much of this is racist drivel intended to stoke fear and promote scapegoating to blame the most vulnerable among us. We are told that undocumented Mexican immigrants are to blame for unemployment. We are told that Black criminals are to blame for poverty. We are told that Muslim terrorists are to blame for shifting billions of dollars from domestic spending to foreign policy. In effect, we are told that the least powerful and influential among us are the problem, while the millionaires and billionaires who are literally running the government are innocent bystanders.

It can almost be guaranteed that when Trump is unable to deliver on his promises to make America great again, he and his administration will double down on racism and disorder. They will use that as a pretext to justify repression. We can already see this taking shape. The executive orders dealing with immigration and law enforcement are designed to stoke fear while rapidly expanding the powers of all police and law enforcement agents. Trump wants to give local police the power of immigration control agents, not necessarily to deport the eleven million people living in this country without papers, but to stoke fear and suspicion, to turn neighbor against neighbor, classmate against classmate, worker against worker.

But it is not just immigration control. It is not a coincidence that the attempts to expand police powers (including the signaling from the misnamed Department of Justice that police departments will face no scrutiny) coincide with what will be an austere, cruel budget that casts poor and working-class people to fend for themselves. Policing in this context will be the public policy of last resort, intended to contain crime to certain neighborhoods, not actually stop it. In a country where both political parties ignore structural factors in the perpetuation of poverty, both parties are then hostile to the kinds of social and public programs necessary to keep people out of poverty. For the Republicans this is obvious, but we should not forget that 2016 marked the twentieth-year anniversary of the Democratic Party's crusade to end welfare as an entitlement to poor people. In other words, these are bipartisan attacks on programming intended to raise the quality of life for ordinary people. And when federal, state, and city leaders have no intention of creating or funding programs necessary to keep people out of poverty, the police are dispatched to manage the crisis. Police violence, brutality, and murder are built into a system that has no answers to the poverty and inequality that it constantly generates. This is why police reform is so hard. We should not be naïve to believe that a country that can put a man on the moon cannot rein in its own police forces. But the reason why mayors and councilpersons regularly turn a blind eye to brutal policing is because it is simply the cost of doing business. And the cost of doing business is quite high.

In Chicago alone, the city has spent $500 million over the last ten years to settle or pay out lawsuits against the city for police brutality and wrongful death suits. The NYPD has averaged $100 million in settlements for police brutality and wrongful death lawsuits a year, since 2007, adding up to $1 billion. The ten cities with the largest police departments paid out $248 million last year in settlements and court judgments in police misconduct cases, up 48 percent from 2010. In the last five years, those same ten cities have paid out $1.2 billion. Any other public institution that incurs this kind of expense has its budgets and services shrunken, or the institution is shut down. When, in 2013, the Chicago Board of Education claimed it was running a billion-dollar deficit, it simply closed fifty-two public schools and never looked back.

The expansion of policing powers of the state is also intended to lay the foundation for the repression of the growing resistance movement. The Trump administration is well aware of the opposition and resistance it has provoked. They have been met with unprecedented protests. The day after Trump was inaugurated, an estimated four million people participated in protests directed at his administration. In the aftermath of his illegal Muslim travel ban, dozens of spontaneous protests erupted at the nation's airports, involving tens of thousands of ordinary people—many of whom were not directly affected by the ban itself. There is organizing happening in every corner of the United States. Some of it is brand new. Some of it is building on campaigns that have been under way for years now. Despite whatever delusions the Trump administration engages in in repeating the lie that it has massive public support, it knows that its political agenda will continue to inspire protest, and so it wants to create the conditions to help repress the social movements. Indeed, Republican governors and supporters of Trump in five states have proposed legislation to ban or curtail protests.

This is not a call for retreat, but the suggestion that we must retool. To begin with, it means that we need larger and more effective protests. Some have asked whether or not protests and demonstrations matter. What can protests do? Black Lives Matter is only one example to look to when understanding the importance of protests themselves. Police brutality was not a new issue in 2014. It is a very old issue in African American life in this country. But the rebellion in Ferguson, when Mike Brown was killed in August 2014, drew national attention to the phenomenon of police murder and judicial misconduct. It also provided a model for communities to know how to respond to police violence—through protest, activism, and organizing. At a time when the political establishment, led by Barack Obama, believed that it could get the movement off the streets by seducing activists with roundtable meetings and seats on commissions, protests and rebellion in Baltimore eight months later reminded the political establishment, and indeed the world, that the entire Black movement would not be bought off with cheap flattery and the appearance of reform. Protests force the mass media, and then the public, to have a deeper engagement with issues that elected officials would like to sweep away or minimize. The Black Lives Matter movement changed the conversation about police brutality in the United States. It provided language for people to articulate their frustrations with police violence and abuse. It provided an analysis for why this violence was happening.

But the Black Lives Matter movement also shows the limitations of social movements that do not advance beyond exposing injustice. Knowledge alone of abuse, injustice, and oppression will not actually change those conditions. The issue is, how do we use that knowledge to draw in the thousands of people that are necessary for an effective mass movement? How do we create the entry points into struggle, the organizations necessary to coordinate struggles? We can only even begin to imagine a movement on that scale when individuals move beyond the specific issue that directly affects them to also seeing the relationship or connection between oppressions.

While it can appear as if we are a long way from that kind of struggle, when individuals are demonstrating and confronting the political status quo, people are suddenly open to new ideas and approaches that they may not have considered at an earlier time, when organizing was more difficult or when an individual did not consider themselves political. In moments like the one we are living through, political consciousness can develop very quickly and people's ideas and expectations can change rapidly.

But more importantly, we have to stop constraining our own political imagination into what is deemed pragmatic and possible. No social movement has ever begun with the question of what is realistic. Black people in the South called what we now refer to as the "civil rights movement" the "freedom movement." When that movement did not go far enough, Black organizers in the south and north engaged in what they called the "Black Liberation Movement." Even though these struggles included all kinds of people who had different ideas of how to achieve these goals, the point was that we have to say what we want. This is especially true today when there are those who will insist that we quiet down and be reasonable. Yes, we have to fight battles in the here and now but we also have to fight for what we want. We must also build independent organizations and political parties that are not connected to the Democratic Party, that do not rise and fall with the electoral cycle. We have to build organizations that are democratic, multiracial, and militant with a foundation in solidarity—"solidarity" meaning that even if you don't experience a specific oppression, you understand that as ordinary people our fates are tied together and that one group's liberation is dependent on the liberation of all the oppressed and exploited.

This year marks the fortieth anniversary of the publication of one of the most important political statements to come out of the Black Liberation Movement of the 1960s. I want to quote from it because, to me, it embodies the spirit of solidarity and the struggle that is necessary to get to the world we want to live in. The Combahee River Collective was a Black feminist collective and political organization of Black and brown women that formed in the early 1970s and emerged as a radical left wing of the women's movement of the era. They were not content with talk of shattering glass ceilings; rather, they wanted to shatter a system built on the exploitation and oppression of Black people, and especially Black women:

We realize that the liberation of all oppressed peoples necessitates the destruction of the political-economic systems of capitalism and imperialism as well as patriarchy. We are socialists because we believe that work must be organized for the collective benefit of those who do the work and create the products, and not for the profit of the bosses. Material resources must be equally distributed among those who create these resources. We are not convinced, however, that a socialist revolution that is not also a feminist and antiracist revolution will guarantee our liberation.

In other words, we must fight a system based on the exploitation and theft of labor and resources, but we must also have the struggle against oppression, in all its forms, at the center of the struggle—or indeed there will be no struggle at all.

Another world is possible, but it is an altogether different world from the one we are living in today. A world free of racism, nationalism and borders, religious bigotry, sexism, homophobia is possible—but it is a world that must be organized and fought for.

THE MISOGYNIST-IN-CHIEF

The Stakes for Women's Rights in the Trump Era

Elizabeth Schulte

Lying in my bed this morning, I began to cry, not for myself but for the future girls who would someday have this feeling. For the girls headed to college this time next year, who will be facing a culture of misogyny that has been excused by Trump's campaign and now validated by his victory.

—Anonymous

This is how a sexual assault survivor described her feelings in the pages of *Teen Vogue* the day after Donald Trump won the election. People all over the country shared her shock and fear, as the reality sunk in that someone who bragged about sexual assault was about to become leader of the "world's greatest democracy."

Just weeks before the election, a 2005 tape of Trump bragging about using his celebrity to "do anything" to women, including grabbing them "by the pussy," was released.[1] Trump laughed off the incident, claiming that it was being blown out of proportion, that this was just "locker room banter." That, however, wasn't everyone's reaction to the leaked tape of Trump joking about sexual assault. In the days after the tape's release, the call volume to the Rape, Abuse, and Incest National Network hotline increased about 35 percent.[2]

Trump's misogyny and contempt for women is in keeping with the anti-women policies he intends to carry out. During his first hundred days in office, he hit the ground running on a series of attacks on women's rights. In his first month, he nominated conservative "constitutionalist" judge Neil Gorsuch to the Supreme Court and antiabortion Republican Georgia representative Tom Price as secretary of health and human services. In April, he announced he was discontinuing US funding for the United Nations Population Fund, which provides reproductive healthcare around the world.

As part of the administration's proposal to "repeal and replace" the Affordable Care Act in March 2017, "Trumpcare" included a provision to defund Planned Parenthood, the women's healthcare provider that is the target of Republican lawmakers because it offers abortion services. This would have an impact not only on women seeking abortion services but on the millions of people who rely on Planned Parenthood for contraception and other healthcare.

On March 27, 2017, "Equal Pay Day," Trump revoked the Fair Pay and Safe Workplaces order, which was instituted in 2014 to ensure that federal contractors don't discriminate against women employees. And he remains completely unrepentant on the issue of sexual assault, publicly defending Fox News "personality" Bill O'Reilly, who was forced to resign amid charges of sexual harassment.[3]

The Trump administration's attack on women is linked to the other facets of its multipronged assault on working people—like the victims of domestic abuse who dropped their cases because they were undocumented and afraid they would be spotted by Immigration and Customs Enforcement agents at court and be deported;[4] or the Muslim airline employee wearing a hijab who was harassed and kicked by a Trump supporter who told her "Trump is here now. He will get rid of all of you";[5] or the fast-food workers protesting a pattern of sexual harassment in their workplaces who could have faced a Labor Department headed by Carl's Jr. CEO Andrew Puzder.[6] These are just a few of many fronts in Trump's war on working people.

Attacking Women's Reproductive Rights

Through the years, Trump's personal opinions about abortion have been hard to pin down—for example, in 1999, he told NBC's Tim Russert, "I'm very pro-choice"—but he made his stance clear during the presidential campaign. When MSNBC's Chris Matthews pressed him on his actual position on abortion, Trump responded that he was "pro-life" and "there has to be some form of punishment" for women who have illegal abortions.[7]

Since Ronald Reagan, Republican candidates have relied on the support of the conservative religious right for votes, and that means candidates must oppose women's right to choose. Trump isn't the first to reverse his position on abortion—George H. W. Bush did the same when he ran for president, which only underscores the fact that the Republicans' anti-choice platform has less to do with "morality" or being "pro-life" and everything to do with cynical political calculations.

But this isn't the only reason. The antiabortion stance fits nicely with a larger worldview shared by Trump and rest of the right, who would like nothing better than to turn back the clock on the gains of the women's movement of the late 1960s and 1970s, and women's reproductive rights in particular. One of Trump's first acts was an executive order that bans federal money going to international groups that perform or provide information on abortions. The "global gag order" will have a terrible impact on poor women around the world who depend on these funds to obtain necessary healthcare.

Trump's win also gave the green light to congressional Republicans who immediately rolled out their plan to ban federal funds to Planned Parenthood, and, in the states, anti-choice lawmakers couldn't wait to get started with dozens of new restrictions on abortion services and abortion providers. As of January 12, 2017, at least forty-six antiabortion bills had already been introduced or were pending in fourteen states, according to the Guttmacher Institute. Fifteen of them were all in the state of Missouri alone.[8] And many more are expected to come.

In recent years, the anti-choice right's focus has been on laws claiming to "protect" women, like those that impose burdensome regulations on abortion facilities and doctors, or Targeted Regulation of Abortion Providers (TRAP) laws. However, the anti-choice tactic may be changing, as the bills focus more on the "rights" of the fetus or the beginning of conception. "More legislation we're seeing now is focusing on the fetus and really ignores the woman and her situation completely," said Elizabeth Nash at the Guttmacher Institute in January 2017. She added that activists expected to see "several hundred more provisions" before the first three weeks of Trump's presidency had passed.[9]

These restrictions will have terrible and even deadly consequences for women, particularly working-class and poor women, who will have a harder time gaining access to abortion services. These restrictions on reproductive rights also attempt to reinforce the idea the women can't be trusted to make decisions about their own bodies and scapegoats them in many ways, like the divide-and-conquer policies that target immigrants and Muslims. On top of this, anti-choice activists demonstrated new confidence after Trump's election to take their anti-women message to the streets, when they organized a day of action on February 11, 2017, that targeted Planned Parenthood clinics to demand they be defunded.

These attempts to restrict women's control over their bodies go hand in hand with other attacks on working-class women. By almost any measure—wages, housing, access to healthcare, discrimination, and harassment on the job—women are a long way from achieving equality. Let's take the example of women with children, a group conservatives must at least claim they care about. According to the National Women's Law Center, mothers who work outside the home make 71 percent of every dollar a man makes, Black mothers are paid 51 percent, and Latina mothers make just 46 percent.[10] Now consider the fact that women are the sole or primary source of income in 40 percent of households with children, according to the Pew Research Center.[11]

Emboldening the Right Wing

In a broader sense, Trump's polices emboldens the right, like the protests against Planned Parenthood, and also contributes to a general atmosphere that denigrates women and doesn't take their liberation seriously, minimizing the effects of sexism and discrimination. It contributes to the fear felt by people like the anonymous rape survivor writing in *Teen Vogue* that sexist behavior and violence against women could become more acceptable with an unapologetic misogynist like Trump in power.

In fact, just weeks after Trump's election, there were some sickening examples of this, including a Greenwich, Connecticut, Republican politician named Christopher von Keyserling who grabbed a woman by the genitals and pinched her after telling her, "I love this new world, I no longer have to be politically correct." The woman said von Keyserling—who was charged with fourth-degree sexual assault—told her, "It would be your word against mine, and nobody will believe you."[12]

Part of the fear is fed by the knowledge that millions of people actually voted for Trump and supported the sexist and racist ideas that he spouted during his campaign. While in the end Trump lost the popular vote by almost three million, he did win enough votes to make it a narrow race against Hillary Clinton, someone the Democratic Party leadership and the media and political pundits all thought couldn't possibly lose against Trump. His campaign rhetoric aimed to appeal to people's anger and frustration over the status quo in Washington and the enormous gap between the people in the halls of power and the majority of people they claim to serve.

Hillary Clinton on the other hand represented the model establishment candidate—decades in service of the Democratic Party, the ultimate insider whose response to Trump's "Make America Great Again" slogan was to claim that "America is already great." For millions of people, Clinton's slogan rang hollow and was a perfect example of how out of touch her campaign, and the Democratic Party establishment, were with working people, even those on whom the party ordinarily depends for votes. This was the Democratic Party leadership's choice for candidate—she sat on the board of Walmart in the 1980s, backed the crime bill and welfare reform in the 1990s, and supported a coup in Honduras in the 2000s, along with the Iraq War and covert drone warfare.

And while Trump used a phony outsider populist pose to try to appeal to an audience fed up with business as usual in Washington, he also tried to appeal to another layer of people by providing scapegoats to their problems, appealing to them on the basis of racist, anti-immigrant, Islamophobic, and sexist ideas. He let the sexist comments fly, and if anyone called him on this filth, he replied that they should stop taking this so seriously. Gross sexist attacks aimed at Clinton were a central part of Trump's campaign. At Trump's speaking events, some supporters wore sexist T-shirts and buttons directed at Clinton—like the one that read "Trump That Bitch."

For many people making a choice in the 2016 election, and not just Trump supporters but those who looked to other alternatives like Bernie Sanders or the Green Party's Jill Stein, Clinton symbolized the political establishment that has presided in Washington, an elite enriching itself while the working class's living standards stagnated or declined. When that critique of Clinton came from people on the left, it explained why so many people were dissatisfied with Clinton and the Democratic Party and were looking for an alternative to both major parties. But in the hands of Trump, who added women-hating rhetoric to the mix, the bitterness toward Clinton became a toxic brew of class anger diverted into sexism—with feminism being attacked as one of the root problems of society.

As Trump attacked Clinton for "playing the woman card" or laughed off accusations of sexual harassment, he was also taking aim at feminism generally, especially the gains of the women's rights movement of the 1960s and 1970s, which was responsible for many of the rights that women have today and completely transformed the way that women are viewed in society. In the eyes of Trump and his supporters, that movement went "too far," but the daily realities of working class women show the opposite—they still have a very long way to go.

One of the alarming outcomes of the 2016 election was that some women actually turned out to vote for Trump. According to polling data released just after the election by *FiveThirtyEight*, among white women voters, Clinton lost to Trump by 10 percentage points, and among white women voters without a college degree by 28 points.[13] In an interview just before the election, historian Stephanie Coontz explained how women facing economic precariousness were often hostile to a woman like Clinton, whose fortunes were rising as theirs were falling. "When they hear feminists talk about the glass ceiling, they don't see that as the main issue," Coontz said.[14]

Coontz situated Trump's popularity in the deterioration of the living standards for the working-class family since the 1950s and 1960s, alongside the increasing fortunes of those at the very top of American society. These conditions made some low-paid workers an audience for ideas about how immigrants or Blacks were taking away their jobs, as well as conservative ideas about the traditional family. "The fact remains that women who have the fewest opportunities to compete successfully in the labor market are the ones who are much more likely to support the policies and values that reward a traditional division of labor in the household," Coontz said.

The Trump administration is likely on a collision course with many of these supporters, who may have voted for Trump with the hope of some kind of change and will see more attacks on their living standards and rights. Already, Trump's budget promises to slice and dice at programs that benefit working families, such as heating and food assistance.

While the Clinton campaign emphasized breaking the glass ceiling and voting for the first woman president, it had nothing to offer working women. By and large, the problem wasn't how popular Trump was but how deeply unpopular Clinton and the party she represents turned out to be.

Clinton and the Democratic Party Strategy

It's impossible to explain the result of the election without taking into account how, among a layer of people, support for Trump coincided with a rejection of Clinton and the politics she represented. While women who voted by and large chose Clinton over Trump—including 94 percent of Black women and 68 percent of Latina women—Clinton failed to turn them out in the numbers she needed to win.[15]

As *The Democrats: A Critical History* author Lance Selfa pointed out in an interview after the election, "Women composed about 52 percent of the electorate—about equal to their percentage of the voting-eligible population. In 2012, however, women made up 54 percent of the electorate—higher than their share of the voting-eligible electorate. So, women turned out to be one more group that Clinton couldn't motivate to the polls in the numbers they did for Obama."[16]

So, as Trump fed red meat to his supporters, Clinton didn't lift a finger to invigorate supporters and, to quote *Listen, Liberal!* author Thomas Frank, played the role of the "complacency candidate," sure that the promise of the status quo was enough to win the election.[17] Instead of offering something positive for the left to vote for, Clinton offered more of the same, and because she was so sure that people would vote for her because she wasn't Trump, the lesser-evil Clinton offered very little to working-class voters, including women.

The major middle-class women's organizations, such as the National Organization for Women (NOW), NARAL Pro-Choice America, and Planned Parenthood, fell in line behind Clinton. More left-wing voters who dared to support Democrat Bernie Sanders were either condemned as "brocialists" who didn't care about sexism or, worse, spoilers who would be responsible for Trump's taking the White House. The reality, however, is that it wasn't just white males who supported Sanders and his message. According to an April 2017 Harvard-Harris Poll, 73 percent of African Americans, 68 percent of Hispanics, 62 percent of Asian Americans, and 58 percent of women approved of Sanders.[18]

The Democratic Party establishment responded with what could be called "identity politics from above"—shaming people into voting for Clinton with the argument that only the most privileged could even consider not voting for the only candidate that could defeat Trump. The same threats applied to supporters of Green Party candidate Jill Stein, because even though she was a woman, she wasn't *the* woman, Hillary Clinton.

According to the Democratic Party, women had no choice but to vote for Clinton, because if they didn't, women's rights would be in peril. Relying on revulsion toward Trump and the fear of what his presidency would mean for women's rights, Clinton refused to put forward demands that would actually have an impact on working-class women and, in fact, opposed these demands, including a federal fifteen-dollar minimum wage.

What the Clinton campaign failed to understand, or ignored, was that a growing number of people, including women, were repelled by Trump but also by the Democratic Party status quo that Clinton exemplified. They decided to sit out the election. Many voters, among them women, didn't want to vote for a candidate with such a long history of enriching Corporate America at the expense of workers. They were also fed up with a party that manipulated supporters' fear of what could happen to women's rights if a Republican won, yet did nothing to actually fight for these rights itself.

Democratic Party leaders, however, drew their own conclusions from the election. Their takeaway from their pathetic failure to mobilize support for their candidate was *not* that they needed to find ways to appeal to their traditional liberal support, but, instead, to attract Trump supporters. Some have concluded that the party is too closely associated with hot-button social issues like abortion rights and should begin focusing on purely "economic" issues (as if having a child doesn't have a profound economic effect on a woman).

As part of its "Come Together, Fight Back" tour in April, the Democratic National Committee (DNC) made a stop to lend support to anti-choice Democratic Omaha mayoral candidate Heath Mello. Ilyse Hogue of NARAL Pro-Choice America pointed out that the DNC decision made this "fight back tour" look more like "a throwback tour for women and our rights. . . . If Democrats think the path forward following the 2016 election is to support candidates who substitute their own judgement and ideology for that of their female constituents, they have learned all the wrong lessons and are bound to lose. It's not possible to have an authentic conversation about economic security for women that does not include our ability to decide when and how we have children."[19]

The Resistance to Trump

This was the backdrop to Trump's taking office in January. And while the Democratic Party politicians and the liberal organizations that support them fought fiercely to coerce people on the left into voting for Clinton, they didn't have much fight in them once Trump was actually elected.

Hillary Clinton set the tone the day after the election when she told supporters, "I still believe in America, and I always will. And if you do, we must accept this result. We owe him an open mind and the chance to lead." More Democratic politicians followed her lead, as did several trade union leaders. Women's organizations like NOW followed their lead and, despite their huge mailing lists, didn't call a protest in response to Trump's election in the immediate aftermath of the election.

But that doesn't mean that there wasn't a response. Within weeks, a Facebook invitation started by a grandmother in Hawaii grew into a much larger call for a march in Washington, DC, on inauguration weekend, involving experienced activists who saw the importance of putting the demands of women of color at the center of the march. The resulting statement of principles included decidedly progressive demands for equal pay; paid family leave; freedom from sexual violence; the "dismantling" of the gender and racial inequities within the criminal justice system; the expansion and protection of LGBTQ rights; and reproductive justice, including access to safe, legal, affordable abortion and birth control for all people.[20]

When January 21, 2017, came, some four million protesters took the streets in Washington, DC, and in local demonstrations around the United States. Described as the largest day of demonstrations in US history, and far outpacing anyone's expectations, it revealed an important truth about Trump's America—there are people who not only are angry about what Trump might do in the White House but also are ready to be counted in the streets. The messages of the homemade signs that protesters brought to the Women's Marches showed not only their anger at the Trump administration but also their diverse concerns: "Women's rights are human rights," "No human is illegal," "Black Lives Matter," "No means no," and "This is not normal." Many of the signs reflected a thirst for solidarity and showed the potential to organize a fightback against Trump's many-fronted war—from defending reproductive rights to ending deportations to defending Arabs and Muslims to fighting for LGBTQ rights.

Similar early signs of a willingness and eagerness to protest were demonstrated on February 11, 2017, when thousands of women turned out to counterprotest anti-choice forces demanding that the federal government defund Planned Parenthood. In most cases, the political wing of Planned Parenthood tried to stop the counterprotests from happening, but women still came out to defend their clinic. As one protester explained, "I'm tired of being told to write letters that never get read. I'm done with writing letters!"[21] One could imagine what would have happened if Planned Parenthood had called demonstrations itself.

As women's rights supporters look down the barrel of four years of Donald Trump and an emboldened right wing, there will be a lot of fights ahead. There are also a number of important debates about the best way to organize that struggle. For several decades, focusing on electing Democrats to protect women's rights has been the dominant strategy of liberal women's organizing. In the process, these groups have echoed the positions of the Democratic Party.

So, for instance, as Democratic politicians like Bill and Hillary Clinton changed the conversation away from the confident defense of women's right to abortion that existed during the reproductive rights struggles of the 1960s and 1970s, so did liberal women's organizations. In the 1990s, the Clintons' refrain was that abortions should be "safe, legal, and rare" and that Democrats should even seek "common ground" with those who opposed abortion. Instead of challenging this position, liberal women's groups took up this message as their own. Instead of acting as groups that pressure the Democrats to do the right thing, they were the ones that were pressured—into doing the wrong thing.

Meanwhile, the Democratic Party has taken women's votes for granted and done very little to earn them. During his 1992 campaign for president, Bill Clinton vowed to help enact the Freedom of Choice Act (FOCA), which would have codified *Roe v. Wade* in federal law. In the first year of his administration—and with Democratic control of both the Senate and House—the measure died without reaching the floor of either chamber. Barack Obama made the same promise to enact FOCA before he got into office; he also broke that promise.

There's a potential to build a movement to take on Trump, and it's a good time to start a conversation about what will make our movement stronger. With the sides in this fight so clear, there has been no better time in years for activists to make a confident defense of women's rights, including the right to safe, legal, and affordable abortion. Activists can't allow the Democratic Party to dictate our demands to suit the party's electoral ambitions.

The Women's Marches provided an important snapshot of what public opinion really looks like in the United States—a largely spontaneous outpouring of anger and resistance to Trump's election. After decades of the mainstream women's organizations prioritizing campaigning for Democrats over an unapologetic defense of women's rights, you could see the potential for more grassroots organizing for women's rights in the streets, expanding on recent campaigns like those of campus activists who demanded that their university administrations take sexual assault seriously or fast-food workers who shone a light on sexual harassment at work.

The Women's Marches—as well as the many other protests that followed in the weeks and months after the inauguration, like the protests against Muslim bans at the airports and, in spring 2017, marches for science and for climate justice—also showed the widespread eagerness to express solidarity with those under attack. As the Trump administration continues, it will take careful and determined organizing to build the kind of networks and organizations that will be strong enough to stand up to Trump's attack on our rights and create a political climate where sexists like Donald Trump are protested, not elected president. In the process, we can build the groundwork for a resistance, and a left, strong enough to start putting its own demands for equality and liberation on the table.

TRUMP, ISLAMOPHOBIA, AND US POLITICS

An Interview with Deepa Kumar

Donald Trump is no lone wolf. Islamophobia can be found across the political mainstream. In the first few months after Trump's election, hate crimes against Muslims and those who "look Muslim" spiked.[1]

In the first week of the Trump administration, Trump issued an executive order banning the entry of all refugees and travelers from seven Muslim-majority countries into the United States. Spontaneous mass demonstrations and several court decisions blocked Trump's "Muslim ban," but the administration's Islamophobic policies continued in other ways.

*As **Deepa Kumar**, the author of* Islamophobia and the Politics of Empire, *reminds us, to dismiss Trump as a crank overlooks the pervasiveness of Islamophobia and how its conservative and liberal variants have reinforced one another. This interview, a version of which first appeared in* Jacobin *in December 2015,*[2] *discusses how US politics came to this point.*

Kumar refers to several incidents contemporary to the time of the interview: the coordinated attacks in Paris by gunmen claiming loyalty to the Islamic State of Iraq and Syria (ISIS) in November 2015, killing 130; a mass shooting of attendees at a public health department holiday party in San Bernardino, California, by a married couple of immigrants from Pakistan in December 2015; and an antiabortion extremist's late November 2015 assault on a Planned Parenthood clinic in Colorado Springs, Colorado, killing three.

We're seeing a toxic rise in Islamophobia that reaches its apex on the far right, but also extends to the center left. The same week that Donald Trump proposed halting all Muslim immigration in December 2015, for instance, the liberal writer Michael Tomasky effectively called on Muslims in the United States to prove that they're good Americans. What do you make of the current climate? How worried should we be about the uptick in this sort of rhetoric?

We should worry for at least two reasons. First, we have seen an escalation of Islamophobia and the hate crimes that accompany it in the aftermath of San Bernardino and Paris. Glenn Greenwald has compiled a list of threats and attacks on Muslims over just a one-week period, and it is quite alarming. I know of friends who, for the first time since 9/11, are wearing hoodies over their hijabs because they are fearful of attacks by random strangers.

While racist and xenophobic attacks are not new, they have been intensifying. We have seen waves of this kind of backlash since 9/11, such as during the "Ground Zero mosque" controversy and the Boston Marathon bombing, to name just two, and with every new incident the rhetoric reaches new heights. This is the new reality of the "war on terror," with Islamophobia integrated into the very fabric of US society because it serves to justify empire and the bloated national security state.

The second reason we should be concerned is the timing. First, the upsurge of anti-Muslim rhetoric comes on the heels of the Paris attacks, and the already polarized international climate that those attacks created. Second, it has been swept into election-year politics, with the Republicans jumping onto the Islamophobia bandwagon to score political points, as they have in previous election years.

The far right and the well-funded Islamophobic network have espoused blatantly racist ideas for some time now, but their rhetoric can spill over into the mainstream only when mainstream politicians and figures echo their talking points. What we have seen since the Paris attacks is that far-right ideas produced by a global Islamophobic network, or what has been called the "counterjihad movement," have been echoed and amplified by various Republican presidential candidates, Trump being the most vitriolic of them.

A recent report from a UK-based group on the counterjihad movement documents the global scope of this movement and how their ideas have moved from the margins to the mainstream. People like Trump play an instrumental role in facilitating this process.

Now, many people have denounced Trump for his comment about halting Muslim immigration, including the other Republican candidates. The general consensus in the political establishment, and among pundits, is that he went too far and should be disqualified from running for the presidency.

Trump countered by saying that his plan is not unlike what President Roosevelt did in 1942 following the attack on Pearl Harbor, when he signed an executive order authorizing the internment of 110,000 Americans of Japanese descent (of which over 60 percent were American-born). Indeed, Trump is correct in pointing out that both Democrats and Republicans have made use of racist policing to help consolidate the national security state and promote US imperialism, from the era of the Cold War to the war on terror. In fact, one could make a strong case that the connection between the two phenomena dates to the very founding of the country itself.

But Trump need not have looked to 1942, or earlier, for a historical precedent. His internment proposal has already been in process, albeit in different forms, since 9/11, with tens of thousands of Muslim immigrants and citizens having passed through the prison-industrial complex.

Immediately after 9/11, about twelve hundred Muslim citizens and noncitizens were summarily arrested and questioned by the FBI and various state and local law enforcement agencies. Despite the fact that *not even one* of these twelve hundred was found to have connections to 9/11 or terrorism, the pattern of detention and deportation has only grown since then. Mosques, community centers, and even children's sports leagues have been subjected to surveillance, during both the Bush and the Obama presidencies.

When Trump called for a database to register all Muslims, Hillary Clinton tweeted that this was "shocking rhetoric." Yet, she ignored similar processes that have been at work for over a decade, such as the 2002 National Security Entry-Exit Registration System, which had its origins in her husband's 1996 terrorism bill. The system requires that male immigrants aged sixteen and older from twenty-five different countries be photographed, fingerprinted, and interviewed, and their financial information declared. Already by fall 2003, more than eighty-three thousand immigrant residents were registered through this system.

So, we have to remember that we are in this situation today because both Democrats and Republicans have contributed to it. Donald Trump is playing today the kind of role that Enoch Powell once played in the United Kingdom with his infamous "Rivers of Blood" speech, which included racist, anti-immigrant rhetoric and made him a politically polarizing figure.

A. Sivanandan described Powell's effect as follows: "What Enoch Powell says today, the Conservative Party says tomorrow, and the Labour Party legislates on the day after." We have seen a similar dynamic in the United States since the late 1970s, which is why the range of political discussion is so narrow in this country. This is why one cannot dismiss Trump as a crank or a lone wolf who will have little impact on the system.

When Michael Tomasky called for Muslim Americans to prove their loyalty, he was simply reinforcing what President Obama had said in his December 6, 2015, speech. Obama argued that because "an extremist ideology has spread within some Muslim communities," it is the responsibility of Muslims to "confront, without excuse" this problem.

Presumably, in Obama's book, an example of such an excuse is the argument that Muslims are no more to blame for San Bernardino than white Christians are for the actions of Robert Dear, the Planned Parenthood shooter. Yet, we know that Dear is an evangelical Christian who idolizes the Army of God, an antiabortion group that is responsible for numerous bombings and murders, and that right-wing terrorists have been responsible for more murders since 9/11 than jihadists.

Why then are white Christians not being called upon to take "responsibility" for the far right, and why has all attention shifted from Dear's crimes to those in San Bernardino? When Obama states that it is "the responsibility of Muslims around the world to root out misguided ideas that lead to radicalization," he is articulating a liberal version of Islamophobia, according to which Islam is culpable for violence committed by Muslims, even if most Muslims are "peaceful."

Thus, following every controversy, the range of debate remains restricted to right-wing and liberal variants of Islamophobia, although with an overall steady shift to the right. Hence, just as it is correct to point out that Republican denunciations of Trump's rhetoric ring hollow, given strong Republican support for the logic that underpins it, the same applies to Democratic denunciations of Republicans, and for the same reasons.

While the right views all Muslims as a problem and as a fifth column in Western nations, the liberal establishment sounds more reasonable in that it differentiates between terrorists and the majority of Muslims—between "good" and "bad" Muslims. But it nevertheless holds an entire group of people responsible. This is why establishment liberals believe that "moderate Muslims" should "take responsibility" for denouncing the terrorists, that leftists and antiracists should get over their political correctness, and that everyone should join them in supporting the war on terror and its practices of war, surveillance, indefinite detention, and drone strikes.

Absent from the discussion is the context of empire, i.e., what imperial intervention produces abroad, how those interventions produce blowback on US soil, what they mean for racialized subjects, and what role the entire US political establishment has long played in advancing imperialist intervention and provoking violence both at home and abroad.

What role do the media play in stoking this sort of panic and bigotry?

There is a lot of discussion about how Trump's crazy rhetoric is getting so much play only because the corporate media have devoted so much attention to it. There is some truth to this, of course.

The corporate media eagerly cover controversial and sensational material because it draws larger audiences and serves to pad the bottom line. Trump's horrific rhetoric—e.g., his calls to deport millions of Latino/a immigrants or to bring back waterboarding—is thus seen as newsworthy for this reason. The major broadcasting companies therefore certainly have a financial interest in cheering on the Trump phenomenon.

But it would be wrong to see the escalation of Islamophobia as simply the product of Donald Trump or the corporate media by themselves. In my book on Islamophobia, I examine what I call the "matrix of Islamophobia," which outlines the structures and institutions responsible for shaping anti-Muslim ideology and practice. These include the political establishment (including both Democrats and Republicans), the national security apparatus, and universities and think tanks—all of which contribute to the production of the two strands of Islamophobia (liberal and conservative).

The key arena in which these ideas are propagated to the public is in the mainstream media. They amplify the rhetoric from these other institutions, but also play a part in limiting the range of debate between the liberal and conservative poles. It is only on rare occasions that anyone to the left of the permissible range can enter this space, and those occasions are almost always the product of protests and social movements that are strong enough to force the media to broaden the range of debate (a phenomenon I examined in my book on the 1997 UPS strike).

After receiving pushback for his Muslim ban, Trump snorted that the media do not report on terrorist attacks. He stated that "radical Islamic terrorists are determined to strike our homeland, as they did on 9/11, as they did from Boston to Orlando to San

Bernardino and all across Europe," and that "it's gotten to a point where it's not even being reported, and in many cases, the very, very dishonest press doesn't want to report it."

This is exactly the opposite of the truth, as a study at Georgia State University found. Researchers studied all attacks between 2011 and 2015, and found that even though a minority are committed by Muslims, Muslims received disproportionate media coverage. In fact, the corporate media not only report on a continuous loop every attack committed by a Muslim in the West, they also cover fake terror plots instigated by the FBI with great zeal. As Fairness and Accuracy in Reporting (FAIR) has repeatedly documented, sting operations by the FBI, where undercover agents or informants recruit vulnerable individuals to carry out attacks, are covered extensively by the media, who fail to reveal that without the help of the FBI the "terrorist plot" would not have come into being in the first place.

In the absence of attacks, other events carried out by the national security state—such as the apprehension of high-profile terrorism suspects or the execution of leaders of various jihadist groups through drone strikes or other such methods around the world—become major news stories and serve as reminders that the world is a dangerous place and that the United States is a guarantor of global safety and security. Each of these moments—the attacks on Western targets, the announcements of arrests, the assassination of jihadist leaders, and the prevention of real and fake terror plots, all covered extensively by the corporate media—serves to entrench US imperialism and to sustain the war on terror.

A December 2015 mass shooting/suicide in San Bernardino, California, led police to talk about the gunman's "radicalization" into a jihadist, and led politicians to call for halts to Muslim immigration into the United States. How have the media covered San Bernardino and other acts of violence committed by Muslim Americans compared to those committed by non-Muslims?

First off, let me say a few things about gun violence, which, by the way, is as American as apple pie. The Centers for Disease Control and Prevention has reported that 406,496 Americans have been killed by firearms on US soil since 2001, in comparison to 3,380 killed *worldwide* due to terrorism. In the United States, jihadists have killed forty-five people since 9/11—in other words, a ratio of almost ten thousand to one between deaths from gun violence and those from terrorism.

In cases of school shootings or other mass shootings, the perpetrators are overwhelmingly white men and boys. Yet, when a Muslim American is involved in this most American of traditions, as we saw with San Bernardino, it becomes the occasion to justify war, empire, and the national security state.

There are two different frames used to cover violent acts in the United States, one that is applied to white perpetrators and another to Muslims. In the first case, the causes of violence are seen as individual (e.g., the product of mental illness), the solution to which lies in apprehending the perpetrator and bringing him or her (though usually him) to justice.

In the case of Muslims, violence is explained as a product of the "clash of civilizations," to which war on entire groups of people is seen as the only appropriate response. This is what Albert Memmi, the French philosopher, meant when he talked about the "mark of the plural," in which the acts of racialized others are seen to be generalizable to entire groups, while those of whites are limited to the individual.

This logic is true not only of those we call conservatives, but also of liberals. Proponents of liberalism, which champions individual rights and freedoms, have long denied individuality—and therefore rights—to racialized "others," whether in the metropole or in the colony.

What impact has Trump's anti-Muslim racism and immigrant-bashing had on national politics?

The Trump effect, as I noted earlier, is very much like the Enoch Powell effect. There is a codependent relationship that exists between the Democratic and Republican parties.

On the one hand, the Democrats' complicity in the war on terror, the construction of the national security state, and the systematic discrimination against Muslims not only serves to legitimize the Republicans' own role in these developments, but also gives the latter the freedom to adopt ever more extreme positions.

On the other hand, as the Republicans move further and further to the right, the Democrats are able not only to obscure their own culpability by pointing fingers at Republican extremism, but also to adopt more extreme measures themselves, albeit with less incendiary rhetoric and accompanied by assurances that they're only after "bad" Muslims.

In this respect, Donald Trump represented a political godsend for the Democratic Party establishment, a bogeyman whom they could use to frighten voters into supporting an "anybody-but-Trump" option in the 2016 general election. This strategy failed, and Clinton lost in an election that was widely regarded as a contest between the two most unpopular candidates in a generation, if not all time. Since then, with an eye towards the 2018 congressional elections and the 2020 presidential election, the liberal establishment has denounced Trump as a fascist. While Trump's agenda is vile and reprehensible, to call him a fascist plays into the hands of the Democrats, because the whole notion of a united front against fascism gives the Democratic Party greater freedom to carry out its own imperialist agenda, unencumbered by any criticism from its left.

To be sure, Trump does represent a frightening turn in US politics. However, to see him as an anomaly in US politics is to downplay and misunderstand the no-less-frightening political dynamic that makes Trump possible, a dynamic that is a product of the political system in its entirety. It bears reiterating that we need to understand this phenomenon in *systemic* terms—not as the product of a single individual or a single political party.

For instance, Trump's anti-immigrant bashing, whether directed at Mexicans or Muslims, fits into a long-established pattern of scapegoating. Like virtually all members of his class, Trump understands that immigrants are a source of cheap labor that has long been integral to the US economy, and that is especially true today. He also understands that keeping immigrants vulnerable keeps them cheap, while scapegoating them serves to distract attention from the dismal conditions affecting the US working class as a whole.

And here, too, we would be remiss to ignore the role that US administrations have long played both in generating displacement and immigration (e.g., NAFTA, the wars in the Middle East, the drug war in Mexico and Central America) and in subjecting immigrants to punitive treatment (e.g., Obama's policies of mass deportation). All of this is a reminder that racism is a product of the class oppression and imperialist domination that are integral to the history of capitalist development.

I would add that, at least in part, the obsession with Russian meddling in the US elections is a reflection of the liberal establishment's attempt to place blame elsewhere, outside the fundamentally flawed US electoral system. The logic is that it must be the Russians, otherwise a character like Trump would never have come to power in the "exceptional" United States. To admit otherwise would be a blow to US exceptionalism, the idea that the United States is a beacon of democracy and an example to the rest of the world—an image, moreover, that has served to justify US imperialism.

How should we think about Islamophobia and the far right in the United States and in Europe?

The relationship of the far right to Islamophobia is, in fact, different in Europe. The main difference is that Europe has a long colonial history in the Middle East, North Africa, and South Asia. What this means is that racist discourses about Muslims are much more entrenched both ideologically and in practice in various European countries.

In the case of France, Napoleon's invasion of Egypt in 1798 and France's later conquest of Algeria were instrumental in the production of racist and Orientalist rhetoric. France also created systematic discrimination through the Code de l'indigénat, a set of laws first applied in Algeria and later to other French colonies, where the native population was accorded inferior status. Even after decolonization, racist ideas and practices continued. The National Front is a reflection of this longer historical process.

In the United States, however, the history of Islamophobia is more recent. It is only after the United States took over the imperial reins from France and Britain in the Middle East and North Africa following World War II that it had seriously to contend with the region. US Orientalism and Islamophobia have also been shaped by its close relationship with Israel. The production of the "terrorist threat" began in the 1970s, with the 1979 Iranian Revolution playing a key role in shaping this construction. As I have argued elsewhere, the neocon-Likud alliance shaped the development of the "Islamic threat" in the 1980s.

Thus, it was only in the 1990s that the far right in the United States began to engage with Islamophobia, and even then it was only after 9/11 that it started to get some traction around it. This is in part because anti-immigrant rhetoric in the United States does not neatly line up with Muslim immigrants, as in Europe. It is primarily Latino/a immigrants who are scapegoated here in the United States. That said, the US far right collaborates with and learns from its European counterparts and vice versa in this global counterjihad movement.

The far right in Europe has also seen much more electoral success using anti-Muslim rhetoric than its counterpart here. The key turning point was 2010, when far-right-wing parties across Europe, using anti-Muslim and anti-immigrant rhetoric, made unprecedented electoral gains both domestically and in the European Parliament elections.

The British National Party, which has its roots in fascist parties of the past, got almost a million votes and its first two seats in the

European Parliament. Geert Wilders' Party for Freedom in Holland made significant gains as well. Even in countries considered liberal, such as Holland and Sweden, far-right-wing parties had breakthroughs. In Sweden, the Sweden Democrats gained power in the parliament running on a blatantly anti-Muslim campaign. Its leader, Jimmie Akesson, called for restricting immigration and stated that Islam was the greatest threat facing the Swedish nation.

The European far right has made gains in the context of a prolonged economic crisis, once again illustrating the connection between the diminished life conditions of the working class and the salience of racist appeals. European governments responded through imposing austerity measures and attacking the most vulnerable. Unfortunately, traditional left parties have failed to offer an alternative. In this political vacuum, the right has been able to tap into voter anxiety by scapegoating Muslim immigrants.

In 2010, France's upper house voted almost unanimously to ban the burqa. When the vote passed in the lower house, the left parties (the Socialists, Greens, and Communists) abstained. Rather than put up a principled defense of Muslims and try to defeat the measure, they decided to sit out the vote instead. The Socialist Party then came forward and stated that it too objected to the veil, but didn't support constitutional measures banning it. This pathetic response from the left has only strengthened the far right.

How do those similarities and differences from Europe affect how we organize against racism and Islamophobia? What should the left in the United States and elsewhere be doing to combat the increase in Islamophobia?

The first lesson from Europe is that we cannot fight the right from the center. In the face of hyperbolic rhetoric that blatantly demonizes Muslims, a weak-kneed response that attempts to be moderate only strengthens the far right. This is what the Democrats have done in the United States, which paved the way for a Trump victory.

The second lesson is that the right is facing resistance from ordinary people, sometimes organized by smaller far-left groups who
have tied together anti-austerity with antiracism. The nonmain-
stream left in various European nations has a historical memory of
what it takes to fight the right.

For instance, the Anti-Nazi League in Britain that successfully
pushed back the fascist National Front, the precursor to the British
National Party, organized on two fronts. First, they articulated a
principled defense against racism. And second, they also articulated a broader politics that situated racism within the broader political economy, thereby putting forward a systematic critique and a
progressive alternative.

Brexit and the Trump victory represent racist and xenophobic solutions to the crisis of neoliberal globalization. While Geert
Wilders and Marine Le Pen couldn't reproduce the Trump victory
in the Dutch and French elections in 2017, their parties nonetheless gained significantly. What is noteworthy is that far-left parties
also did well in these elections.

The lessons for us in the United States is to build a left, independent of the Democratic Party, around a program that opposes
racism in all its forms and offers a positive solution to the crisis
of neoliberalism. We need a strategy that not only deals with the
immediate threats posed by the far right emboldened by Donald
Trump but also addresses the root causes that make these (and other) threats possible. In other words, we need to learn how to walk
and chew gum at the same time, devising short-term tactics that
put out fires in the present but without undermining the prospects
for long-term change and thereby forcing us to confront even larger and more frequent fires in the medium- to long-term.

For too long, this has been the central weakness of the left—too
often opting for short-term tactics born in a moment of fear and
divorced from any clear sense of what got us here, much less where
we want to go or how we're going to get there.

Thus, in order to combat Islamophobia, or racism more generally, it is going to take a great deal more than uniting in opposition

to its most egregious manifestations (whether a single individual or a single political party). Far more important is dismantling the institutional and structural foundations upon which Islamophobia is built and which provide sustenance to both its liberal and conservative variants.

In other words, it is going to require a radical approach, one that gets at the very root of the problem, and that means, at a minimum, putting an end to the war on terror, dismantling the national security state, and undoing the class power that underpins that apparatus. That, in turn, is going to require a politics in which the strengthening of mass social movements, the building up of class struggle, and the democratization of our political system is paramount.

This may seem like a tall order, but if we set our sights on anything short of that, we would be underestimating the real threat that we and the rest of the world face at this moment and how best to fight it.

FROM "DEPORTER-IN-CHIEF" TO XENOPHOBIA UNLEASHED

Immigration Policy under Trump

An Interview with Justin Akers Chacón

Justin Akers Chacón is an activist, writer, and educator in the San Diego–Tijuana border region. He is a professor of Chicana and Chicano studies at San Diego City College. His previous work includes No One Is Illegal: Fighting Racism and State Violence on the U.S.-Mexico Border *(with Mike Davis). His forthcoming book,* Radicals in the Barrio, *uncovers the lost history and rich tradition of political radicalism behind some of the twentieth century's most important social movements, documenting the ways that migrant workers carried with them radical political ideologies, new organizational models, and the shared experience forged in the flames of intense class struggle in Mexico as they crossed the border into the southwestern United States during the first three decades of the twentieth century. This interview appeared originally in* International Socialist Review *105, published in spring 2017.*

Trump has made attacking immigrants, Muslims, and refugees central to his presidency. What impact is this having on immigrants?

The Trump administration issued an executive order that explicitly restricts the entry of Muslim travelers from Iran, Libya, Somalia,

Sudan, Syria, and Yemen to the United States, imposing a three-month ban on those seeking to apply for a visa. It also places a similar four-month comprehensive ban on refugees, by suspending the already woefully inadequate United States Refugee Admissions Program. The rationale for the targeted exclusions is, according the order, "each of these countries is a state sponsor of terrorism, has been significantly compromised by terrorist organizations, or contains active conflict zones."

Iraq was originally included but then removed, after it became apparent that significant Iraqi military and political personnel working alongside US military forces, the CIA, and private contractors as part of the continuing US occupation would not be able to travel to Washington for training and debriefing. What the order fails to mention is that the United States government has already been targeting these predominantly Muslim nations through aerial bombings, proxy wars, drone attacks, and a variety of other forms of clandestine warfare as part of the larger "War on Terror"—a generational effort to project its power and influence in the Arab and Muslim world. While claiming that this order is to "protect . . . citizens from terrorist attacks, including those committed by foreign nationals," the administration ignores the fact that no citizens from these countries have committed any acts of terrorism on US soil. Rather, this is part of a long tradition in the United States of using immigration policy as another type of weapon in the empire's arsenal.

There is no doubt in my mind that Trump and his inner circle of advisors are patently racist Islamophobes. In practice, though, the administration's mounting attack on Muslims is not a departure from, but rather an intensification of, the ideological war on people who have been the immediate subjects in the crosshairs of US imperialism over the last two decades. Characterizing Yemeni refugees as potential terrorists legitimizes the US government's ongoing drone assassinations in that country and reinforces support for a bloody invasion and sustained bombing campaign against the Yemeni population by the US-allied and armed Saudi Arabian government.

It should be noted that Trump's attempted bans on people from countries such as Syria and Iraq reveal the depths of hypocrisy in US politics, as refugees from these countries are fleeing US-led wars in their countries. In 2015 and 2016, according to the Council on Foreign Relations, the United States dropped over forty-seven thousand bombs on Syria and Iraq alone, killing untold thousands. On March 17, 2017, for example, a US-led airstrike killed over two hundred people huddled in a bomb shelter in a residential district in Mosul, Iraq, after allegedly targeting ISIS positions. Claiming Syrian and Iraqi refugees are therefore a "threat to national security" is the ultimate irony, as millions of Syrians and Iraqis have been displaced as a result of US policies.

A second front on this attack targets undocumented Mexican and Central American immigrants within the United States. Again, the order falsely characterizes this population as a threat, claiming, "Aliens who illegally enter the United States without inspection or admission present a significant threat to national security and public safety.... Among those who illegally enter are those who seek to harm Americans through acts of terror or criminal conduct. Continued illegal immigration presents a clear and present danger to the interests of the United States." Researchers have long dispelled the notion of the "criminal immigrant," including researchers who collect crime data for police departments and the FBI, but that is not the point.

The order rhetorically affirms the continuation of the trajectory of immigration politics and policy from Reagan to Clinton, and from Bush to Obama: increased militarization of border enforcement and further expansion of the already-existing six-hundred-mile wall, augmentation of enforcement personnel and their authority, police participation in immigration enforcement, and expansion of the detention and deportation capacities. While Congress must approve the funding for Trump's increased expenditures for the Department of Homeland Security (already $65 billion in 2016), the proposals are based on existing policy statutes that enable such increases. The presidents of both parties have made use of these statutes to ratchet up enforcement over the last generation.

The most immediate threatening act of the Trump Administration has been a series of rule changes ("guidance memos") that are currently being implemented by the Department of Homeland Security (DHS) under executive authority. The memos give a broader mandate for Immigration and Customs Enforcement (ICE) agents to arrest, detain, and deport undocumented people, as well as authorizing them to act on their own impulses and target people more generally in the course of conducting their "duties," without restriction or checks.

Under the new rules, if someone can't prove that they have been living in the United States continuously for two years, they are eligible for "expedited removal," that is, without the opportunity for legal consultation or a court hearing. Previously, this was limited in practice to those apprehended within one hundred miles of the border and who had arrived within the past two weeks. This rule is designed to allow the Border Patrol, ICE agents, and the bureaucrats of the DHS themselves to become the handmaidens of mass deportation. Deportations in the first year of the Trump presidency are already projected to surpass the annual average for the last two years of the Obama administration.

Trump has also ominously stripped federal privacy protections for undocumented youth who registered with the federal government in order to qualify for the Obama administration's Deferred Action for Childhood Arrivals (DACA). This program has shielded over 750,000 people from deportation and allowed them to apply for work permits. By repealing the privacy provisions, the Trump administration is indicating that their names and information could be turned over to immigration agents if DACA is repealed.

It should be noted that the union representing the Border Patrol officially endorsed the candidacy of Donald Trump, showing the alignment of thinking with the twenty-thousand-member armed border force. The national police union, the Fraternal Order of Police, also endorsed Trump. In other words, this order is designed to allow more impunity to the federal border police, a federal agency already accused of widespread human rights abuses, as well as police auxiliaries in cities that work with immigration agencies. In effect, the Trump administration is unleashing and encouraging the policing agencies to go on the offensive and unleash a more far-reaching reign of terror on undocumented immigrants, which will undoubtedly increase and intensify high rates of state violence and abuse.

The Arizona-based human rights organization No More Deaths, for instance, produced a comprehensive report that documents thirty thousand incidents where human rights abuses occurred between fall 2008 and spring 2011. Since 2010, according to the Southern Border Communities Coalition, forty-six people have been killed on the border. Another study conducted by the Kino Border Initiative, a binational organization promoting humane immigration policies, found that about "40 percent of Mexican migrants deported from the United States said Border Patrol agents violated their human rights, and two-thirds said their families were returned to Mexico separately." These daily abuses were committed during a period when the border police had at least minimal restrictions on their policing tactics.

ICE agents operating within the interior are no different, although their patterns of arrest have been more selective and targeted. Even though their stated purpose is to catch and deport "criminals," the initial results under Trump show a different reality. Guadalupe Garcia de Rayos, an Arizona-based worker and mother of two, was detained and deported after an annually required "check-in" with ICE. She had previously, during a workplace raid in 2008, been arrested for using false documents to work and charged with "identity theft" under the regime of notoriously racist Sheriff Joe Arpaio; she spent one year in prison.

In the era of Trump, such injustices have the potential to be even more political, as illustrated by the fact that another early detainee in the interior of the country was DREAM activist Daniela Vargas. A twenty-two-year-old DACA college student, Vargas was arrested moments after speaking publicly at an immigrant-rights rally in Jackson, Mississippi, and transferred to a detention center in Jena, Louisiana.

Enrique Balcazar, Zully Palacios, and Alex Carillo-Sánchez, community and labor organizers with Migrant Justice, a workers' rights organization in Vermont, were also arrested in late March. Since they had no deportation orders, criminal records, or any other factor that would have brought them to the attention of ICE, this shows that they were surveilled, arrested, and detained by regional agents for no other reason than for their immigrant-rights advocacy.

Not only are the armed enforcers of Trump's immigration orders animated by their new license to target immigrants, but the far right is also emboldened. For example, racists in the well-funded, right-wing information production industry are jubilant. The fake think tank "Center for Immigration Studies," an overt anti-immigrant organization that produces bogus research to justify exclusion and receives access to practically every mainstream media outlet, rejoiced at the new rules. Director of the group, Mark Krikorian, claimed that "the message is: The immigration law is back in business." After declining in the first few years of the Obama administration, when it was believed that immigration reform would pass through a Democratic "supermajority" in Congress, the number of anti-immigrant hate groups and membership is once again on the rise.

The political attack on immigrants has also increased the confidence of racist hate groups and individuals to commit acts of violence and terrorism. Encouraged by the rhetoric of Trump and the ratcheting up of state repression, the far right has increased its activities. The Southern Poverty Law Center documented more than seven hundred incidents of hate crimes in the first week of the Trump administration alone, and further attacks have targeted a broad spectrum of people including immigrants, African Americans, Jewish people, South and Central Asians, and others. For instance, in late February, a racist gunman in Kansas walked into a bar near Kansas City and opened fire on two Indian men, killing Srinivas Kuchibhotla while yelling, "Get out of my country!" This is the violence of the anti-immigrant and anti-Muslim policies at the center of US politics in its most unfiltered, toxic form.

Much of this was under way before Trump, under Obama, so much so that Obama was termed the "deporter-in-chief." What did Obama do and how did this pave the way for Trump? Given that Obama and the Democrats have been party to the war on immigrants, how should activists and the left relate to the Democratic Party in today's struggle?

Immigration reform was an issue Obama promised Latino groups he would take up within his first "hundred days" in office. That didn't happen. The narrative of the Democratic Party attributes the failure to Republican opposition and congressional gridlock. But a closer examination shows that the Democratic Party leadership allowed the Republican Party to determine the narrative and to effectively kill the possibility for legalization. After this failure, the administration walked away from its promise for legalization and instead became the most aggressive enforcer of restrictions in modern presidential history.

The Democratic Party strategy under Obama was doomed from the start. During the campaign, Obama outlined the emerging strategy that would unfold under his administration. According to a campaign email, he believed that immigration reform must include a "three-pronged response": 1) strengthen border security; 2) establish a path to legalization that includes fines and adherence to the rule of law for immigrants and their families who may have entered the United States illegally but are now contributing and responsible members of society; and 3) create a "guest-worker" program, whereby American businesses can temporarily recruit foreign workers for jobs that American workers cannot or refuse to fill.

The Democratic Party's prescription for "reform" was hardly discernable from the mainstream of the Republican Party, although the right preferred to ditch even the extremely vicarious "path to legalization." When the Obama administration introduced its policy guidelines, it bypassed the House and pushed the issue through the Senate first.

According to Democratic Speaker of the House Nancy Pelosi, this was carried out ostensibly to protect "vulnerable Democrats" who might lose in more conservative districts if they tangled with such a thorny issue. In reality, it was an effort to preempt and sideline efforts by Congressman Luis Gutierrez and the Congressional Hispanic Caucus to introduce a bill considered "too liberal" by Democratic leaders.

The Democratic leadership's vision for immigration policy followed a carefully worded script that would not allow for deviation. Like with the debacle over the passage of Obamacare, the Democrats squandered the opportunity to use their practical super-majority status in both houses of Congress to push for substantial reform, mobilize public support, and force the Republicans on the defensive. Instead, they conceded leadership to the minority-status Republicans in 2009, stating that any bill would have to pass through committee with "bipartisan" support.

Their unilateral commitment to bipartisanship allowed the Republican minority to steer the negotiation. This was despite the fact that Republicans running on an anti-immigrant platform took heavy losses in the 2006 and 2008 elections, as well as in the Republican presidential primaries of 2008. Given that context, the Democrats had a golden opportunity to carry out a legalization program, with or without Republican support.

Given this opportunity to lead on the issue, the Republicans torpedoed any possibility for reform and the Democrats dutifully conceded. Through the negotiations, the proposal was loaded with repressive, enforcement-only measures. When the Republicans called for the legalization component to be postponed, in order to "secure the border first," the effort collapsed.

A similar effort again tanked after Obama's reelection. Following the same path of "bipartisanship"—albeit after the Democrats lost their majority in the House and maintained only a slight majority in the Senate—the next attempt at immigration policy reform crashed even more abruptly. The Republicans learned that even as a defeated minority they could win, so why even bother with bipartisanship?

In the meantime, the Obama administration enhanced the machinery of immigrant repression in the United States during Obama's tenure. Between 2005 and 2012, a period spanning the second term of George W. Bush and the first completed term of Obama, the Customs and Border Protection budget was nearly doubled, from $6.3 billion to $11.7 billion. The ICE budget increased from $3.1 billion to $6.3 billion, and total enforcement personnel increased from 41,001 to over 61,354, including the vast expansion of ICE offices, field operations, and detention centers throughout the interior of the country.

This helps explain why detentions and deportations accelerated under Obama, reaching a record of over three million over the course of his tenure, a majority of which were connected to no crime whatsoever. The ramping up of repression, even while the Obama administration claimed to be championing the rights of immigrants and striving for humane reform, only goaded the Republicans and conservative Democrats to take an even harder line against any relief for undocumented workers. Furthermore, this ninety-degree shift led liberal supporters to become muted, lower their expectations, or even drop the issue altogether as a policy priority.

The failure of the Democrats to make more than a symbolic gesture at immigration reform greatly demoralized the prolegalization base of the Democratic Party who showed up at the polls in fewer numbers in the elections of 2010 and 2012. This failure energized the hard-right Tea Party, which mobilized bigoted, anti-immigrant sentiment to get to the polls in greater numbers in 2010 and 2012, helping to pave the way for the Republican Party and Trump to ascend on a reactionary and racist platform once again centered on attacking immigrants.

The Democratic Party has failed, on a national level, to present any coherent or principled opposition to Trump's initial policies. While governors of the predominantly liberal states with substantial immigrant populations, like New York and California, have rhetorically postured against the federal government, a new round of deportations has commenced with little actual outcry beyond immigrant-rights activists. A new movement in defense of immigrants will need to hold Democrats and their auxiliaries accountable when they are complicit or silent, put massive pressure on them to take public stances against Trump and Republican immigrant-bashing policies, and block Trump and the Republicans by all means at their disposal. At the same time, this new movement will need to retain complete independence from the Democratic Party, resisting its multifaceted capabilities to coopt, divide, and demobilize social movements.

How have immigrant-rights activists responded to this assault?

One of the first responses took place before Trump even assumed office. Across the country, student activists began organizing to get their school administrations to declare themselves "sanctuary campuses." While the definition of "sanctuary" varies, it generally involves the campus administration making a public declaration to refuse to comply with immigration enforcement on the campus, to not share student information with federal immigration agents, and to keep campus police from collaborating or assisting in any form of immigration policing.

Perhaps the most impressive response since the inauguration was the airport protests following the executive order imposing a travel ban on Muslims. Immediately after the ban was announced, an estimated one hundred people had arrived from the banned countries and were detained at various airports across the country. In an amazing display of opposition to the ban, and in support for those detained, tens of thousands of people converged at airports across the country on short notice, from San Diego to New York City, to confront overzealous ICE agents and demand that detainees be released. The outpouring undoubtedly cajoled a group of federal judges to overturn the order in a matter of days.

To defend undocumented workers, immigrant-rights activists across the county have returned to the strategy that was developed after previous waves of repression unleashed by the Bush administration in the wake of the May 1, 2006, protests and in Arizona in 2010. Namely, they are forming, or reactivating, "emergency response networks" to mobilize rapidly to protest and protect immigrants being targeted.

In Arizona, for instance, when Guadalupe Garcia de Rayos was detained during her "check-in," a group of about two hundred activists affiliated with the long-standing immigrant-rights organization "Puente Movement" quickly gathered at the Phoenix offices of ICE. For several hours, until they were physically repressed by the Phoenix police, they blocked federal vehicles attempting to leave with Garcia de Rayos. In other parts of the country, similar networks are forming or reconnecting and conducting legal workshops and civil disobedience trainings, establishing communication networks, and setting up other strategies to intervene on behalf of targeted people and communities.

Scattered immigrant-rights marches have been organized in different parts of the country. Where immigrant-rights organizations have some continuity and connection to the labor movement, such as in Milwaukee, the actions have been impressive. On February 13, 2017, for instance, a crowd estimated at thirty thousand marched through the Latino-majority south side of the city in response to the call for "a day without an immigrant," and for people not to work, shop, or go to school. This protest also directed its message of opposition to Milwaukee County Sheriff David Clarke, a Trump partisan who has stated his intention to volunteer local police to assist in federal roundups. These actions show the possibility for larger and coordinated mass actions as organizations and networks take shape. The dominant slogan that has emerged from these protests—"No Ban, No Wall, Sanctuary for All!"—shows how a new generation of activists is making the convergence of struggle against Islamophobia and a reinvigorated anti-immigrant right.

The last time immigrants were attacked in such a frontal manner was back in 2006, with the Sensenbrenner-King Bill. That provoked mass marches and work shutdowns called "A Day Without an Immigrant." How does today's situation compare with that response?

What happened in 2006 was very important, and worth recalling. The House of Representatives approved the reactionary Sensenbrenner-King Bill in December 2005, named after congressmen James Sensenbrenner from Wisconsin and Peter King from New York. Its provisions would have turned twelve million undocumented immigrants and anyone who aided them into felons. Millions of immigrant workers, their families, and supporters were pushed into opposition, flocking to protests called by small groups. Since no national structure existed, few were prepared for the size of the protests. Nevertheless, organizations were created and grew significantly during this period.

Following a mass protest of twenty thousand people in Washington, DC, at least three hundred thousand protesters took to the streets of Chicago on March 10, 2006. This was the largest protest in Chicago history, and it shut down the city as workers left their jobs and students walked out of schools to join the human streams that jammed several city blocks. Entire families marched together, and the vast majority had clearly never been to a protest in their lives.

After Chicago, the dam broke. Mass protests of immigrant workers took place in more than fifty cities within two weeks. About 150,000 people crowded onto Denver's streets, 50,000 marched through the streets of Phoenix, and over 30,000 took to the streets in Milwaukee. In Atlanta, more than 80,000 protesters heeded a call to not go to work. In Tulsa, Oklahoma, 5,000 people came out to oppose anti-immigrant legislation; 15,000 marched across the Brooklyn Bridge in New York; 3,000 took to the streets of Fort Smith, Arkansas; and thousands more clogged the downtowns in a constellation of other cities and towns across the country. The turnout reached new heights in Los Angeles, where over one million people transformed the downtown area into a human sea, every open space commandeered by the otherwise hidden workforce of the city's vast street-level economy.

These demonstrations also inspired student actions. Sons and daughters of the Latino working class shut down schools across the country in protest against anti-immigrant racism. In California, tens of thousands of students walked out of classes across the state. In Dallas, four thousand walked out of school, with another two thousand in El Paso, three thousand in Las Vegas, and a thousand in Aurora, Illinois. In Tucson, a thousand middle-school students walked out of their schools, showing that many young teens were keenly aware of what's at stake and were making their voices heard.

Some union organizations also got on board, joining with the National Council of La Raza and other civic and religious organizations calling for a day of protest. On April 9, 2006, half a million more came out in Dallas, one hundred thousand in San Diego, and twenty thousand in Salt Lake City. Protests also sprouted in smaller towns and in rural regions. Three thousand people converged on the small agricultural community of Garden City, Kansas. Thousands more turned out in South Bend, Indiana; Portland, Maine; Harrisburg, Pennsylvania; and Lake Worth, Florida.

On April 10, protests continued in ninety-four cities. Half a million came out in New York City, thirty thousand in Boston, and ten thousand in Madison, Wisconsin. More than fifty thousand came out in Atlanta, and an equal number in Phoenix, ten thousand protested in Boston, and another ten thousand in Omaha. The protest movement culminated in the call for a general strike and economic boycott on May 1, 2006, when an estimated two to three million people left their homes, work, and schools to participate in the single largest protest action in US history. In response to this popular outpouring of opposition, the repressive bill was killed.

Many of the immigrants' rights organizations that were developed during the mass marches, strikes, and boycotts of 2006 have disappeared or were dismantled after the successful election of Obama and the Democrats in 2008. With Democrats in power, many believed some form of immigrant legalization was imminent. When it didn't materialize—and when the persecution persisted and intensified—the largest organizations, which were aligned with the Democratic Party, organized little public opposition.

This included liberal membership groups, nongovernmental organizations, labor unions, church groups, and think tanks. With the exception of DREAM activist networks, which went against the stream and intensified their activism, including repeated sit-ins at Democratic Party offices, disruption at several of Obama's speeches, and other high-profile actions, the opposition demobilized under the Democrats and has yet to recover. Nevertheless, some of these groups are once again emerging and coalescing. It will also be important that the veteran organizers in the unions and on the left who played a pivotal role in the mass movement of 2006 bring their experience and organizational networks back onto the field of struggle.

In 2017, the Trump administration is determined to terrorize immigrant working-class communities and to undermine opposition as much as possible. It's worth recalling that George W. Bush authorized a national campaign of workplace raids in the weeks following the mass actions in 2006, which set back the movement as people understandably retreated from the streets in fear.

How has the labor movement responded to the attack on immigrants? What should labor militants be demanding from their unions?

Unfortunately, there has been no substantial, positive response from the national leadership of labor. Shamefully, the AFL-CIO leadership under Richard Trumka has set the wrong tone for labor, bending to Trump instead of resolutely, on principle, opposing his policies. Trumka recently met with Trump—hat in hand—claiming a desire to "work with him," especially on renegotiating trade deals and immigration. Trumka also appeared on Fox News right after Trump's first address to Congress, stating that the speech, in which Trump declared his intention to publish a list of immigrant "criminals" as part of his larger war on immigrants, "was one of his finest moments."

He further went on to congratulate Trump for including "legal immigrants" as well as "undocumented immigrants" being "used to drive down wages." Aligning himself with Trump, he concluded, "We partner with him to write the rules of immigration, absolutely." Cozying up to Trump and trying to align unions with his anti-immigrant project will be a poison pill for organized labor. Trump's criticism of "free trade" isn't that it is unjust for workers; rather, he believes trade rules can be "improved" so that they are less regulatory, provide even fewer rights for workers, and give even more power to corporate profiteers. Any immigration policy that this president presides over will be designed to oppress immigrant workers more, to further isolate them, to stoke more racism, and to widen the divides in the working class along racial and national lines as part of a larger strategy to weaken and break unions.

The organization and incorporation of immigrant workers, documented and undocumented, is essential to rebuilding labor unions in this country. Unions have been in a state of perpetual decline and represent the lowest percentage of workers in modern history. The failure to take a consistent stand to combat the anti-immigrant policies embedded in both capitalist parties has allowed for the current recycling of right-wing reactionaries into the highest echelons of government. To reverse course, unions will need to build on previous gains made in defending and organizing the immigrant workforce.

In California, the state that boasts the largest immigrant worker population, immigrant workers have been the fastest growing segment of organized labor over the last few decades. Nationally, the Service Employees International Union (SEIU) has become the largest and fastest growing labor union in the United States, claiming a membership of 1.9 million, with immigrant workers accounting for two-thirds of that figure. In the Midwest and South region, the United Food and Commercial Workers (UFCW) union now represents over 250,000 workers, nearly half of them Latino immigrants. Unions and locals at the state and regional levels will need to take action, in some cases despite their own leadership.

Right now, we are witnessing the largest migration in human history, with over sixty million people in flight from their countries. Why has this happened?

War and violence have played a role. As previously mentioned, the US-led "War on Terror" has had a major destabilizing impact on the Middle East, displacing millions in the region. In Mexico and Central America, the US-led "War on Drugs" has amounted to the militarization of the drug trade. Regional policies pushed by Washington, such as Plan Mérida Initiative (in Mexico) and similar efforts in Central America, have allocated billions of dollars of military support and equipment to repressive state regimes to supposedly fight drug cartels, but in practice are also used against the population.

In Mexico, over 100,000 people have been killed as a result of the conflict since it began in 2006, and 25,000 have been "disappeared," including the missing forty-three students from Ayotzinapa, Guerrero.[1] According to the Mexican think tank Parametria, over 2 million people have been displaced. In Central America, a study conducted by the Internal Displacement Monitoring Center estimates that over 850,000 people have been displaced by state repression and drug-war violence from El Salvador, Honduras, and Guatemala.

Even larger numbers are displaced by the economic logic of world capitalism. Global economic integration along neoliberal lines—where corporations write the rules of trade, investment, and regulation in their own interest—has destabilized laboring classes internationally. As a predictable result, labor itself has become internationalized. By 2013, an estimated 231.5 million people migrated and took up residence in a foreign country. If that number was the population of a country, it would be the fifth-largest in the world, roughly larger than the population of each of the remaining 189 other countries. In the United States, the Pew Research Center estimates that forty-two million residents, primarily workers and their families, were born in another country. This number has more than doubled over the last three decades.

Displaced workers that cannot be absorbed within their own national economies as a result of corporate-led trade policies have been compelled to cross boundaries into foreign labor markets where they can find work. This has altered workforce demographics internationally, from Qatar to the Dominican Republic, from Japan to the United States. The end result of US-led free-trade policies exported south has been destructive for the laboring classes of Mexico, Central America, and the Caribbean nations, dislodging millions of small agricultural producers and urban workers made redundant through skewed competition, "debt-servicing," privatization of state industry, and the downsizing of the welfare state.

Migration has flowed in reverse through these same channels from poorer to richer capitalist nations, as workers follow the profit streams that translate into disproportionate job creation or opportunities in other nations. Once drawn into US labor markets, undocumented workers are regulated not by the "invisible hand of the free market," but by immigration enforcement and employers themselves.

Most recently, thousands of Haitians have been entering Mexico with the hopes of crossing into the United States. Haiti, a country where three-quarters of the people live on less than two dollars a day, has been wracked by US-led military intervention and destabilizing economic policies. For example, the US government passed the Haitian Hemispheric Opportunity through Partnership Encouragement Act of 2006 under the existing Caribbean Basin Trade Partnership Act. This policy gives garments manufactured on the island duty-free access to US markets. As a result, US-based corporations such as Levi Strauss, Haneswear, Nautica, Dockers, and others have relocated production to the island to take advantage of lower wages alongside the corporate tax breaks, with assembled garments now comprising 90 percent of the country's exports. These companies, with the support of the State Department operating through the Haitian embassy, helped block a planned minimum-wage increase from being implemented in the garment industry in 2009, which would have tripled the minimum wage of $1.75 a day to over $5 a day. As a result of pressures placed on the Haitian government, including the threat of capital flight, the garment industry was exempted and limited to an increase of only $3 per day.

After the great earthquake of 2010, which devastated the already poor country, the lack of significant and meaningful international aid further accelerated an exodus of migrants from Haiti. Many went to Brazil, while others flowed into Tijuana, hoping to apply for a type of refugee status under a humanitarian parole provision granted after the earthquake. Then, in September 2016, the Obama administration reversed its policy, denying Haitians entry and vowing to deport them if they entered the country without authorization. By Trump's inauguration, over five thousand Haitians were still languishing in the Mexican border region, largely housed in privately run shelters, since the Mexican government of Enrique Peña Nieto has ignored their plight.

What should the left agitate for in terms of demands in the short term as well as in the long term?

In the immediate term, the left will need to stand shoulder to shoulder with all those willing to struggle to defend targeted communities, and the undocumented immigrant workers, students, and their family members facing arrest and deportation. This will likely require a higher level of militancy and confrontation with emboldened and empowered agents of the state.

In the current social environment, politically polarized along class, racial, and generational lines, a mass opposition to Trump and the right has already emerged and has quickly situated itself to the left of the Democratic Party. Millions of people have already registered some form of action against or discontent with the reactionary turn in US politics and the ideological bankruptcy of the Democratic Party. In the first two months of Trump's presidency alone, there has been some visible convergence between anti-Trump, feminist, and pro-immigrant sectors of the protest movement. This will have to be strengthened and expanded if there is to be any substantial challenge from the left to the scale of the attacks yet to come.

Even small victories can galvanize a sustained resistance and draw wider segments of the population into active opposition. This will be necessary to build a revitalized left that can sustain long-term social movement opposition, especially important in order to build a more powerful base of opposition rooted in the labor unions. Building that more powerful base is crucial because "Trumpism" is providing an opening for the Republican establishment to advance its reactionary agenda, while also nurturing the resurgence of the far right and fascist movements in the streets. Any long-term possibilities for the left depend on how fast and how well we can organize and sustain active opposition over the next four years.

THE END OF PROGRESSIVE NEOLIBERALISM

Nancy Fraser

The election of Donald Trump represents one of a series of dramatic political uprisings that together signal a collapse of neoliberal hegemony. These uprisings include the Brexit vote in the United Kingdom, the rejection of the Renzi reforms in Italy, the Bernie Sanders campaign for the Democratic Party nomination in the United States, and rising support for the National Front in France, among others. Although they differ in ideology and goals, these electoral mutinies share a common target: all are rejections of corporate globalization, neoliberalism, and the political establishments that have promoted them. In every case, voters are saying "No!" to the lethal combination of austerity, free trade, predatory debt, and precarious, ill-paid work that characterize financialized capitalism today. Their votes are a response to the structural crisis of this form of capitalism, which first came into full view with the near meltdown of the global financial order in 2008.

Until recently, however, the chief response to the crisis was social protest—dramatic and lively, to be sure, but largely ephemeral. Political systems, by contrast, seemed relatively immune, still controlled by party functionaries and establishment elites, at least in powerful capitalist states like the United States, the United Kingdom, and Germany. Now, however, electoral shockwaves reverberate throughout the world, including in the citadels of global finance. Those who voted for Trump, like those who voted for Brexit and against the Italian reforms, have risen up against their political masters. Thumbing their noses at party establishments, they have repudiated the system that has eroded their living conditions for the last thirty years. The surprise is not that they have done so, but that it took them so long.

Nevertheless, Trump's victory is not solely a revolt against global finance. What his voters rejected was not neoliberalism tout court, but progressive neoliberalism. This may sound to some like an oxymoron, but it is a real, if perverse, political alignment that holds the key to understanding the US election results and perhaps some developments elsewhere too. In its US form, progressive neoliberalism is an alliance of mainstream currents of new social movements (feminism, antiracism, multiculturalism, and LGBTQ rights), on the one side, and high-end "symbolic" and service-based business sectors (Wall Street, Silicon Valley, and Hollywood) on the other. In this alliance, progressive forces are effectively joined with the forces of cognitive capitalism, especially financialization. However unwittingly, the former lend their charisma to the latter. Ideals like diversity and empowerment, which could in principle serve different ends, now gloss policies that have devastated manufacturing and what were once middle-class lives.

Progressive neoliberalism developed in the United States over the last three decades and was ratified with Bill Clinton's election in 1992. Clinton was the principal engineer and standard-bearer of the "New Democrats," the US equivalent of Tony Blair's "New Labor." In place of the New Deal coalition of unionized manufacturing workers, African Americans, and the urban middle classes, he forged a new alliance of entrepreneurs, suburbanites, new social movements, and youth, all proclaiming their modern, progressive bona fides by embracing diversity, multiculturalism, and women's rights. Even as it endorsed such progressive notions, the

Clinton administration courted Wall Street. Turning the econ-omy over to Goldman Sachs, it deregulated the banking system and negotiated the free-trade agreements that accelerated dein-dustrialization. What fell by the wayside was the Rust Belt—once the stronghold of New Deal social democracy, and now the re-gion that delivered the electoral college to Donald Trump. That region, along with newer industrial centers in the South, took a major hit as runaway financialization unfolded over the course of the last two decades. Continued by his successors, including Barack Obama, Clinton's policies degraded the living conditions of all working people, but especially those employed in industrial production. In short, Clintonism bears a heavy share of responsi-bility for the weakening of unions, the decline of real wages, the increasing precarity of work, and the rise of the two-earner family in place of the defunct family wage.

As that last point suggests, the assault on social security was glossed by a veneer of emancipatory charisma, borrowed from the new social movements. Throughout the years when manufacturing cratered, the country buzzed with talk of "diversity," "empower-ment," and "nondiscrimination." Identifying "progress" with meri-tocracy instead of with equality, these terms equated "emancipation" with the rise of a small elite of "talented" women, minorities, and gays in the winner-takes-all corporate hierarchy instead of with the latter's abolition. These liberal-individualist understandings of "progress" gradually replaced the more expansive, anti-hierarchical, egalitarian, class-sensitive, anti-capitalist understandings of emanci-pation that had flourished in the 1960s and 1970s. As the new left waned, its structural critique of capitalist society faded, and the country's characteristic liberal-individualist mindset reasserted itself, imperceptibly shrinking the aspirations of "progressives" and self-proclaimed leftists. What sealed the deal, however, was the coincidence of this evolution with the rise of neoliberalism. A party bent on liberalizing the capitalist economy found its perfect mate in a meritocratic corporate feminism focused on "leaning in" and "crack-ing the glass ceiling."

The result was a "progressive neoliberalism" that mixed together truncated ideals of emancipation and lethal forms of financialization. It was that mix that was rejected in toto by Trump's voters. Prominent among those left behind in this brave new cosmopolitan world were industrial workers, to be sure, but also managers, small businessmen, and all who relied on industry in the Rust Belt and the South, as well as rural populations devastated by unemployment and drugs. For these populations, the injury of deindustrialization was compounded by the insult of progressive moralism, which routinely cast them as culturally backward. Rejecting globalization, Trump voters also repudiated the liberal cosmopolitanism identified with it. For some (though by no means all), it was a short step to blaming their worsening conditions on political correctness, people of color, immigrants, and Muslims. In their eyes, feminists and Wall Street were birds of a feather, perfectly united in the person of Hillary Clinton.

What made possible that conflation was the absence of any genuine left. Despite periodic outbursts such as Occupy Wall Street, which proved short-lived, there had been no sustained left presence in the United States for several decades. Nor was there in place any comprehensive left narrative that could link the legitimate grievances of Trump supporters with a fulsome critique of financialization, on the one hand, and with an antiracist, anti-sexist, and anti-hierarchical vision of emancipation, on the other. Equally devastating, potential links between labor and new social movements were left to languish. Split off from one another, those indispensable poles of a viable left were miles apart, waiting to be counterposed as antithetical.

At least until the remarkable primary campaign of Bernie Sanders, who struggled to unite them after some prodding from Black Lives Matter. Exploding the reigning neoliberal common sense, Sanders's revolt was the parallel on the Democratic side to that of Trump. Even as Trump was upending the Republican establishment, Bernie came within a hair's breadth of defeating Obama's anointed successor, whose apparatchiks controlled every lever of power in the Democratic Party. Between them, Sanders and Trump galvanized a huge majority of American voters. But only Trump's reactionary populism survived. While he easily routed his Republican rivals, including those favored by the big donors and party bosses, the Sanders insurrection was effectively checked by a far less democratic Democratic Party. By the time of the general election, the left alternative had been suppressed. What remained was the Hobson's choice between reactionary populism and progressive neoliberalism. When the so-called left closed ranks with Hillary Clinton, the die was cast.

Nevertheless, and from this point on, this is a choice the left should refuse. Rather than accepting the terms presented to us by the political classes, which oppose emancipation to social protection, we should be working to redefine them by drawing on the vast and growing fund of social revulsion against the present order. Rather than siding with financialization-cum-emancipation against social protection, we should be building a new alliance of emancipation and social protection against financialization. In this project, which builds on that of Sanders, emancipation does not mean diversifying corporate hierarchy, but rather abolishing it. And prosperity does not mean rising share value or corporate profit, but the material prerequisites of a good life for all. This combination remains the only principled and winning response in the current conjuncture.

I, for one, shed no tears for the defeat of progressive neoliberalism. Certainly, there is much to fear from a racist, anti-immigrant, anti-ecological Trump administration. But we should mourn neither the implosion of neoliberal hegemony nor the shattering of Clintonism's iron grip on the Democratic Party. Trump's victory marked a defeat for the alliance of emancipation and financialization. But his presidency offers no resolution of the present crisis, no promise of a new regime, no secure hegemony. What we face, rather, is an interregnum, an open and unstable situation in which hearts and minds are up for grabs. In this situation, there is not only danger but also opportunity: the chance to build a new new left.

Whether that happens will depend in part on some serious soul-searching among the progressives who rallied to the Clinton campaign. They will need to drop the comforting but false myth that they lost to a "basket of deplorables" (racists, misogynists, Islamophobes, and homophobes) aided by Vladimir Putin and the FBI. They will need to acknowledge their own share of blame for sacrificing the cause of social protection, material well-being, and working-class dignity to faux understandings of emancipation in terms of meritocracy, diversity, and empowerment. They will need to think deeply about how we might transform the political economy of financialized capitalism, reviving Sanders's catchphrase "democratic socialism" and figuring out what it might mean in the twenty-first century. They will need, above all, to reach out to the mass of Trump voters who are neither racists nor committed right-wingers but themselves casualties of a "rigged system," who can and must be recruited to the anti-neoliberal project of a rejuvenated left.

This does not mean muting pressing concerns about racism or sexism. But it does mean showing how those long-standing historical oppressions find new expressions and grounds today, in financialized capitalism. Rebutting the false, zero-sum thinking that dominated the election campaign, we should link the harms suffered by women and people of color to those experienced by the many who voted for Trump. In that way, a revitalized left could lay the foundation for a powerful new coalition committed to fighting for all.

ACKNOWLEDGMENTS

A number of the articles in this collection appeared in print in other publications. All the authors have given their approval for the reprinting of their work here. In most cases, they have revised or updated the original texts for this collection.

Sharon Smith, "Chickens Coming Home to Roost for the Democratic Party? How Neoliberalism Quietly Devastated the US Working Class," is original to this collection.

Charlie Post, "We Got Trumped!," appeared in *International Socialist Review* 104, Spring 2017. It has been revised and edited for this collection.

Kim Moody, "Who Put Trump in the White House?," appeared in *Against the Current* 186, January–February 2017.

A version of Mike Davis, "The Great God Trump and the White Working Class," appeared in *Jacobin*, February 7, 2017.

Neil Davidson, "Choosing or Refusing to Take Sides in an Era of Right-Wing Populism," appeared in *International Socialist Review* 104, Spring 2017. It has been revised and edited for this collection.

Lance Selfa, "From Hope to Despair: How the Obama Years Gave Us Trump," is revised and updated from chapter 4 in *The Democrats: A Critical History*, 2nd ed. (Haymarket Books, 2012) and from "Sanders and the Left: Where Do We Go from Here?," published in *International Socialist Review* 104, Spring 2017.

Keeanga-Yamahtta Taylor, "Black Politics in the Trump Era," is original to this collection.

Elizabeth Schulte, "The Misogynist-in-Chief: The Stakes for Women's Rights in the Trump Era," is original to this collection.

"Trump, Islamophobia, and US Politics: An Interview with Deepa Kumar" appeared as "The Roots of Islamophobia" in *Jacobin*, December 21, 2015.

"From 'Deporter-In-Chief' to Xenophobia Unleashed: An Interview with Justin Akers Chacón" appeared in *International Socialist Review* 105, Summer 2017.

Nancy Fraser, "The End of Progressive Neoliberalism," appeared in *Dissent*, January 2, 2017.

CONTRIBUTOR BIOGRAPHIES

Sharon Smith is the author of *Women and Socialism: Class, Race, and Capital* and *Subterranean Fire: A History of Working-Class Radicalism in the United States*, both published by Haymarket Books (2005 and 2006, respectively), as well as many articles on women's liberation and the US working class. Her writings appear regularly in *Socialist Worker* newspaper and the *International Socialist Review*.

Charlie Post is a longtime socialist activist who teaches at the City University of New York. He is the author of *The American Road to Capitalism* (Haymarket Books, 2012). Post has published essays on the trajectory of the Republican Party in *New Politics, Jacobin, Cultural Dynamics*, the *Brooklyn Rail*, and the *International Socialist Review*.

Kim Moody was a founder of *Labor Notes* and is a member of the National Union of Journalists. He is currently a Visiting Scholar at the University of Westminster in London and the author of *On New Terrain: How Capital Is Reshaping the Battleground of Class War in the United States* (Haymarket Books, forthcoming).

Mike Davis is the author of several books, including *Prisoners of the American Dream, City of Quartz, Magical Urbanism, Late Victorian Holocausts, Planet of Slums* (Verso Books, 2000, 2006, 2001, 2017, 2017, respectively, and *In Praise of Barbarians* (Haymarket Books, 2007). He is the recipient of the MacArthur Fellowship and the Lannan Literary Award. He lives in San Diego.

Neil Davidson currently lectures in sociology with the School of Social and Political Science at the University of Glasgow. He is the author of *The Origins of Scottish Nationhood* (Pluto Press, 2000); *Discovering the Scottish Revolution* (Pluto Books, 2003), for which he was awarded the Deutscher Memorial Prize; *How Revolutionary Were the Bourgeois Revolutions?* (Haymarket Books, 2012 and 2017); *Holding Fast to an Image of the Past* (Haymarket Books, 2014); *We Cannot Escape History* (Haymarket Books, 2015); and *Nation-States: Consciousness and Competition* (Haymarket Books, 2016). Davidson is a member of rs21 at the UK level and of RISE: Scotland's Left Alliance and the Radical Independence Campaign in Scotland.

Keeanga-Yamahtta Taylor writes on Black politics, social movements, and racial inequality in the United States. Her articles have been published in *Souls: A Critical Journal of Black Politics, Culture and Society*, *Jacobin*, *New Politics*, *Guardian*, *In These Times*, *Black Agenda Report*, *Ms.*, *International Socialist Review*, *Al Jazeera America*, and other publications. Taylor is assistant professor in the department of African American studies at Princeton University. She is the author of *From #BlackLivesMatter to Black Liberation* (Haymarket Books, 2016).

Lance Selfa is a frequent contributor to the *International Socialist Review* and writes a column on US politics for *Socialist Worker*. He is the author of *The Democrats: A Critical History* (Haymarket Books, 2012).

Elizabeth Schulte is a journalist at *Socialist Worker*, writing frequently on US politics and women's rights. Her articles have also appeared in the *International Socialist Review*, *Jacobin*, and *Truthout.*

Deepa Kumar is an associate professor of media studies and Middle East studies at Rutgers University. She is the author of *Islamophobia and the Politics of Empire* (Haymarket Books, 2012) and *Outside the Box: Corporate Media, Globalization, and the UPS Strike* (University of Illinois Press, 2008). She has offered her analysis on Islamophobia to numerous outlets around the world, including the BBC, *USA Today*, *Philadelphia Inquirer*, Mexico's *Proceso*, China International Radio, and Gulf News from Dubai.

Justin Akers Chacón is an activist, writer, and educator in the San Diego-Tijuana border region. He is a professor of Chicana and Chicano studies at San Diego City College. His previous work includes *No One Is Illegal: Fighting Racism and State Violence on the U.S.-Mexico Border* (with Mike Davis) (Haymarket Books, 2009). His forthcoming book *Radicals in the Barrio* (Haymarket Books, expected 2018) uncovers the lost history and rich tradition of Mexican and Mexican American political radicalism and labor militancy in the United States, forged in the flames of intense class struggle in Mexico and carried across the border into the Southwest during the first three decades of the twentieth century.

Nancy Fraser is Henry A. and Louise Loeb Professor at the New School for Social Research, president-elect of the American Philosophical Association, Eastern Division, and holder of an international research chair at the Collège d'études mondiales, Paris. Her new book, *Capitalism: A Critical Theory*, coauthored with Rahel Jaeggi, will be published by Polity Press in autumn 2017. Fraser's work has been translated into more than twenty languages and was cited twice by the Brazilian Supreme Court (in decisions upholding marriage equality and affirmative action).

NOTES

Introduction

1. "Resistance and Reaction in the Time of Trump," editorial, *ISR,* 104 http://isreview.org/issue/104/resistance-and-reaction-time-trump-0.
2. Nate Cohn, "Why Trump Won: Working-Class Whites," *New York Times,* November 9, 2016; George Packer, "Head of the Class," *New Yorker,* May 16, 2016; and Joan C. Williams, "Why the White Working Class Voted for Trump," *Harvard Business Review,* November 18, 2016, are a few examples of literally hundreds of articles in this genre.
3. Eric Sasson, "Blame Trump's Victory on College-Educated Whites, Not the Working Class," *New Republic,* November 15, 2016; Nate Silver, "The Mythology of Trump's 'Working Class' Support," *FiveThirtyEight,* May 3, 2016, https://fivethirtyeight.com/features/the-mythology-of-trumps-working -class-support/.
4. Brent Griffiths, "Sanders Slams Identity Politics as Democrats Figure Out Their Future," *Politico,* November 21, 2016, www.politico.com/story/2016 /11/bernie-sanders-democrats-identity-politics-231710; Craig Mills, "Here's Why Democrats Must Not Abandon Identity Politics," *Daily Beast,* December 12, 2016, www.thedailybeast.com/heres-why-democrats-must -not-abandon-identity-politics; Michelle Goldberg, "Democratic Politics Have to Be Identity Politics," *Slate,* November 22, 2016, www.slate.com /articles/news_and_politics/politics/2016/11/democratic_politics_have _to_be_identity_politics.html; Shuja Haider, "Safety Pins and Swastikas," *Jacobin,* January 5, 2017, www.jacobinmag.com/2017/01/safety-pin-box -richard-spencer-neo-nazis-alt-right-identity-politics.

Chickens Coming Home to Roost for the Democratic Party?

1. Jim Tankersley, "How Trump Won: The Revenge of Working-Class Whites," *Washington Post,* November 9, www.washingtonpost.com/news/wonk

/wp/2016/11/09/how-trump-won-the-revenge-of-working-class-whites/.

2. Jill Filipovic, "The Revenge of the White Man," *Time*, November 10, 2016, http://time.com/4566304/donald-trump-revenge-of-the-white-man/.

3. Alec MacGillis, "Revenge of the Forgotten Class," *ProPublica*, November 10, 2016, www.propublica.org/article/revenge-of-the-forgotten-class.

4. Helena Bottemiller Evich, "Revenge of the Rural Voter," *Politico*, November 13, 2016, www.politico.com/story/2016/11/hillary-clinton -rural-voters-trump-231266.

5. Nate Cohn, "Why Trump Won: Working-Class Whites," *New York Times*, November 9, 2016, www.nytimes.com/2016/11/10/upshot/why-trump -won-working-class-whites.html.

6. Nate Silver, "The Mythology of Trump's 'Working Class' Support," *FiveThirtyEight*, May 3, 2016, https://fivethirtyeight.com/features/the -mythology-of-trumps-working-class-support/.

7. Konstantin Kilibarda and Daria Roithmayr, "The Myth of the Rust Belt Revolt," *Slate*, December 1, 2016, www.slate.com/articles/news_and _politics/politics/2016/12/the_myth_of_the_rust_belt_revolt.html.

8. Nate Cohn, "Why Trump Won."

9. See, for example, Richard Fording and Sanford Schram, "'Low Information Voters Are a Crucial Part of Trump's Support," *Washington Post*, November 7, 2017, www.washingtonpost.com/news/monkey-cage/wp/2016/11/07 /low-information-voters-are-a-crucial-part-of-trumps-support/?utm _term=.a61c954832d5.

10. Markos "Kos" Moulitsas, "Be Happy for Coal Miners Losing Their Health Insurance. They're Getting Exactly What They Voted For," *Daily Kos*, December 12, 2016, www.dailykos.com/stories/2016/12/12/1610198/-Be -happy-for-coal-miners-losing-their-health-insurance-They-re-getting -exactly-what-they-voted-for.

11. Mark Lilla, "The End of Identity Liberalism," *New York Times*, November 18, 2016, www.nytimes.com/2016/11/20/opinion/sunday/the-end-of -identity-liberalism.html.

12. Bryanna Cappadona, "Here's What Bernie Sanders Had To Say About Transgender Bathroom Rights," Boston.com, May 27, 2016, www.boston .com/culture/tv/2016/05/27/heres-bernie-sanders-say-transgender -bathroom-rights.

13. William H. Frey, "Five Charts That Show Why a Post-White America Is Already Here," *New Republic*, November 21, 2014, newrepublic.com /article/120370/five-graphics-show-why-post-white-america-already-here.

14. Nate Cohn, "How the Obama Coalition Crumbled, Leaving an Opening for Trump," *New York Times*, December 23, 2016, www.nytimes.com /2016/12/23/upshot/how-the-obama-coalition-crumbled-leaving-an -opening-for-trump.html.

15. Robert Dreyfuss, "How the DLC Does It," *American Prospect*, December 19, 2001, http://prospect.org/article/how-dlc-does-it.

16. Feliz Solomon, "Hillary Clinton Called for Strikes on Syrian Airfields Shortly before Trump's Announcement," *Time*, April 6, 2017, http://time .com/4730416/syria-missile-attack-hillary-clinton-assad/.

17. Daniel Strauss, "Clinton Haunted by Coal Country Comment, *Politico*, May 10, 2016, www.politico.com/story/2016/05/sanders-looking-to-rack-up -west-virginia-win-over-clinton-222952.

18. Mitt Romney, "Let Detroit Go Bankrupt," *New York Times*, November 18, 2008, www.nytimes.com/2008/11/19/opinion/19romney.html.

19. Nate Cohn, "How the Obama Coalition Crumbled."

20. Christian Parenti, "Listening to Trump," *CommonDreams*, November 21, 2016, www.commondreams.org/views/2016/11/21/listening-trump.

21. "Election 2016: Exit Polls," CNN Politics, November 23, 2016, www.cnn .com/election/results/exit-polls.

22. See, for example, Akhil Reed Amar, "The Troubling Reason the Electoral College Exists," *Time*, November 08, 2016 [updated November 10, 2016], http://time.com/4558510/electoral-college-history-slavery/.

23. Sean McElwee, "The Income Gap at the Polls: The Rich Aren't Just Megadonors. They're Also Dominating the Voting Booth," *Politico*, January 7, 2015, www .politico.com/magazine/story/2015/01/income-gap-at-the-polls-113997.

24. Sean McElwee, *Why the Voting Gap Matters*, Demos, October 23, 2014, www.demos.org/publication/why-voting-gap-matters.

25. Linda Qiu, "Bernie Sanders Said Poor People Don't Vote," *PolitiFact*, April 24, 2016, www.politifact.com/truth-o-meter/statements/2016 /apr/24/bernie-s/bernie-sanders-said-poor-people-dont-vote/.

26. Maria Murriel, "Millions of Americans Can't Vote for President Because of Where They Live," Public Radio International, November 1, 2016, https:// www.pri.org/stories/2016-11-01/millions-americans-cant-vote-president-because-where-they-live.

27. Jean Chung, "Felony Disenfranchisement: A Primer," The Sentencing Project, May 10, 2016, www.sentencingproject.org/publications/felony -disenfranchisement-a-primer/.

28. Sean McElwee, *Why the Voting Gap Matters*.

29. Ron Fonger, "Weaker Democratic Support in Detroit, Flint Made Trump Stronger in Michigan," MLive, November 9, 2016, www.mlive.com /news/index.ssf/2016/11/detroit_flint_voting_muscle_we.html.

30. Sean McElwee, *Why the Voting Gap Matters*.

31. Lauren McCauley, "Pro-Clinton Probe of 2016 Reveals That, Yes, Democrats Have a 'Wall Street Problem,'" *CommonDreams*, May 1, 2017, www.commondreams.org/news/2017/05/01/pro-clinton-probe-2016 -reveals-yes-democrats-have-wall-street-problem.

32. Erik Sherman, "America Is the Richest, and Most Unequal, Country," *Forbes*, September 30, 2015, http://fortune.com/2015/09/30/america-wealth -inequality/.

33. "Declining Trust in Government Is Denting Democracy: According to a

New Index, America's Democracy Score Deteriorated in 2016," *Economist*, January 25, 2017, www.economist.com/blogs/graphicdetail/2017/01 /daily-chart-20; Elena Holodny, "The US Has Been Downgraded to a 'Flawed Democracy,'" *Business Insider*, January 25, 2017, www.businessinsider.com/economist-intelligence-unit-downgrades-united-states-to-flawed -democracy-2017-1.

34. *Business Week* quoted in Ken Silverstein, "Labor's Last Stand: The Corporate Campaign to Kill the Employee Free Choice Act," *Harper's*, July 2009, https://harpers.org/archive/2009/07/labors-last-stand/2/.

35. Kim Moody, *On New Terrain: How Capital Is Reshaping the Battleground of Class War in the United States* (Chicago: Haymarket Books, forthcoming).

36. Bureau of Labor Statistics, US Department of Labor, "Economic News Release: Work Stoppages Summary," February 9, 2017, www.bls.gov/news .release/wkstp.nr0.htm.

37. Bureau of Labor Statistics, US Department of Labor, "Union Membership Rate 10.7 Percent in 2016," *The Economics Daily*, February 9, 2017, www.bls.gov /opub/ted/2017/union-membership-rate-10-point-7-percent-in-2016.htm.

38. The figure on the percent of young workers who belong to unions comes from Charity Jackson, "18 to 29 Things You Didn't Know About Young Workers," Working America, March 12, 2015, http://blog.workingamerica .org/2015/03/12/18-to-29-things-you-didnt-know-about-young-workers/. The estimate of the favorability of unions among younger workers comes from Elizabeth Bruenig, "Even Conservative Millennials Support Unions, *New Republic*, May 1, 2015, https://newrepublic.com/article/121688/ pew-releases-new-labor-survey-millennials-supports-unions.

39. Andy Kiersz, "America Is No. 1 in Low-Paying Jobs," *Business Insider*, September 23, 2014, www.businessinsider.com/oecd-low-wage-paying -jobs-by-country-2014-9.

40. Paul Mason, "The Strange Case of America's Disappearing Middle Class," *Guardian*, December 14, 2015, www.theguardian.com/commentisfree/2015 /dec/14/the-strange-case-of-americas-disappearing-middle-class.

41. Steve Benen, "Poverty Goes Down, Coverage Goes Up, and America Gets a Raise," MSNBC, September 13, 2016, www.msnbc.com/rachel-maddow -show/poverty-goes-down-coverage-goes-and-america-gets-raise.

42. Prairie News Service, "ND Child Poverty Data Highlights Local Racial Disparities," KFGO, September 20, 2016, http://kfgo.com/news/articles /2016/sep/20/nd-child-poverty-data-highlights-local-racial-disparities/.

43. Kristi Tanner, "Michigan Posts Its Largest Income Gain since the Recession," *Detroit Free Press*, September 15, 2016, www.freep.com/story /news/local/michigan/2016/09/15/michigan-posts-its-largest-income -gain-since-recession/90308316/.

44. Claire Zippel, "As DC Has Grown, So Has Its Racial Prosperity Gap," Greater Greater Washington, September 22, 2016, https://ggwash.org/view /42944/as-dc-has-grown-so-has-its-racial-prosperity-gap.

45. Andrew Woo, "How Have Rents Changed Since 1960?" Apartmentlist.com, June 14, 2016, www.apartmentlist.com/rentonomics/rent-growth-since-1960/.

46. Tom Gerencer, "The Exploding Cost of Childcare in the U.S.," *MoneyNation,* September 1, 2015, http://moneynation.com/exploding-cost-childcare-u-s/.

47. Andrew Siddons, "Deductibles Rise in Employer-Sponsored Health Plans," *Washington Health Policy Week in Review,* September 19, 2016, www .commonwealthfund.org/publications/newsletters/washington-health-policy -in-review/2016/sep/september-19-2016/deductibles-rise-in-employer -sponsored-health-plans.

48. Georgetown University, Center on Education and the Workforce, McCourt School of Public Policy, *America's Divided Recovery: College Haves and Have-Nots 2016,* June 2016, https://cew.georgetown.edu/cew-reports/americas -divided-recovery/.

49. Neil Irwin, "Why American Workers without Much Education Are Being Hammered," *New York Times,* April 21, 2015, www.nytimes.com/2015/04/22 /upshot/why-workers-without-much-education-are-being-hammered.html.

50. David R. Howell, *The Collapse of Low-Skill Wages: Technological Change or Institutional Failure?,* National Jobs for All Coalition, February 1998, http://njfac .org/index.php/us13/.

We Got Trumped!

1. Charlie Post, "The Republicans Have Been Trumped," *Jacobin,* October 14, 2016, www.jacobinmag.com/2016/10/trump-gop-republicans-tea -party-populism-fascism/.

2. Center for Responsive Politics, "Hillary Clinton," www.opensecrets.org /pres16/industries?cycle=2016&id=N00000019; Center for Responsive Politics, "Donald Trump," www.opensecrets.org/pres16/industries ?id=N00023864&cycle=2016&type=f&src=b.

3. Gregory Wallace and Robert Yoon, "Voter Turnout at 20-Year Low in 2016," CNN, November 12, 2016, www.cnn.com/2016/11/11/politics /popular-vote-turnout-2016/.

4. This data is drawn from the running total on Atlas of U.S. Presidential Elections (website), uselectionatlas.org.

5. Voter participation by demographic group for 2008 and 2012 is drawn from the Roper Center for Public Opinion Research at Cornell University, http://ropercenter.cornell.edu/polls/us-elections/how-groups-voted/how -groups-voted-2008/ and http://ropercenter.cornell.edu/polls/us-elections /how-groups-voted/how-groups-voted-2012/. Data for 2016 is drawn from CNN Exit Polls, www.cnn.com/election/results/exit-polls.

6. Sabrina Tavernise, "Many in Milwaukee Neighborhood Didn't Vote—and Don't Regret It," *New York Times,* November 20, 2016, www.nytimes.com /2016/11/21/us/many-in-milwaukee-neighborhood-didnt-vote-and

-dont-regret-it.html?_r=0. Matt Karp points out that similar shifts took place in other predominantly Black areas of major cities like Detroit, St. Louis's northwestern wards, West and North Philadelphia, and East Flatbush in New York: "Fairfax County, USA," *Jacobin*, November 28, 2016, www.jacobinmag .com/2016/11/clinton-election-polls-white-workers-firewall/.

7.   US Census Bureau, "Income and Poverty in the United States, 2014," www.census.gov/library/publications/2015/demo/p60-252.html.

8.   Kevin Uhrmacher, Kevin Schaul, and Dan Keating, "These Obama Strong-holds Sealed the Election for Trump," *Washington Post*, November 9, 2016, www.washingtonpost.com/graphics/politics/2016-election/obama -trump-counties/?tid=ss_mail; Loren Collingwood, "The County-By -County Data on Trump Voters Shows Why He Won," *Washington Post*, November 19, 2016, www.washingtonpost.com/news/monkey-cage/wp /2016/11/19/the-country-by-county-data-on-trump-voters-shows-why -he-won/?postshare=6041479586306602&tid=ss_fb-bottom.

9.   Konstantin Kilibarda and Daria Roithmayr, "The Myth of the Rust Belt Re-volt," *Slate*, December 1, 2016, www.slate.com/articles/news_and_politics /politics/2016/12/the_myth_of_the_rust_belt_revolt.html.

10. Eric Sasson, "Blame Trump's Victory on College-Educated Whites, Not the Working Class," *New Republic*, November 15, 2016, https://newrepublic.com /article/138754/blame-trumps-victory-college-educated-whites-not -working-class.

11. See Christian Parenti's excellent analysis, "Garbage In, Garbage Out: Turns Out Clinton's Ground Game Sucked," *Jacobin*, November 18, 2016, www.jacobinmag.com/2016/11/clinton-campaign-gotv-unions -voters-rust-belt/. Also see Karp, "Fairfax County, USA."

12. Quoted in Jim Geraghty, "Chuck Schumer: Democrats Will Lose Blue-Collar Whites but Gain in the Suburbs," *National Review*, July 28, 2016, www.nationalreview.com/corner/438481/chuck-schumer-democrats-will -lose-blue-collar-whites-gain-suburbs.

13. Karp, "Fairfax County, USA."

14. Much of the following draws on Post, "The Republicans Have Been Trumped"; "Why the Tea Party?," *New Politics* 14, no. 1 (Summer 2012): 75-82, http://new-pol.org/content/why-tea-party; and "Whither the Republican Party? The 2014 Election and the Future of Capital's 'A' Team," *Brooklyn Rail*, December 18, 2014, www.brooklynrail.org/2014/12/field-notes/whither-the-republican-par-ty. Eric Sasson makes a similar point in "Blame Trump's Victory."

15. Michael A. McCarthy, "The Revenge of Joe the Plumber," *Jacobin*, October 26, 2016, www.jacobinmag.com/2016/10/trump-small-business-whites -xenophobia-immigration/.

16. Some left-wing commentators, like Sasha Breger Bush in the most recent issue of *Dollars & Sense* ("Trump and National Neoliberalism," January–February 2017, http://dollarsandsense.org/archives/2017/0117bregerbush .html), argue that Trump's victory marks a move by segments of the capi-

talist class away from "globalism" but not neoliberalism. However, her case in "Trump and National Neoliberalism" is not based on an analysis of the actual positions taken by any capitalist political advocacy organization.

17. While he correctly points to Trump's ability to win the vote of the Christian right in 2016, Mike Davis mistakenly labels this a "cynical covenant," underestimating the populist radicalization of these layers of the population. "Not a Revolution—Yet," *Verso Blog*, November 15, 2016, www .versobooks.com/blogs/2948-not-a-revolution-yet

18. For the European populist right, see F. Leplat, ed., *The Far Right in Europe*, (London: Resistance Books, 2015).

19. Theda Skocpol and Vanessa Williamson, *The Tea Party and the Remaking of Republican Conservatism* (New York: Oxford University Press, 2013).

20. Arlie Russell Hochschild, *Strangers in Their Own Land: Anger and Mourning on the American Right* (New York: New Press, 2016).

21. Philip Bump, "Donald Trump Got Reagan-Like Support from Union Households," *Washington Post*, November 10, 2016, www.washingtonpost.com/news /the-fix/wp/2016/11/10/donald-trump-got-reagan-like-support-from -union-households/.

22. Johanna Brenner and Robert Brenner, "Reagan, the Right and the Working Class," *Against the Current* (Old Series) 2 (Winter 1981): 30.

23. "Why Do White Working-Class People Vote against Their Interests? They Don't," *Nation*, November 16, 2016, www.thenation.com/article/why -do-white-working-class-people-vote-against-their-interests-they-dont/.

24. See Richard C. Longworth, "Disaffected Rust Belt Voters Embraced Trump—They Had No Other Hope," *Guardian*, November 21, 2016, www .theguardian.com/commentisfree/2016/nov/21/disaffected-rust-belt-voters -embraced-donald-trump-midwestern-obama; Rick Rommel, "In Western Wisconsin, Trump Voters Want Change," *Milwaukee Journal Sentinel*, November 27, 2016, www.jsonline.com/story/news/politics/elections/2016/11/26 /western-wisconsin-trump-voters-want-change/94436384/. For an excellent analysis of Trump's appeals to working-class voters, see Christian Parenti, "Listening to Trump," *Jacobin*, November 22, 2106, www.jacobinmag.com /2016/11/trump-speeches-populism-war-economics-election/.

25. Lauren McCauley, "Ugly and Unprepared, 'Knife Fight' Breaks Out in Trump Transition," *CommonDreams*, November 15, 2016, www.commondreams .org/news/2016/11/15/ugly-and-unprepared-knife-fight-breaks-out-trump -transition; Julie Hirschfeld Davis, Mark Mazzetti, and Maggie Haberman, "Firings and Discord Put Trump Transition Team in a State of Disarray," *New York Times*, November 15, 2016, www.nytimes.com/2016/11/16/us/politics /trump-transition.html; Michael D. Shear, "Trump Says Transition's Going 'Smoothly,' Disputing Disarray Reports," *New York Times*, November 16, 2016, www.nytimes.com/2016/11/17/us/politics/donald-trump-administration -twitter.html.

26. Michael D. Shear, "Donald Trump Picks Reince Priebus as Chief of Staff

and Stephen Bannon as Strategist," *New York Times*, November 13, 2016,
www.nytimes.com/2016/11/14/us/politics/reince-priebus-chief-of-staff
-donald-trump.html.

27. Julia Hahn, "Michael Savage Warns Donald Trump: 'Rinse' Reince; He's
'Everything the Voters Rejected,'" Breitbart, November 13, 2016,
www.breitbart.com/2016-presidential-race/2016/11/13/michael-savage
-warns-donald-trump-rinse-reince-priebus/.

28. Allum Bokhari and Milo Yiannopoulos, "An Establishment Conservative's
Guide to the Alt-Right," Breitbart, March 29, 2016, www.breitbart.com
/tech/2016/03/29/an-establishment-conservatives-guide-to-the-alt-right/.

29. Alan Rappeport and Noah Weiland, "White Nationalists Celebrate 'an Awak-
ening' after Donald Trump's Victory," *New York Times*, November 19, 2016,
www.nytimes.com/2016/11/20/us/politics/white-nationalists-celebrate
-an-awakening-after-donald-trumps-victory.html?_r=0; Joseph Goldstein,
"Alt-Right Exults in Donald Trump's Election with a Salute: 'Heil Victory,'"
New York Times, November 20, 2016, www.nytimes.com/2016/11/21
/us/alt-right-salutes-donald-trump.html?ref=todayspaper. Trump, in his
interview with the *New York Times* ("Donald Trump's *New York Times* Interview: Full Transcript," *New York Times*, November 23, 2016, www.nytimes
.com/2016/11/23/us/politics/trump-new-york-times-interview-transcript
.html), distanced himself from the white nationalists, saying, "I don't want to
energize the group," while claiming that Bannon was not a racist.

30. Virgil, "How A Newly Elected Republican President Can Gain 17 Points in
His Reelection Campaign," Breitbart, November 18, 2016, www.breitbart.com
/big-government/2016/11/18/virgil-how-a-newly-elected-republican
-president-can-gain-17-points-in-his-re-election-campaign/; "It's On! The
Battle for Blue Collar America: Remembering the Forgotten Man," Breitbart, November 21, 2016, www.breitbart.com/big-government/2016/11/21
/virgil-battle-blue-collar-america-remembering-forgotten-man/.

31. Michael Wolff, "Ringside with Steve Bannon at Trump Tower as the
President-Elect's Strategist Plots 'An Entirely New Political Movement,'"
Hollywood Reporter, November 18, 2016, www.hollywoodreporter.com
/news/steve-bannon-trump-tower-interview-trumps-strategist-plots-new
-political-movement-948747.

32. Julia Hahn, "Day before Election Paul Ryan Said GOP Not Trump's Party,"
Breitbart, November 12, 2016, www.breitbart.com/big-government
/2016/11/12/day-election-paul-ryan-said-gop-not-trumps-party/; "GOP
Lawmakers Work behind Closed Doors to Stop Donald Trump's Mandate,"
Breitbart, November 15, 2016, www.breitbart.com/2016-presidential-race
/2016/11/15/gop-lawmakers-work-behind-closed-doors-to-stop-donald
-trumps-mandate/.

33. "Donald Trump is Choosing His Cabinet: Here's the Latest List," *New York
Times*, December 7, 2016.

34. Reed Abelson, "Health Insurers List Demands If Affordable Care Act Is

Killed," *New York Times*, December 6, 2016, www.nytimes.com/2016/12
/06/business/health-insurers-obamacare-republicans.html?emc=eta1.

35. Binyamin Appelbaum, "Terry Branstad, Iowa Governor, Is Trump's Pick as China Ambassador," *New York Times*, December 7, 2016, www.nytimes.com /2016/12/07/us/politics/terry-branstad-china-ambassador-trump.html ?emc=eta1.

36. David E. Sanger, "Tillerson Leads from State Department Shadows as White House Steps In," *New York Times*, March 11, 2017, www.nytimes.com /2017/03/11/us/politics/rex-tillerson-trump-white-house.html?emc=eta1.

37. US Chamber of Commerce, "US Chamber President Comments on Election Results," press release, November 9, 2016, www.uschamber.com /press-release/us-chamber-president-comments-election-results.

38. A Better Way website, http://abetterway.speaker.gov/.

39. Pam Key, "Ryan: Border Security Is Our Focus, Not Mass Deportations," Breitbart, November 13, 2016, www.breitbart.com/video/2016/11/13 /ryan-border-security-focus-not-mass-deportations/; Julia Hahn, "Paul Ryan: No Deportations," Breitbart, November 13, 2016, www.breitbart.com /video/2016/11/13/ryan-border-security-focus-not-mass-deportations/; Julia Hahn, "GOP Rep: Paul Ryan's Immigration Policy Not 'In Best Interest of America,'" Breitbart, November 14, 2016, www.breitbart.com/2016 -presidential-race/2016/11/14/gop-congressman-mo-brooks-paul-ryans -position-immigration-not-best-interest-america/; Ezra Klein, "Senate Republicans Can Save the Country—and Their Party—from Trump," *Vox*, November 28, 2016, www.vox.com/policy-and-politics/2016/11/28 /13758376/senate-republicans-trump.

40. Julia Hahn, "Dave Brat Urges Delay on Speaker Vote: A 'Better Way" Did Not Animate This Historic Election," Breitbart, November 14, 2016, www.breitbart.com/big-government/2016/11/14/dave-brat-urges-delay-on -speaker-vote-a-better-way-did-not-animate-this-historic-election/.

41. Landon Thomas Jr., "Investors Make Bullish Bet on Trump, and an Era of Tax Cuts and Spending," *New York Times*, November 21, 2016, www.nytimes.com /2016/11/21/business/dealbook/investors-make-bullish-bet-on-trump -and-an-era-of-tax-cuts-and-spending.html?ref=todayspaper.

42. Henry Fountain and Erica Goode, "Trump Has Options for Undoing Obama's Climate Legacy," *New York Times*, November 25, 2016, www.nytimes.com /2016/11/25/science/donald-trump-obama-climate.html?ref=todayspaper.

43. Bob Herbert, "Get Ready for War on the Poor," *Nation*, November 22, 2016, www.thenation.com/article/get-ready-for-a-war-on-the-poor/.

44. Marisa Franco and Carlos Garcia, "The Deportation Machine Obama Built for President Trump," *Nation*, June 27, 2016, www.thenation.com /article/the-deportation-machine-obama-built-for-president-trump/; Elliot Young, "The Hard Truths About Obama's Deportation Priorities," *Huffington Post*, March 1, 2017, www.huffingtonpost.com/entry/hard-truths -about-obamas-deportation-priorities_us_58b3c9e7e4b0658fc20f979e.

45. Amy Chozick, "Trump Appears to Soften on Deporting Thousands of Young Immigrants," *New York Times,* December 7, 2016, www.nytimes.com /2016/12/07/us/immigration-dreamers-trump.html?emc=eta1

46. National Right to Work Committee, "National Right to Work Act," https://nrtwc.org/facts-issues/national-right-to-work-act/. See also Harold Meyerson, "Donald Trump Can Kill the American Union," *Washington Post,* November 23, 2016, www.washingtonpost.com/posteverything/wp /2016/11/23/donald-trump-could-kill-the-american-union/?postshare =6271479932172355&tid=ss_mail&utm_term=.29ed659b93ab.

47. Leon Neyfakh, "Can the 'Secret Government' Save Us?," *Slate,* November 14, 2016, www.slate.com/articles/news_and_politics/politics/2016/11/can _the_secret_government_save_us_from_donald_trump.html.

48. Jennifer Steinhauer, "Senate Democrats' Surprising Strategy: Trying to Align with Trump," *New York Times,* November 16, 2016, www.nytimes.com /2016/11/17/us/politics/democrats-house-senate.html; Jared Bernstein, "Trump's Misguided Flirtation with Keynesianism," *Politico,* November 21, 2016, www.politico.com/magazine/story/2016/11/trumps-misguided -flirtation-with-keynesianism-214468.

49. Demetri Sevastopulo and David J. Lynch, "Trump Reverses Course on Core Campaign Promises," *Financial Times,* November 22, 2016; Michael D. Shear, Julie Hirschfeld Davis, and Maggie Haberman, "Trump, in Interview, Moderates Views but Defies Conventions," *New York Times,* November 22, 2016, www.nytimes.com/2016/11/22/us/politics/donald-trump-visit.html. The permanent staff of the CIA opposed the reintroduction of waterboarding. Michael Hayden, the former CIA director, said that Trump should "bring his own bucket" if he wants to bring back waterboarding. Matt Apuzzo and James Risen, "Donald Trump Faces Obstacles to Resume Waterboarding," *New York Times,* November 28, 2016, www.nytimes.com/2016/11/28/us /politics/trump-waterboarding-torture.html.

50. Larry Buchanan, Alicia Parlapiano, and Karen Yourish, "How Hard (or Easy) It Will Be for Trump to Fulfill His 100-Day Plan," *New York Times,* November 24, 2016.

51. Carl Hulse, "Trump's Next Battle: Keeping These Republican Senators Happy," *New York Times,* November 26, 2016, www.nytimes.com/2016/11 /26/us/politics/donald-trumps-republicans-senate.html; Klein, "Senate Republicans Can Save the Country"; Nelson D. Schwartz, "Wary Corporate Chiefs Keep an Ear Turned to Trump's Messages," *New York Times,* December 7, 2016, www.nytimes.com/2016/12/07/business/donald-trump -corporate-chiefs.html?emc=eta1.

52. Among other recent articles, see Eduardo Porter, "Trump Campaign's Easy Answers Confront Hard Reality," *New York Times,* November 15, 2016, www.nytimes.com/2016/.11/16/business/economy/trump-campaigns -easy-answers-confront-hard-reality.html; David E. Sanger, "From Iran to Syria, Trump's 'America First' Approach Faces Its First Tests," *New York*

Times, November 17, 2016, www.nytimes.com/2016/11/18/us/politics
/from-iran-to-syria-trumps-america-first-approach-faces-its-first-tests.html;
Neil Irwin, "What Will Trump's Trade Policy Actually Look Like? Three
Possibilities," *New York Times*, November 22, 2016, www.nytimes.com/2016
/11/22/upshot/what-will-trump-trade-policy-actually-look-like-three
-possibilities.html; Eduardo Porter, "A Trade War against China Might Be a
Fight Trump Couldn't Win," *New York Times*, November 22, 2016,
www.nytimes.com/2016/11/22/business/a-trade-war-against-china-might
-be-a-fight-trump-couldnt-win.html; Nelson D. Schwartz, "Wary Corporate
Chiefs Keep an Ear Turned to Trump's Messages," *New York Times*, December 7, 2016, www.nytimes.com/2016/12/07/business/donald-trump
-corporate-chiefs.html?emc=eta1.

53. For an excellent discussion of these obstacles, see Kevin Young, Tarun Ba-
nerjee, and Michael Schwartz, "Who's Calling the Shots?," *Jacobin*, February
6, 2017, www.jacobinmag.com/2017/02/trump-banks-protests-carrier
-business-gop/.

54. For the full transcript of Trump's speech, see CNN, March 1, 2017, www.cnn.
com/2017/02/28/politics/donald-trump-speech-transcript-full
-text/. The notion that protective tariffs would allow the United States to
industrialize without producing a deskilled and degraded industrial working class was a mainstay of the worldview of the US industrial capitalist
class for the century before the Great Depression of the 1930s. See Allen
Kaufman, *Capitalism, Slavery, and Republican Values: American Political Econo-
mists, 1819-1948* (Austin: University of Texas Press, 1982), chaps. 4–5.

55. See the National Immigration Forum website, immigrationforum.org.

56. Robert Pear and Thomas Kaplan, "House Republicans Unveil Plan to Replace Health Law," *New York Times*, March 6, 2017, www.nytimescom/2017
/03/06/us/politics/affordable-care-act-obamacare-health.html?emc=eta1.

57. Jeremy W. Peters, "Why Republicans Are Battling Republicans On
Obamacare Repeal," *New York Times*, March 9, 2017, www.nytimes.com
/2017/03/09/us/politics/why-republicans-are-battling-republicans
-on-obamacare-repeal.html?emc=eta1; Carl Hulse, "GOP Desire to Keep
Party Feuds Private Breaks Down Over Health Care," *New York Times*,
March 12, 2017, www.nytimes.com/2017/03/09/us/politics/why
-republicans-are-battling-republicans-on-obamacare-repeal.html?emc=eta1.

58. Abby Goudnough, Robert Pear, and Thomas Kaplan, "Health Groups De-
nounce GOP Bill as Its Backers Scramble," *New York Times*, March 8, 2017,
www.nytimes.com/2017/03/08/us/politics/affordable-care-act-obama-care
-health.html?emc=eta1.

59. Thomas Kaplan and Robert Pear, "Health Bill Would Add 24 Million Uninsured but Save $337 Billion, Report Says," *New York Times*, March 13, 2017,
www.nytimes.com/2017/03/13/us/politics/affordable-care-act-health
-congressional-budget-office.html?ref=todayspaper.

60. See Paul Heideman, "It's Their Party," *Jacobin*, February 4, 2016,

www.jacobinmag.com/2016/02/democratic-party-realignment-civil
-rights-mcgovern-meany-rustin-sanders/.

61.   Michael Kruse, "What Trump Voters Want Now," *Politico*, November 18,
      2016, www.politico.com/magazine/story/2016/11/donald-trump-voters
      -pennsylvania-blue-collar-214466; Sherryl Gay Stolberg, "Trump's Prom-
      ises Will Be Hard to Keep, but Coal Country Has Faith," *New York Times*,
      November 28, 2016, www.nytimes.com/2016/11/28/us/donald-trump
      -coal-country.html.

62.   Hatewatch Staff, "Update: Incidents of Hateful Harassment since Election
      Day Now Number 701," *Hatewatch* (blog), Southern Poverty Law Center,
      November 18, 2016, www.splcenter.org/hatewatch/2016/11/18/update-in-
      cidents-hateful-harassment-election-day-now-number-701.

Who Put Donald Trump in the White House?

1.   Nate Silver, "The Mythology of Trump's 'Working Class' Support," *Five
      ThirtyEight*, May 3, 2016, http://fivethirtyeight.com/features/the-mythology
      -of-trumps-working-class-support/; "Election 2016, Exit Polls," CNN Politics,
      November 23, 2016, www.cnn.com/election/results/exit-polls.

2.   US Census Bureau, "Educational Attainment of the Population 18 Years
      and Over, by Age, Sex, Race, and Hispanic Origin: 2014," Table 1, 2014,
      www.census.gov/data/tables/2014/demo/educational-attainment/cps
      -detailed-tables.html.

3.   National Small Business Association, *NSBA 2016 Politics of Small Busi-
      ness Survey* (Washington, DC: National Small Business Association), 4–6;
      US Small Business Administration, Office of Advocacy, *SBA Demographic
      Characteristics of Business Owners and Employees: 2013* (Washington, DC: Small
      Business Administration), 1; Bureau of Labor Statistics, "May 2015 National
      Occupational Employment and Wage Estimates United States," www.bls
      .gov/oes/current/oes_nat.htm#00-000; "Small Business Owner Salary,"
      Indeed, www.indeed.com/small-business-owner.htm.

4.   "Election 2016, Exit Polls; President," CNN Politics, November 23, 2016,
      www.cnn.com/election/results/president, www.cnn.com/election/results
      /exit-polls.

5.   Bureau of Labor Statistics, "Occupational Employment, Job Openings and
      Worker Characteristics," Table 1.7, 2014, www.bls.gov/emp/ep_table_107.htm.

6.   The Data Team, "Where Donald Trump's Support Really Comes From,"
      Economist, April 20, 2016, www.economist.com/blogs/graphicdetail
      /2016/04/daily-chart-14?zid=297&ah=3ae0fe266c7447d8a0c7ade5547d62ca.

7.   Harry Enten, "How Much Do Democrats Depend on the Union Vote?,"
      FiveThirtyEight, July 1, 2014, http://fivethirtyeight.com/datalab/supreme
      -court-ruling-wounds-both-democrats-and-unions-neither-fatally/; "Election
      2016, Exit Polls; President."

8. Kim Moody, *US Labor in Trouble and Transition: The Failure of Reform from Above, the Promise of Revival from Below* (London: Verso, 2007), 145.

9. Roper Center, "How Groups Voted," 1980, 2014, http://ropercenter.cornell .edu/polls/us-elections/how-groups-voted/how-groups-voted/; "Election 2016, Exit Polls."

10. Roper Center, "How Groups Voted," 1996, 2000, http://ropercenter.cornell .edu/polls/us-elections/how-groups-voted/how-groups-voted/.

11. Sean McElwee, "Why Non-Voters Matter," *Atlantic*, September 15, 2015, www.theatlantic.com/politics/archive/2015/09/why-non-voters-matter/405

12. David Wasserman, "2016 National Popular Vote Tracker," *Cook Political Report*, December 15, 2016, http://cookpolitical.com/story/10174; US Electoral College, "2012 Presidential Election," www.archives.gov/federal -register/electoral-college/2012/popular-vote.html; "Election Center: President: Ohio," CNN Politics, December 10, 2012, www.cnn.com /election/2012/results/state/OH/president/#exit-polls and www.cnn.com /election/2012/results/state/OH/president/.

13. Wasserman, "2016 National Popular Vote Tracker"; US Electoral College, "2012 Presidential Election."

14. "Election Center: President: Ohio."

15. "President, 100% Reporting," *New York Times*, http://elections.nytimes .com/2-12/results/states/ohio; US Census, "QuickFacts, Lorain County, Ohio," 2016, www.census.gov/quickfacts/table/PST045215/39093.

16. Russel Saltamontes, "A Union County," *Jacobin*, October 6, 2014, www .jacobinmag.org/2014/a-union-county; US Census, "QuickFacts, Lorain County."

17. Lorain County Board of Elections, "2016 Primary Election," http:media.wix.com/ugd/2568d0_45e5b97f36b54098befa5ee19cb7f8e3.pdf.

18. Lorain County Board of Elections, "2012 General Election," http:media .wix.com/ugd/2568d0_45e5b97f36b54098befa5ee19cb7f8e3.pdf; Lorain County Board of Elections, "Lorain County 2016 General Election Results," November 8, 2016, www.loraincounty.com/government/2016-general/; US Census, "QuickFacts, Lorain City, Ohio," 2016, www.census.gov/quickfacts /table/PST045215/3944856; US Census, "QuickFacts, Elyria City, Ohio, 2016, www.census.gov/quickfacts/table/PST045215/3925256.

19. Donald Green and Michael Schwam-Baird, "Mobilization, Participation, and American Democracy: A Retrospective and Postscript," *Party Politics* 22, no. 2 (2016): 158–64; National Conference of State Legislatures (NCSL), "Voter Identification Requirements / VoterID Laws," www.ncsl.org/re-search/elections -and-campaigns/voter-id.aspx.

20. "Campaigns and Voter Information: Elections in a Digital Age," Politics & Policy, http://politicsandpolicy.org/article/campaigns-and-voter -information-elections-digital-era; Max Willens, "Election 2016 Ads: Xaxis Will Target Voters Using Their Digital and Real-Life Data," *International*

Business Times, November 9, 2016, www.ibtimes.com/election-2016-political
-ads-xaxis-will-target-voters-using-their-digital-real-life-2176196; DSPolitical, "Voter Targeted Digital Ads Now at Fingertips of Thousands of
Democratic Campaigns," http://dspolitical.com/press-releases/voter
-targeted-ads-now-fingertips-thousands-democratic-campaigns; Hari
Sreenivasan, "The Digital Campaign" transcript, PBS, 2012, www.pbs.org
/wgbh/frontline/film/digital-campaign/transcript/.

21. Harry Davies and Danny Yadron, "How Facebook Tracks and Profits from
Voters in a \$10bn Election," *Guardian*, January 28, 2016, www.theguardian
.com/us-news/2016//jan28/facebook-voters-us-election-fed-cruz-targeted
-ads-trump; Green and Schwam-Baird, "Mobilization, Participation, and
American Democracy," 158–64; Willens, "Election 2016 Ads"; DSPolitical,
"Voter Targeted Digitial Ads."

22. Davies and Yadron, "How Facebook Tracks and Profits from Voters."

23. John Nichols, "Hillary Clinton's Popular-Vote Victory Is Unprecedented—
and Still Growing," *Nation*, November 17, 2016, www.thenation.com
/article/hillary-clintons-popular-vote-victory-is-unprecedented-and
-still-growing/; "Election 2016: New York Results," *New York Times*, August
1, 2017, www.nytimes.com/elections/results/new-york.

24. United States Elections Project, "2016 November General Election
Turnout Rates," 2016, www.electproject.org/2016g; Thom File, *Who Votes?
Congressional Elections and the American Electorate: 1978–2014* (Washington DC:
US Department of Commerce, 2015), 3.

25. Sean McElwee, "Why The Voting Gap Matters" Demos, October 23, 2014,
www.demos.org/publication/why-voting-gap-matters; Sean McElwee,
"Why Non-Voters Matter"; Pew Research Center, "The Party of Nonvoters," October 31, 2014, www.people-press.org/2014/10/31/the-party
-of-nonvoters-2/.

26. US House of Representatives, "Party Divisions of the House of Representatives," http://history.house.gov/Institution/Party-Divisions/Party
-Divisions/; Thom File, "Who Votes?"; NCSL, "2009 State and Legislative
Partisan Composition," National Conference of State Legislatures,
www.ncsl.org/documents/statevote/legiscontrol_2009.pdf.

27. NCSL, "2009 State and Legislative Partisan Composition"; NCSL, "2015
State and Legislative Partisan Composition," National Conference of State
Legislatures, www.ncsl.org/documents/statevote/legiscontrol_2015.pdf.

28. Rick Perlstein, "It Goes Way, Way Back," *New Republic*, June 14, 2016,
https://newrepublic.com/article/133776/split; Aaron Bycoffe, "The Endorsement Primary," *FiveThirtyEight*, 2016, http://projects.fivethirtyeight.
com/2016-endorsement-primary/; Radiowalla, "Many Progressive Caucus
Members Have Endorsed Hillary and Here's the Corrected List," *Daily Kos*,
October 1, 2015, www.dailykos.com/story/2015/10/11/1430646/-Many
-Progressive-Caucus-members-have-endorsed-Hillary-and-here-s-the
-corrected-list; Tote, "New York City Council Member Jumaane Williams

Endorses Bernie Sanders at Prospect Park Rally," *Daily Kos*, April 18, 2106, www.dailykos.com/story/2016/4/17/1516643/-BREAKING-NY-City -Council-Member-Jumaane-Williams-Endorses-Bernie-Sanders-at -Prospect-Park-Rally. See the following pages on the Congressional Progressive Caucus website: "About Us," "Caucus Members," "Seeking Global Security: Rethinking National Security and Defence Policy," "The People's Budget," https://cpc-grijalva.house.gov/.

29. Thom File, "Who Votes?," 1–4.

The Great God Trump
and the White Working Class

1. According to the Pew Research Center, there were 10.7 million more eligible voters in 2016 than in 2012. "More than two-thirds of net growth in the US electorate during this time has come from racial and ethnic minorities." Jens Manuel Krogstad, "2016 Electorate Will Be the Most Diverse in U.S. History," *Fact Tank* (blog), Pew Research Center, February 3, 2016, www .pewresearch.org/fact-tank/2016/02/03/2016-electorate-will-be-the-most -diverse-in-u-s-history/.

2. Jeremy Carl, "The Red Wall," *National Review*, December 5, 2016. "By the presidential election of 2020, Census Bureau projections indicate that non-Hispanic whites will be down to around 61 percent of the population. By 2050 that share will have dropped to almost exactly half." Depending on which criterion is used (education or occupation) the white working class will be 41 or 37 percent of the adult population in 2020. Alternatively, using an income-based definition, "yields an estimate of 20 percent of families qualifying as white working class." Alan Abramowitz and Ruy Teixeira, "The Rise of a Mass Upper-Middle Class," in Ruy Teixeira, ed., *Red, Blue, and Purple America: The Future of Election Demographics* (Brookings Institution, Washington, DC: 2008), 133–34.

3. Craig Gilbert, "Great Lakes Battlegrounds Turned Tide to Trump," *Milwaukee Journal Sentinel*, November 9, 2016.

4. Vanessa Williamson and Carly Knight, "Choose Your Own Election Postmortem: Part Two," Brookings, November 16, 2016.

5. All statistics are derived from Ballotpedia; the *New York Times* (county data 100 percent count); the *Cook Political Report* (raw votes); and the Atlas of U.S. Elections website, http://uselectionatlas.org. Caveat emptor: all 2016 figures are subject to final count figures (not yet available at time of writing) and in some of the tables have been rounded off to the nearest thousandth or tenth of a percent.

6. "The Most Extreme Republican Platform in Memory," editorial, *New York Times*, July 18, 2016, www.nytimes.com/2016/07/19/opinion/the-most -extreme-republican-platform-in-memory.html.

7. Kenneth Vogel, "The Heiress Quietly Shaping Trump's Operation," *Politico*, November 21, 2016.

8. In Pew exit polls, a majority of self-identified white, evangelical voters said they were voting against Clinton, not for Trump. See Kate Shellnutt, "Trump Elected President, Thanks to 4 in 5 White Evangelicals," *Christianity Today*, November 17, 2016, www.christianitytoday.com/news/2016/november /trump-elected-president-thanks-to-4-in-5-white-evangelicals.html.

9. The flip side is that 147 million voters in thirty-five nonswing states, plus the District of Columbia, were "sidelined and largely bypassed by the national campaigns." Nonprofit Vote and US Elections Project, *America Goes to the Polls: A Report on Voter Turnout in the 2016 Election*, March 2017, p. 12, www.nonprofitvote.org/documents/2017/03/america-goes-polls-2016.pdf.

10. Where Clinton did win previously red suburbs, most notably in metropolitan Atlanta (Cobb and Gwinnett counties) and Houston (Fort Bend County), the key factor may have been recent increases in the minority population more than disaffected Republican women.

11. Quoted in Eleanor Clift, "How Macomb County Created and Killed the Clinton Machine," *Daily Beast*, 28 November 2016.

12. Roger Stone, *The Making of the President 2016: How Donald Trump Orchestrated a Revolution* (Skyhorse Publishing: New York, 2017), 312.

13. She also outperformed Obama in some strategic suburban counties around DC, Philadelphia, and Milwaukee, but in the latter two cases it was not enough to overcome Trump's margins in small cities and rural areas. See Amy Walter, "The Story of the Suburbs," *Cook Political Report*, November 14, 2016.

14. According to the *Miami Herald*, while total voter turnout was up 3 percent in Florida, the share of voters identifying as Democrats fell from 35 to 32 percent. Patricia Mazzei, "Gobsmacked by Election, Florida Democrats Try to Refocus," *Miami Herald*, November 12, 2016, www.miamiherald.com /news/politics-government/election/article114255783.html..

15. John Russo, "Why Democrats Lose in Ohio," *American Prospect*, February 2, 2017, http://prospect.org/article/why-democrats-lose-ohio.

16. Mark Muro and Sifan Liu, "Another Clinton-Trump Divide: High-Output America versus Low-Output America," Brookings Brief, November 29, 2016.

17. Brennan Center for Justice, "New Voting Restrictions in Place for 2016 Presidential Election," www.brennancenter.org/sites/default/files/analysis/ New_Restrictions_2016.pdf.

18. Paul Krugman, "The Populism Perplex," *New York Times*, November 25, 2016.

19. Carl, "The Red Wall." Carl quotes from a memo he wrote in 2015: "According to the modelling done here, if [Candidate X] could win white voters at Reagan 1984 percentages (66 percent) and at Bush 2004 turnout levels (67 percent) and we assume African American turnout was to return to historical levels and percentages for Democrats, we could win the presidency without winning a single Hispanic, Asian, Native American, or Arab vote. Think about that, because it is a staggering statement and it's a true one."

20. Clift, "How Macomb County Created."
21. It's important to recall that Ohio, the key to Bush's 2004 victory, swung dramatically to the Democrats in 2006, in part because of plant closures and job losses. The rest of the Midwest, except Missouri, followed in 2008. The Democrats had a clear mandate to address the region's distress and, as with Appalachia, failed to produce major policy initiatives—apart from Obamacare—to support local Democrats. The 2009 auto bailout's political impact faded with the flight of the auto parts industry to Mexico.
22. Karl Rove, "The GOP Targets State Legislatures," *Wall Street Journal*, March 4, 2010, www.wsj.com/articles/SB10001424052748703862704575099670689398044.
23. Quoted in David Daley, *Rat F**ked: The True Story behind the Secret Plan to Steal America's Democracy* (New York: Liveright, 2016), 86–87.
24. Andy Kroll, "Behind Michigan's 'Financial Martial Law': Corporations and Right-Wing Billionaires," *Mother Jones*, March 23, 2011.
25. See Chris MacKenzie, *Outside Influence: Out of State Money in the 2016 Senate Elections*, US PIRG Education Fund, October 2016; Ian Vandewalker, *Election Spending 2016*, Brennan Center for Justice, New York University.
26. Alan Abramowitz and Steven Webster, "The Rise of Negative Partisanship and the Nationalization of US Elections in the 21st Century," *Electoral Studies* 41 (2016): 21.
27. Peter Worsley, *The Trumpet Shall Sound: A Study of 'Cargo' Cults in Melanesia*, 2nd ed. (New York: MacGibbon & Kee, 1957; New York: Schocken Books, 1968), 136, 153. Citations refer to the Schocken edition.
28. Worsley, *The Trumpet Shall Sound*, 153. Worsley, a Communist anthropologist, collaborated with the famed CP Historians Group, especially with Hobsbawm with whom he shared similar interests in millenarian movements, and was one of the founders of the *New Left Review*. His important contributions have been overlooked in most accounts of these two germinal milieus of contemporary left thought.
29. In addition to the Rust Belt and its outliers (Pueblo, Colorado, for instance), we might also include a few other regions dominated by formerly unionized extractive industries, such as the eight coastal timber counties in the Pacific Northwest that were flipped by Trump—an approximately 20,000-vote shift. In Oregon, Clinton won eight counties including metro Portland, but popular Democratic senator Ron Wyden won these and ten more.
30. "White Voters: What's Going On," *Economist*, November 5, 2016, 24.
31. Trip Gabriel, "How Erie Went Red: The Economy Sank, and Trump Rose," *New York Times*, November 12, 2016; Devin Henry, "Company Announces Closure of Ohio Coal Plants," *The Hill*, July 22, 2016; and Shelley Hanson, "Local Plant Closings Shock Ohio Valley," *The Intelligencer: Wheeling News-Register*, December 5, 2016.
32. "White Voters," 24.
33. Jack Jenkins, "Appalachia Used to be a Democratic Stronghold," *ThinkProgress*, https://thinkprogress.org/appalachia.

34. Cited in "16 for '16," *Sabato's Crystal Ball* (blog), University of Virginia Center for Politics, November 19, 2016, www.centerforpolitics.org/crystalball/articles/16-for-16.

35. John Gunther, *Inside U.S.A.* (New York: Harper & Brothers, 1947), 811.

36. At stake are birthright citizenship and congressional apportionment by population—both of which are opposed by many Trump supporters.

37. Gunther, *Inside U.S.A.*, 809–12. This almost 1,000-page portrait of immediate postwar America is a time capsule that everyone should find time to open, if only to discover how much the present only recapitulates the past.

38. "Populist-Nationalist Tide Rolls On," Patrick Buchanan – Official Website, November 29, 2016, http://buchanan.org/blog/populist-nationalist-tide-rolls-126086..

Choosing or Refusing to Take Sides in an Era of Right-Wing Populism

1.   Some of what follows draws on chapters 7 and 8 of my *Nation-States: Consciousness and Competition* (Chicago: Haymarket Books, 2016).

2.   See Mark Lilla, "The End of Identity Liberalism," *New York Times*, November 18, 2016, www.nytimes.com/2016/11/20/opinion/sunday/the-end-of-identity-liberalism.html.

3.   Hal Draper [1967], "Who's Going to Be the Lesser Evil in 1968?" Reprinted in *International Socialist Review* 34, April–May, 2004, and also available at the Marxist Internet Archive, at www.marxists.org/archive/draper/1967/01/lesser.htm.

4.   Ellen Meiksins Wood, "The Separation of the Economic and Political under Capitalism," *New Left Review* 127 (1981): 81–82.

5.   Adam Smith [1776], *An Inquiry into the Nature and Causes of the Wealth of Nations*, edited by Edwin Cannan (Chicago: University of Chicago Press, 1976), book 1, chap. 11, 278.

6.   Smith, *An Inquiry*, book 4, chaps. 7, 8.

7.   Karl Marx [1867], *Capital: A Critique of Political Economy*, vol. 1 (Harmondsworth, UK: Penguin Books/New Left Review, 1976), 606–7.

8.   Marx, *Capital*, 610.

9.   Carl Schmitt [1932], "The Concept of the Political," in *The Concept of the Political*, expanded ed. (Chicago: University of Chicago Press, 2007), 63.

10. Joseph Schumpeter [1944], *Capitalism, Socialism and Democracy* (London: Routledge, 1994), 138–39.

11. Hal Draper, *Karl Marx's Theory of Revolution*, vol. 1, *State and Bureaucracy* (New York: Monthly Review Press, 1978), 321–24.

12. Bernard Porter, *Empire and Superempire: Britain, America and the World* (New Haven, CT: Yale University Press, 2006), 49.

13. Fred Block [1977], "The Ruling Class Does Not Rule: Notes on the Marxist

Theory of the State," in *Revising State Theory: Essays in Politics and Postindustrialization* (Philadelphia: Temple University Press, 1987), chap. 3.

14. Eric J. Hobsbawm, "Revolution," in *Revolution in History*, edited by Roy Porter and Mikulas Teich (Cambridge: Cambridge University Press, 1986), 27.

15. Antonio Gramsci [1929–1934], *Selections from the Prison Notebooks*, edited and translated by Quintin Hoare and Geoffrey Nowell Smith (London: Lawrence and Wishart, 1971), 211, Q13§23.

16. Gramsci, *Selections*, 408, Q7§24.

17. Robert Skidelsky, "The Economic Consequences of Mr. Osborne," *New Statesman*, March 14–20, 2014, 29. The reasons for this are too complex to be discussed here, but see my "Neoliberalism as the Agent of Capitalist Self-Destruction," *Salvage* 1 (2015): 81–96.

18. Ha-Joon Chang, *Economics: The User's Guide* (Harmondsworth, UK: Penguin Books, 2014), 190–91; Will Hutton, "Power Is Fragmenting. But What Is the True Cost to Democracy?," *Guardian*, August 25, 2013, 36.

19. Jan-Werner Müller, *What is Populism?* (Philadelphia: University of Pennsylvania Press, 2016, 93.

20. Michael Mann, *Fascists* (Cambridge: Cambridge University Press, 2004, 367–68.

21. Peter Mair, *Ruling the Void: The Hollowing of Western Democracy* (London: Verso, 2013), 45.

22. Leon Trotsky, "What Next?," Marxist Internet Archive, www.marxists.org /archive/trotsky/germany/1932-ger/next01.htm.

23. Neil Davidson, *How Revolutionary Were the Bourgeois Revolutions?* (Chicago: Haymarket Books, 2012), 490–97.

24. Roger Griffin, "Revolution from the Right: Fascism," in *Revolutions and Revolutionary Traditions in the West, 1560–1991*, edited by David Parker (London: Routledge, 2000), 198.

25. Daniele Albertazzi and Duncan McDonnell, "Introduction: The Scepter and the Specter," in *Twenty-First Century Populism: The Spectre of Western European Democracy*, edited by Daniele Albertazzi and Duncan McDonnell (New York: Palgrave Macmillan, 2008), 5.

26. Alexandra Cole, "Old Right or New Right? The Ideological Positioning of Parties of the Far Right," *European Journal of Political Research* 44, no. 2 (2005): 222–23.

27. Ulrich Herbert, "Labor and Extermination: Economic Interest and the Primacy of Weltanschauung in National Socialism," *Past and Present* 138 (1993): 195.

28. Alex Callinicos, "Plumbing the Depths: Marxism and the Holocaust," *Yale Journal of Criticism* 14, no. 2 (2001): 403, 406.

29. Peter Sedgwick, "The Problem of Fascism," *International Socialism* 42 (1970): 34. Callinicos actually ascribes this thought to Joel Geier, who expressed it from the floor during a discussion at Marxism 1993. See Callinicos, "Plumbing the Depths," 413, note 95.

30. Richard Evans, *The Coming of the Third Reich* (London: Allen Lane, 2003), 22–76; Ian Kershaw, *Fateful Choices: Ten Decisions that Changed the World, 1940–1941* (London: Allen Lane, 2007), 438–44; Sabby Sagall, *Final Solutions: Human Nature, Capitalism, and Genocide* (London: Pluto Press, 2013), 196–210.

31. Detlev Peukert [1982], *Inside Nazi Germany: Conformity, Opposition, and Racism in Everyday Life* (Harmondsworth, UK: Penguin Books, 1989), 44.

32. Götz Aly, *Hitler's Beneficiaries: Plunder, Racial War, and the Nazi Welfare State* (New York: Metropolitan Books, 2006).

33. Donny Gluckstein, *The Nazis, Capitalism, and the Working Class* (London: Bookmarks, 1999), chap. 9; Peukert, *Inside Nazi Germany*, 118–25.

34. Tim Mason [1975], "The Primacy of Politics: Politics and Economics in National Socialist Germany," in *Nazism, Fascism and the Working Class*, edited by Jane Caplan (Cambridge: Cambridge University Press, 1995), 74.

35. Peukert, *Inside Nazi Germany*, 176–78; Adam Tooze, *The Wages of Destruction: The Making and Breaking of the Nazi Economy* (New York: Viking, 2006), 358–59, 513–15.

36. Ian Kershaw, *Hitler, 1889–1936: Hubris* (London: Allen Lane, 1998), 563, 567–68, 713.

37. Theodor Adorno [1951], *Minima Moralia: Reflections from Damaged Life* (London: Verso, 1978), 105–6.

38. Chip Berlet and Matthew N. Lyons, *Right-Wing Populism in America: Too Close for Comfort* (New York: Guilford Press, 2000), 347–48.

39. Nigel Harris [1968], *Beliefs in Society: The Problem of Ideology* (Harmondsworth, UK: Penguin Books, 1971), 115–16.

40. Sara Diamond, *Roads to Dominion: Right-Wing Movements and Political Power in the United States* (New York: Guilford Press, 1995), 6.

41. Gramsci, *Selections*, 333–34, Q11§12.

42. Georg Lukács [1923], "Class Consciousness," in *History and Class Consciousness: Essays on Marxist Dialectics* (London: Merlin Press, 1971), 51.

43. Berlet and Lyons, *Right-Wing Populism in America*, 348.

44. Chip Berlet, "The Violence of Right-Wing Populism," *Peace Review* 7, nos. 3/4 (1995): 285.

45. Alexandra Cole, "Old Right or New Right?"

46. Michael Kimmel, *Angry White Men: American Masculinity at the End of an Era* (New York: Nation Books, 2013), 281.

47. Kimmel, *Angry White Men*.

48. Müller, *What is Populism?*, 13.

49. Ed Pilkington, "Immigrants Go into Hiding as Alabama Rules That Looking Illegal Is Enough," *Guardian*, October 15, 2011.

50. American Immigration Council, "Bad for Business: How Alabama's Anti-Immigrant Law Stifles State Economy," November 3, 2011, www .immigrationpolicy.org/just-facts/bad-business-how-alabama's-anti -immigrant-law-stifles-state-economy.

From Hope to Despair

1. Edward Morrisey, "The Catastophic Decline of the Democratic Party," *The Week*, January 11, 2017; Eric Garcia, "Republicans Expand Domination of State Legislatures," *Roll Call*, November 10, 2016.

2. David Frum, "Beware the Democratic Sea-Change," *Financial Times*, February 6, 2008.

3. Ron Suskind, *Confidence Men: Wall Street, Washington and the Education of a President* (New York: HarperCollins, 2011), loc. 5377 of 12,193, Kindle.

4. Andrea Orr, "Tracking the Recovery," Economic Policy Institute, October 6, 2009, www.epi.org/publication/big_banks_seen_as_big_beneficiaries_of _government_economic_policies.

5. Physicians for a National Health Program, "Pro Single-Payer Doctors: Health Bill Leaves 23 Million Uninsured," www.pnhp.org/news/2010 /march/pro-single-payer-doctors-health-bill-leaves-23-million-uninsured.

6. Glenn Greenwald, "The White House as Helpless Victim on Health Care," *Salon*, December 16, 2009, www.salon.com/2009/12/16/white _house_5/.

7. Republicans failed in their first attempt to "repeal and replace" Obamacare under Trump in March 2017. But they committed to keep trying. See Sam Frizell, "The Effort to Repeal Obamacare Is Failing Again. Here's What That Means for the GOP," *Time*, April 6, 2017.

8. Greenwald, "The White House as Helpless Victim."

9. Matt Taibbi, "Obama and Jobs: Why I Don't Believe Him Anymore," *Rolling Stone*, September 6, 2011.

10. See Bernadette D. Proctor, Jessica L. Semega, and Melissa A. Kollar, "Income and Poverty in the United States: 2015," US Census Bureau, September, 2016.

11. For an excellent postmortem on Obama's term, see Perry Anderson, "Passing the Baton," *New Left Review* 104 (2017): 41–64.

12. Guy T. Saperstein, "Trump Didn't Win the Election, Hillary Lost It," *Alternet*, November 12, 2016, www.alternet.org/election-2016/trump-didnt -win-election-hillary-lost-it.

13. Zaid Jilan, "Center for American Progress Advised Clinton Team against $15 Minimum Wage, Leaked Emails Show," *The Intercept*, October 10, 2016, https://theintercept.com/2016/10/10/center-for-american-progress -advised-clinton-team-against-15-minimum-wage-leaked-emails-show/.

14. Luke Savage, "Why Bernie Was Right," *Jacobin*, October 21, 2016, www.jacobinmag.com/2016/10/bernie-sanders-hillary-clinton-podesta -emails-wikileaks/.

15. Liberal pollsters and analysts, like Stanley Greenberg, Celinda Lake, and Ruy Texeira, use this term to describe groups like unmarried women, people of color, and younger voters who have been reliably liberal and Democratic voters when they vote. A good reference for these analyses is the Democratic Strategist website, thedemocraticstrategist.org.

16. On this, see the indispensable report by Jasper Craven, "Once an Organizational Army, Team Sanders Now a Skeleton Crew," *Vermont Digger*, May 16, 2016, http://vtdigger.org/2016/05/16/once-an-organizational-army-team-sanders-now-skeleton-crew/.

17. Edward-Isaac Dovere and Gabriel DeBenedetti, "Bernie Sanders' New Group Is Already in Turmoil," *Politico*, August 23, 2016, www.politico.com/story/2016/08/bernie-sanders-group-turmoil-227297.

18. For a number of examples, see James Hohmann, "The Daily 202: Five Reasons Bernie Sanders Lost Last Night's Democratic Debate," *Washington Post*, March 7, 2016, www.washingtonpost.com/news/powerpost/paloma/daily-202/2016/03/07/daily-202-five-reasons-bernie-sanders-lost-last-night-s-democratic-debate/56dcf1e6981b92a22d730a5d/.

19. Chris Sánchez, "Don't Vote for a Third Party Presidential Candidate in This Election," *Business Insider*, September 17, 2016, www.businessinsider.com/bernie-sanders-dont-vote-third-party-gary-johnson-jill-stein-2016-9.

20. Adolph Reed, "Vote for the Lying Neoliberal Warmonger: It's Important," *CommonDreams*, August 18, 2016, www.commondreams.org/views/2016/08/18/vote-lying-neoliberal-warmonger-its-important.

21. Jeff Stein, "Study: Hillary Clinton's TV Ads Were Almost Entirely Policy-Free," *Vox*, March 8, 2017, www.vox.com/policy-and-politics/2017/3/8/14848636/hillary-clinton-tv-ads.

22. Aziz Rana, "Decolonizing Obama: What Happened to the Third-World Left?" *n+1*, no. 27, Winter 2017, https://nplusonemag.com/issue-27/politics/decolonizing-obama/.

23. Kevin Baker, "Barack Hoover Obama," *Harper's*, July 2009, http://harpers.org/archive/2009/07/barack-hoover-obama/.

The Misogynist-in-Chief

Epigraph source: Anonymous, "Sexual Assault Survivor Reacts to Donald Trump Presidency," *Teen Vogue*, November 10, 2016, www.teenvogue.com/story/sexual-assault-survivor-reacts-to-donald-trump-presidency.

1. "Transcript: Donald Trump's Taped Comments about Women," *New York Times*, October 8, 2016, www.nytimes.com/2016/10/08/us/donald-trump-tape-transcript.html.

2. Gillian Mohney, "Sexual Assault Hotline Calls Up in Wake of Donald Trump Allegations," ABC News, October 14, 2016, http://abcnews.go.com/Health/sexual-assault-hotline-calls-wake-donald-trump-allegations/story?id=42805063.

3. Michael M. Grynbaum and Jim Rutenberg, "Trump, Asked About Accusations Against Bill O'Reilly, Calls Him a 'Good Person,'" *New York Times*, April, 5, 2017, www.nytimes.com/2017/04/05/business/media/trump-oreilly-fox-murdochs.html.

4. Heidi Glenn, "Fear of Deportation Spurs 4 Women to Drop Domestic

Abuse Cases In Denver," NPR, March 21, 2017, www.npr.org/2017/03/21
/520841332/fear-of-deportation-spurs-4-women-to-drop-domestic
-abuse-cases-in-denver.

5. "Businessman at JFK Kicks, Shouts at Muslim Employee, 'Trump Is Here Now,
    He Will Get Rid of All of You,'" New York 4 News, January 26, 2017, www
    .nbcnewyork.com/news/local/Muslim-Employee-Hijab-Delta-Sky-Lounge
    -Kicked-Harassed-Flyer-Shouts-Trump-is-Here-Now-411924555.html.

6. Oliver Laughland and Lauren Gambino, "Restaurants Run by Labor Secre-
    tary Nominee Report 'Disturbing' Rates of Sexual Harassment," *Guardian*,
    January 10, 2017, www.theguardian.com/business/2017/jan/10
    /andrew-puzder-cke-sexual-harassment-labor-secretary. Puzder subse-
    quently withdrew his name from consideration to be labor secretary.

7. Matt Flegenheimer and Maggie Haberman, "Donald Trump, Abortion Foe,
    Eyes 'Punishment' for Women, Then Recants," *New York Times*, March 30, 2016,
    www.nytimes.com/2016/03/31/us/politics/donald-trump-abortion.html.

8. Olivia Becker, "46 Anti-Abortion Bills Are Already in Front of State Legis-
    latures," *Vice News*, January 12, 2017, https://news.vice.com/story/at-least
    -46-anti-abortion-bills-are-already-in-front-of-state-legislatures-in-2017.

9. Becker, "At Least 46 Anti-Abortion Bills."

10. "The Wage Gap for Mothers, State by State," National Women's Law Cen-
    ter, 2016, https://nwlc.org/resources/the-wage-gap-for-mothers-state
    -by-state-2016/.

11. Wendy Wang, Kim Parker, and Paul Taylor, "Breadwinner Moms," Pew
    Research Center, May 29, 2013, www.pewsocialtrends.org/2013/05/29
    /breadwinner-moms/.

12. Ben Guarino, "Police: Conn. Politician Said He No Longer Has to Be
    'Politically Correct,' Pinched Woman's Groin," *Washington Post*, January 17,
    2017, www.washingtonpost.com/news/morning-mix/wp/2017/01/17
    /police-conn-politician-said-he-no-longer-has-to-be-politically-correct
    -pinches-womans-groin/?utm_term=.2aad6758bae8.

13. Clare Malone, "Clinton Couldn't Win Over White Women," *FiveThirty-
    Eight*, November 9, 2016, https://fivethirtyeight.com/features/clinton
    -couldnt-win-over-white-women/.

14. Stephanie Coontz, "Why Women Are Still Voting for Trump, Despite His Mi-
    sogyny," interview by Daniel Denvir, *Vox*, October 25, 2016, www.vox.com
    /conversations/2016/10/25/13384528/donald-trump-women-stephanie
    -coontz.

15. "Election 2016, Exit Polls," CNN Politics, November 23, 2016, www.cnn.
    com/election/results/exit-polls.

16. Lance Selfa, "Who's to Blame for Trump's Victory," interview, *Socialist Worker*,
    November 14, 2016, https://socialistworker.org/2016/11/14/whos-to-blame
    -for-trumps-victory.

17. Thomas Frank, "Why Must the Trump Alternative Be Self-Satisfied, Com-
    placent Democrats?" *Guardian*, May 4, 2016, www.theguardian.com
    /commentisfree/2016/may/04/democrats-acting-elitist-not-progressive

-thomas-frank.

18. Monthly Harvard Poll, April 2017, http://harvardharrispoll.com/wp
-content/uploads/2017/04/Harvard-CAPS-Harris-Poll-April-Wave
-Topline-Favorability-04.18.2017.pdf.

19. NARAL Pro-Choice America, "NARAL Statement on DNC Chair Perez
and Senator Sanders Embracing an Anti-Choice Candidate in Nebraska,"
press release, April 20, 2017, www.prochoiceamerica.org/2017/04/20/
naral-statement-dnc-chair-perez-senator-sanders-embracing-anti-choice
-candidate-nebraska-today/.

20. Christina Cauterucci, "The Women's March on Washington Has Released
an Unapologetically Progressive Platform," *Slate*, January 12, 2017,
www.slate.com/blogs/xx_factor/2017/01/12/the_women_s_march_on
_washington_has_released_its_platform_and_it_is_unapologetically.html.

21. Jen Roesch, "The Lessons of Our Counterprotests," *Socialist Worker*, February
17, 2017, socialistworker.org/2017/02/17/the-lessons-of-our-counterprotests.

Trump, Islamophobia, and US Politics

1. Laura Pitter, "Hate Crimes against Muslims in US Continue to Rise in
2016," Human Rights Watch, May 11, 2017, www.hrw.org/news/2017
/05/11/hate-crimes-against-muslims-us-continue-rise-2016.

2. "The Roots of Islamophobia: An Interview with Deepa Kumar," *Jacobin*,
December 21, 2015, www.jacobinmag.com/2015/12/islamophobia-donald
-trump-syrian-refugees-national-front/.

From "Deporter-in-Chief"
to Xenophobia Unleashed

1. On September 26, 2014, forty-three "normalistas," students training to
become teachers, were abducted and disappeared while they traveled by
bus from the state of Guerrero to Mexico City to take part in protests
commemorating the 1968 Tlatelolco Massacre. Many indications pointed to
the culpability of drug gangs, with collusion of politicians and the Mexican
state, in the disappearance and likely murder of the students. See Francisco
Goldman, "Crisis in Mexico: The Disappearance of the Forty-Three," *New
Yorker*, October 24, 2014, www.newyorker.com/news/news-desk/crisis
-mexico-disappearance-forty-three.

INDEX

ACA. *See* Affordable Care Act (ACA)
Adorno, Theodor, 101
Aetna, 9
Affordable Care Act (ACA), 36, 39,
    40, 41–42, 115–16, 135, 144, 178,
    219n21
Afghanistan, 10, 115
AFL-CIO, 184
African Americans, 3, 6, 9, 31, 33, 38,
    112, 125–41
    and hate crimes against, 42–43, 126,
      176
    politics of, 125–41
    and poverty, 19, 80, 127, 129, 132,
      146
    and voting, 12–13, 27, 28, 52, 54,
      55–58, 65, 67, 134–35, 150,
      218n19
AFT. *See* American Federation of
    Teachers (AFT)
AIG, 9, 115
Alabama poll closures, 69
ALEC. *See* American Legislative Ex-
    change Council (ALEC)
Allianz Global Wealth Report 2015, 14
alt-right. *See under* right (political)
Aly, Götz, 101
American Federation of Teachers
    (AFT), 41
American Legislative Exchange Coun-
    cil (ALEC), 71, 72, 73
American Medical Association, 41
American Prospect, 9, 68

Americans for Prosperity, 73
Anderson, John, 49
Appalachia, 63, 73–81
Arabs, 10, 153
Aristotle (company), 54–55
Arizona, 67, 69, 175
Army of God, 161
Arpaio, Joe, 78, 175
Asian Americans, 11, 56, 150, 176
AT&T, 9

Baker, Kevin, 123–24
Bannon, Steve, 34–35, 64, 125
Barrett, Tom, 68
Beason-Hammon Alabama Taxpay-
    er and Citizen Protection Act
    (HB56), 107–8
Berlet, Chip, 103, 104
Bernanke, Ben, 114
Black Liberation Movement, 140–41
Black Lives Matter, 10, 43, 125–26, 128,
    129, 136, 138–39, 153, 194
Block, Fred, 92
Bossie, David, 64
Branstad, Terry, 36–37
Breitbart, 33–35, 64, 125
Brennan Center for Justice, 69
Brenner, Bob and Johanna, 32
British National Party, 167–68, 169
Brookings Institute, 22
Brooks, David, 69
Buchanan, Pat, 64, 83
Bush, George H. W., 145